Scenic Driving

COLORADO

Stewart Green

FALCON®

HELENA, MONTANA

A FALCON GUIDE ®

Falcon® is continually expanding its list of recreational guidebooks. All books include detailed descriptions, accurate maps, and all information necessary for enjoyable trips. You can order extra copies of this book and get information and prices for other Falcon® guidebooks by writing Falcon, P.O. Box 1718, Helena, MT 59624 or calling toll-free 1-800-582-2665. Also, please ask for a free copy of our current catalog. Visit our website at www.FalconOutdoors.com or contact us by e-mail at falcon@falcon.com.

Cover photo: Mount Yale from Cottonwood Pass
Back cover photo: Cliff Palace at Mesa Verde National Park

All photos by Stewart M. Green

Cataloging-in-Publication Data is on record at the Library of Congress.

CAUTION
Outdoor recreation activities are by their very nature potentially hazardous. All participants in such activities must assume the responsibility for their own actions and safety. The information contained in this guidebook cannot replace sound judgment and good decision– making skills, which help reduce risk exposure, nor does the scope of this book allow for disclosure of all the potential hazards and risks involved in such activities.

Learn as much as possible about the outdoor recreation activities you participate in, prepare for the unexpected, and be safe and cautious. The reward will be a safer and more enjoyable experience.

♻ Text pages printed on recycled paper.

CONTENTS

ACKNOWLEDGMENTS

Colorado, my home state, remains a place of beauty and mystery—for now. It's still a place of pristine views and wide-open spaces. But it is also slowly shrinking. No longer is Colorado a great frontier and an enclave of wildness. Now, like most of the American West, it's a collection of wilderness areas, a few untouched places, and uncluttered scenic views dismembered from a great eco-community. It's a special land that needs, more than ever before, to be loved, respected, and preserved. *Scenic Driving Colorado* celebrates Colorado's unique history.

Nature and guidebook writers have a serious responsibility to address environmental ethics, to interpret natural history, and to bring historical sensitivity to their subjects. By educating and sensitizing visitors, newcomers, and long-time residents to the beauty, wonder, and fragility of a place, a writer and a book can instill a sense of reverence, pride, and preservation in its users. *Scenic Driving Colorado* helps educate its readers by interpreting and caring for this wonderful place. Bring that respectful ethos with you as you travel its ribbons of highway and remember that we are a reflection of this world.

Many thanks to Falcon Press and publisher Bill Schneider for the opportunity to contribute to its marvelous book list. Kudos to editor Randall Green for editing, comments, and direction. Thanks to the USDA Forest Service and National Park Service naturalists and rangers who reviewed portions of the manuscript. Gracias also to my family, Nancy, Ian, and Brett for encouragement, belays, and campfire wisdom and comedy; to Frances and Michael at Bear Paw Books in Norwood; and to traveling companions Erick C. and the Brits Dennis and Yvonne. It was an adventure.

Yuccas poke through fresh snow along Phantom Canyon Road.

Columbine, the state flower.

LOCATOR MAP

N

MAP LEGEND

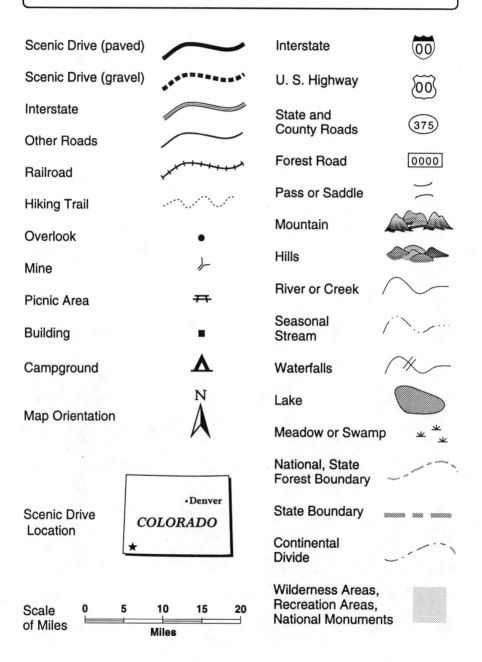

Scenic Drive (paved)		Interstate	
Scenic Drive (gravel)		U. S. Highway	
Interstate		State and County Roads	375
Other Roads		Forest Road	0000
Railroad		Pass or Saddle	
Hiking Trail		Mountain	
Overlook	●	Hills	
Mine		River or Creek	
Picnic Area		Seasonal Stream	
Building	■	Waterfalls	
Campground		Lake	
Map Orientation	N	Meadow or Swamp	
		National, State Forest Boundary	
Scenic Drive Location	•Denver COLORADO ★	State Boundary	
		Continental Divide	
Scale of Miles	0 5 10 15 20 Miles	Wilderness Areas, Recreation Areas, National Monuments	

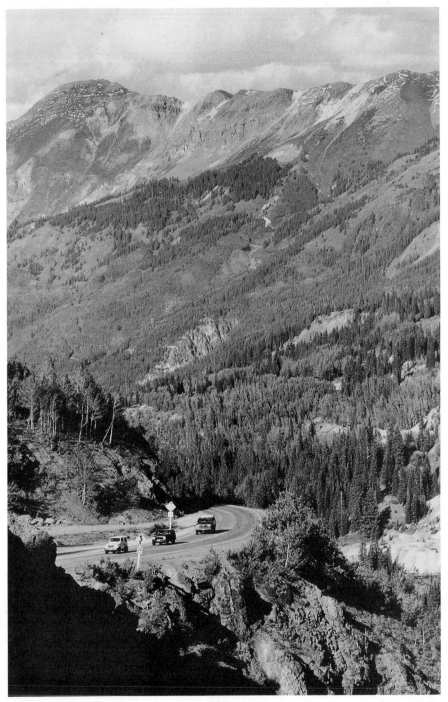

The Million Dollar Highway climbs past mine ruins and tailings to the summit of Red Mountain Pass.

INTRODUCTION

Colorado—it's a state of majestic landscapes, startling panoramas, and an amazing ecological and topographical diversity. It's a land of uncompromising beauty, dominated by lofty, snow-capped peaks, creased by precipitous canyons and broad valleys, and rimmed by distant horizons, mesas, and buttes. Colorado offers a land of extreme contrasts—sere desert and verdant meadow; urban sprawl and rural solitude; granite cliff and aspen woodland; whitewater river thunder and dissected arroyo. The timeless landscape out there, beyond the highway's edge, is filled with hidden places and undiscovered wonders.

Colorado, the eighth-largest state, stretches across North America's midsection. This giant rectangular 104,091-square-mile state bestrides the Continental Divide, the great twisting spine that separates the Atlantic and Pacific watersheds. It's a land of immense topographical variety that ranges from a 3,350-foot low point on the Arkansas River near the Kansas border to the bouldery summit of 14,431-foot Mount Elbert high in the Sawatch Range. In between lies a stunning geography dominated and tempered by its majestic mountain ranges. Geographers divide Colorado into three main physiographic provinces—the Great Plains, Rocky Mountains, and Colorado Plateau. Each distinct province is defined by its geology or earth structure, which, coupled with different climates, dictates the state's diverse ecology, the complex web of relationships between plants and animals and the changing land.

The Great Plains, covering forty percent of Colorado, sweep eastward from the abrupt mountain escarpment to the Kansas border. It's a misnomer to call this region a great plain. This lean land is characterized by undulating hills and interrupted by rock-rimmed mesas, buttes, and escarpments. The broad Arkansas and South Platte river valleys and angular canyons carved by the sparse Purgatoire, Apisapha, and Huerfano rivers seam the shortgrass prairie. Wide fields, watered by snowmelt-laden rivers and groundwater aquifers, are planted with wheat, corn, sorghum, sugar beets, and other crops, while cattle and antelope roam the drier ranges.

The Rocky Mountains abruptly begin where the Great Plains end. The horizontal, 10,000-foot-thick sedimentary rock layers that floor the prairie sharply tilt into steep hogbacks like those seen at Garden of the Gods and Red Rocks parks along the eastern edge of the mountain uplift. Most Coloradans live in large cities scattered along this transition zone. The Continental Divide dominates Colorado's Rocky Mountains, part of the world's longest mountain chain. The Rockies twist from Alaska to Mexico but reach their climax in Colorado with more than fifty separate mountain ranges that include fifty-four of America's sixty-seven 14,000-foot peaks and another 830 summits that top 11,000 feet. The mountains, mostly raised over the last seventy million years, were shaped by volcanism and earthquakes and sculpted by huge glaciers and swift rivers and streams. Colorado is the mother of rivers,

1

The Unaweep-Tabeguache Scenic Drive follows Unaweep Canyon's broad floor beneath abrupt granite crags.

with the Colorado, South and North Platte, Rio Grande, Yampa, Arkansas, San Juan, Gunnison, Dolores, and Purgatoire rivers originating in snowy alpine cirques. Rich mineral deposits, including gold, silver, zinc, lead, copper, and molybdenum, lurk in the Rockies and lured nineteenth-century prospectors that left a historic legacy of roads, trails, mines, towns, and place-names on the mountains.

The plateau region, part of the 150,000-square-mile Colorado Plateau, covers roughly the western quarter of the state. It is a brilliantly colored land of horizontal sedimentary layers, dissected by erosion into canyons, mesas, and cuestas. Deep canyons carved by the Yampa, Green, Colorado, and Dolores rivers slice through the layer-cake rocks. Folding and faulting created huge basins, rolling uplands, and rocky hogbacks in this arid area.

Colorado is an ecological melting pot, a place of unbelievable natural diversity, a place that thrills and startles the naturalist. Famed nature writer Edwin Way Teale wrote in his classic book *Journey into Summer*, "Before us now extended all of Colorado, a state that, like Florida and California, holds endless interest for the naturalist." The Rocky Mountains mold and temper the state's plants and animals, dictating their responses with variable temperatures, precipitation patterns, and elevations. Shortgrass prairie, interrupted by a mosaic of farms, blankets the eastern plains. Verdant ribbons of cottonwoods, willows, tamarisk, and underbrush line sinuous rivers and creeks. Pygmy woodlands of pinyon pine and juniper trees scatter over dry mesas and desert canyons. Dense evergreen forests of ponderosa pine, Englemann spruce, lodgepole pine, and subalpine fir coat mountain slopes, while ancient bristlecone pines, dwarfed by wind and weather, huddle at timberline on snow-shrouded peaks. Immense golden groves of quaking aspen shimmer across the mountains under autumn's bright sun. Alpine tundra, a fragile ecosystem of grass and flowers akin to those of northern Canada and Alaska, lies on the harsh mountainsides above timberline, and above stretches a chilly world of shattered rock and endless winter.

Colorado offers the traveler not only incomparable scenery but a host of natural wonders, historic sites, and outdoor recreation. The state boasts Rocky Mountain and Mesa Verde national parks, two of the nation's most popular parklands, as well as Colorado, Dinosaur, Great Sand Dunes, Hovenweep, Florissant Fossil Beds, and Black Canyon of the Gunnison national monuments, Curecanti and Arapaho national recreation areas, and Bents Fort National Historic Site. Thirty-five state parks and recreation areas are managed for both water and land-based recreation. Eleven national forests and two national grasslands spread across almost 14.5 million acres of public land, while the Bureau of Land Management offers an additional 8.3 million acres. More than eight thousand river-miles and two thousand lakes yield watery opportunities for fishermen and rafters. The 469-mile-long Colorado Trail threads through seven national forests and six wilderness areas between Denver and Durango. Numerous rough roads invite mountain bikers and four-wheel-drive enthusiasts to sample the backcountry.

Scenic Driving Colorado finds the best of Colorado's majestic landscapes and recreational offerings. Its 30 drives traverse 2,250 miles of remote highways and off-the-beaten-track backroads. They discover and explore

Fresh autumn snow caps the Sneffels Range above aspen forests and the Lizard Head Pass Scenic Drive.

3

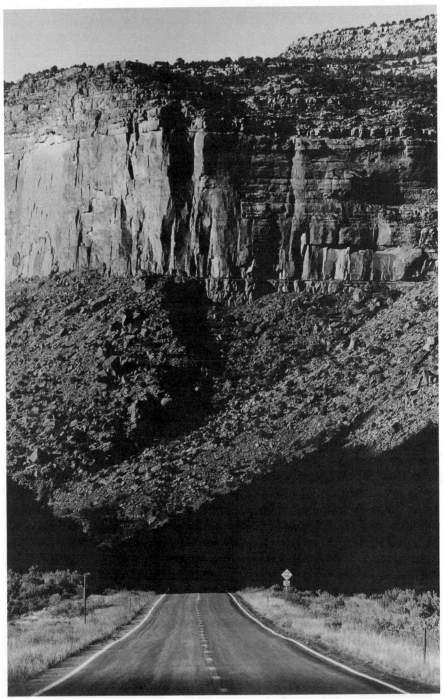

A palisade of Wingate sandstone cliffs lines the Dolores River Canyon along the Unaweep-Tabeguache Scenic Drive.

Horn Peak lifts frosty slopes above the verdant Wet Mountain Valley along the Sangre de Cristo Drive.

Colorado's magnificent landscape, ecological diversity, colorful history, and outdoor activities. Travelers cross lofty mountain passes on Independence Pass and Trail Ridge roads, twist through deep rock-walled canyons along the Dolores and Cache la Poudre rivers, follow the historic Santa Fe Trail, marvel at Mesa Verde's long-deserted Anasazi cities, and climb to the lofty mountain aeries atop Pikes Peak and Mount Evans. The drives leave urban sprawl behind and take to the open road.

These drives are only the start of the adventure. Most of them are paved highways, but some are genuine backroads. Beyond the blacktop and the book hide more scenic drives. After exploring the prime roads detailed here, the intrepid traveler can seek out new tracks. Some of the best include Owl Creek Pass, Ophir Pass, Engineer Pass, the Divide Road on the crest of the Uncompahgre Plateau, Hagerman Pass, Boreas Pass, the twisting road between Buford and New Castle, the Deep Creek Road above Dotsero, and some of those lonely prairie roads like Colorado Highway 71 and the Elbert Highway.

Be prepared when driving Colorado's scenic highways. Make sure your vehicle is in good working condition and the spare tire is properly inflated. Follow the speed limit, particularly on winding mountain roads, stay in your lane, and watch for blind corners. Maintain a safe speed and pull off to allow faster cars to pass. Fickle weather creates changeable driving conditions. Violent summer thunderstorms can impair vision and create hydroplaning situations. Snow and ice quickly slicken mountain highways. Carry chains, a snow shovel, and extra clothes when traveling in winter. Many high passes require chains in winter. Hot summer temperatures and steep mountain slopes can overheat your car. It's best to pull off the road and allow the engine to cool down. Carry extra water in case of breakdown. It's best to top off your gas tank before embarking on remote roads. Know your vehicle and its limits. And above all—use common sense.

The scenic drives cross a mosaic of public and private lands. Respect private property rights by not trespassing. Forest Service and BLM maps designate public lands. Federal laws protect paleontological, archeological, and historic sites, including fossils and bones, Indian sites and artifacts, and historic buildings and structures. It's best to utilize existing campgrounds and campsites to mitigate human impact. Remember to douse all campfires and tote your trash out.

Colorado—it's a word that resounds with images as clear as a mountain stream. Snow-capped peaks sharply etched against an azure sky. A muddy river with a glassy surface runs between dusky red sandstone cliffs. Dark whiskery forests that clot a shaded ravine. An abandoned prairie homestead open to the blazing sun. It's all out there, along the highway shoulder. Follow the roads and drive without destinations. Stop, look, and linger. Every highway bend, every scenic overlook, every canyon crook, and every alpine pass yields a glimpse into the beauty, wonder, and awe of Colorado's natural soul.

Bent's Old Fort National Historic Site, just outside La Junta, reconstructs the Santa Fe Trail's colorful history.

1 SANTA FE TRAIL SCENIC DRIVE
La Junta to Trinidad

General description: This 80-mile-long scenic drive, following the old Santa Fe Trail, crosses the desolate high plains between La Junta and Trinidad.

Special attractions: Santa Fe Trail, Bent's Fort National Historic Site, Comanche National Grassland, Corazon de Trinidad National Historic District, Baca House-Bloom House-Pioneer Museum (Trinidad), scenic views, hiking.

Location: Southeastern Colorado. The drive runs between La Junta and U.S. Highway 50 and Trinidad and Interstate 25.

Drive route number and name: U.S. Highway 350, Santa Fe Trail Scenic and Historic Byway.

Travel season: Year-round.

Camping: No campgrounds lie along the drive. Primitive camping is permitted on the Comanche National Grassland. Nearby campgrounds are at Trinidad State Recreation Area and in San Isabel National Forest.

Services: All services are found in La Junta and Trinidad. No services are found along the drive.

Nearby attractions: Highway of Legends Scenic Byway, Raton Pass, Trinidad State Recreation Area, Stonewall Gap, Cokedale National Historic District, Spanish Peaks Wilderness Area, San Isabel National Forest, Ludlow Monument, Comanche Grasslands Scenic Drive, Purgatoire Canyon.

For more information: La Junta Chamber, P.O. Box 408, La Junta, CO 81050, (719) 384-7411. Trinidad Chamber, 309 Nevada St., Trinidad, CO 81082, (719) 846-9285. Comanche National Grassland,1420 East 3rd, La Junta, CO 81050, (719) 384-2181.

The drive: The limitless prairie brazenly stretches out beneath the blazing sun to a distant line of mountains perched on the horizon. Dusty arroyos, chiseled by quick runoff from occasional thunderstorms, seam broad valleys flanked by rock-rimmed cuestas and undulating hills. A few intermittent creekbeds twist dryly north to the Arkansas River, their water dwindling into sand and re-appearing as occasional bitter pools nestled in sandstone canyons. Out there in southeastern Colorado lies a land of little rain, fierce temperature ranges, and a leaping vault of azure sky. It's a supple, muscular land, an arena of light and space that reminds us that untamed corners still exist.

These rolling plains are Colorado's underdog landscape, a lost place forgotten and almost unseen by those intent on greener mountain pastures. But this brown land south of the river is blanketed by a sea of shortgrass prairie, a delicate and complex ecosystem, and a history older than the

United States. Folsom hunters trod the land 10,000 years ago in pursuit of big game; Comanches and Pawnees battled over its buffalo and water holes; Spanish battalions crossed its bleak wastes in search of golden Cibola; and a scant 150 years ago the caravan wheels of traders bent for Santa Fe creaked across this land. The Santa Fe Trail scenic drive, traversing eighty miles of US 350 between La Junta on the Arkansas River and Trinidad at the foot of the Rockies, follows the old trail and explores this diverse and hidden Colorado corner.

Southeastern Colorado is indeed a land of little rain, and what rain does fall usually drops from violent summer thunderstorms that brew over distant mountains. Annual precipitation ranges between twelve and fifteen inches. Summer brings hot weather, with daily highs climbing into the nineties and above. Carry water and wear a hat if you walk anywhere. Watch for the ubiquitous rattlesnake, they teem among the area's boulders and bluffs. Late September begins the cool down, although hot weather can persist into late October. Expect temperatures in the seventies and eighties. Winter is mild, with light snowfall, warm days, cold nights, and clear skies, although storms can lock in the land in a blizzard of white. Spring is unpredictable. A persistent wind gnaws at the high rangeland, sweeping clouds of dust across Timpas Creek and rattling dry grass on hummocky hills. Light showers dampen the ground and by May, and green grass sprinkled with wildflowers carpets the land. This exquisite bloom lasts but a few weeks before the blast of summer sun arrives to desiccate the prairie.

The drive begins in La Junta, a small town straddling the Arkansas River sixty-four miles east of Pueblo, at the junction of US 50 and US 350. La Junta, Spanish for "the junction," was founded in 1875 at the convergence of the Kansas Pacific and Santa Fe railway lines. History, however, goes back much farther to Bent's Fort, a trading post established in 1834 by brothers Charles and William Bent and Ceran St. Vrain just east of today's La Junta.

Trade with Santa Fe and its remote Mexican colony began in 1821 with Mexico's seccession from Spain and the fall of trade barriers. Missouri trader William Becknell crossed the prairie in 1821 to that lonely northern outpost of a newly independent nation and found an eager market for his trade goods. On his journey to Santa Fe, Becknell had followed the Arkansas River into Colorado and coaxed his mules over rocky Raton Pass, finding the route impractical for wagons. On his second trip he left the Arkansas and cut across waterless plains to the Cimarron River to establish the Cimarron cutoff. A Missouri resident later recalled Becknell's triumphant return: "When the rawhide thongs of the saddlebags were cut, the Spanish dollars rolled into the gutters, causing great excitement." Speculative traders soon found it was cheaper to ship goods to Santa Fe from Missouri than Mexico City, and by 1827 the New Mexico trade had firmly established the 900-mile-long Santa Fe Trail, western America's great road of commerce.

The Bent brothers and St. Vrain cashed in on the lucrative Indian trade in eastern Colorado with their adobe castle perched on the cottonwood-lined banks of the Arkansas River. William Bent concentrated on Indian goods, while Charles Bent and St. Vrain specialized in the lucrative Santa Fe and

Taos trade. The Cimarron cutoff route on the Santa Fe Trail was fast and popular, but mounting Indian attacks and its lack of reliable water forced an increasing number of merchants to follow the longer, but safer, Mountain Branch up the Arkansas River to Bent's Fort. Here they could rest and purchase supplies before heading southwest up arid Timpas Creek to the rough track over Raton Pass. The Bent, St. Vrain & Company mercantile firm thrived until the late 1840s when the enterprise began to unravel. Charles Bent, then the first American governor of the New Mexico Territory, was killed in the 1847 Taos Revolt by rioting Pueblo Indians and shortly afterwards a cholera epidemic swept along the river decimating both Anglos and Indians. The U.S. Army, fighting a war with Mexico between 1846 and 1848, also requisitioned part of Bent's Fort, overgrazed surrounding pastures, and used up what little firewood remained around the fort. In frustration, William Bent abandoned and torched the fort in 1849 and moved downstream to build Bent's New Fort at Big Timber.

The old fort site lay open to the sun and sky until the mid-1970s when the National Park Service, using original plans and scale drawings made in 1846 by army topographical engineer Lieutenant James W. Abert, rebuilt the massive adobe fort. Now open as Bent's Old Fort National Historic Site, the fort offers a glimpse at frontier life in the 1840s when the West was still new. The fort, staffed by interpreters clad in period clothes, including a trader, blacksmith, Mexican laborer, and mountain man, keeps the legacy of Bent's Fort and the Santa Fe Trail alive today. The fort lies a few miles northeast of La Junta on Colorado Highway 194.

The drive begins in western La Junta at the intersection of US 50 and 350.

US 350 and the old Santa Fe Trail follow Timpas Creek up a broad valley.

Head south on quiet residential streets on US 350. The road bends southwest and leaves the town behind after a mile. US 350, nicknamed the National Old Trails Highway, was once a major transcontinental highway between New York and Los Angeles in the days before the interstate system. The trace of the Santa Fe Trail itself, from Franklin, Missouri to Santa Fe, New Mexico, is now preserved as a national historic trail. The eighty-mile section between La Junta and Trinidad follows the Mountain Branch of the Santa Fe Trail. Here the old trail offered passage to trade caravans and later stage, freight, and mail lines before the completion of the railroad in the 1870s. Travel along this segment generally took about four days.

The highway gradually ascends a tilted plain. Short grass coats the flat ground and only an occasional windmill marks the desolate plain. At about five miles an unassuming granite marker sits along the fence on the road's west side. This marker, one of many placed along the trail by the Daughters of the American Revolution (DAR), indicates where the trail crossed today's highway. Sharp eyes can discern wagon wheel ruts etched into the ground west of the marker. Trail ruts, found along much of the drive, appear as long furrowed depressions and are usually heavily vegetated. When traveling flat country like this, wagon caravans spread out three and four abreast creating wide rutted areas. In 1844 teamster Josiah Gregg wrote, "The wagons marched slowly in four parallel columns, in broken lines, often at intervals of many rods between. The unceasing 'crack, crack,' of the wagoners' whips, resembling the frequent reports of distant guns, almost made one believe that a skirmish was actually taking place between two hostile parties." Wagons traveled single file on steep ascents, gouging deep swales into hillsides that are now eroded into sharp arroyos.

Unlike other Santa Fe Trail sections in Colorado and Kansas, the trail stretch followed by the drive remains much as it did when wagons inched across the wide expanse. Eighteen-year-old Susan Shelby Magoffin traveled the trail from Independence, Missouri to Santa Fe with her trader husband Samuel Magoffin in 1846, a boom year when more than one million dollars in goods was hauled over the trail. Magoffin kept a journal recounting her daily experiences that has become a classic tale of the Santa Fe Trail. On Saturday, August 8, she wrote about the trail section southwest of the fort: "The dust is very great, and the vegetation so perfectly parched by the sun that not a blade of *green* grass is to be seen."

After thirteen miles the highway drops over a tawny bluff above Timpas Creek, its dry meanders dotted with cottonwoods. Both the highway and Santa Fe Trail follow the Timpas Creek drainage to its headwaters, some forty miles to the southwest. Distant views unfold west from the bluff-top. The Wet Mountains and Spanish Peaks, over seventy miles away, float on the shimmering horizon like far-off blue clouds. The twin Spanish Peaks, called *Wahatoya* or "Breasts of the World" by the Ute Indians, were long a crucial landmark to the Indians, Spanish, and Santa Fe Trail travelers. The Three Buttes, another trail landmark, lift pointed summits above the cluster of trees marking the abandoned townsite of Timpas. Susan Magoffin traveled here on Saturday, August 9, noting, "Mountains are coming in sight this morning—

we are winding about among large stone hills which finally run into mountains, two of which appear in the distance...."

The road begins a gradual descent into the broad Timpas Creek valley and enters the Timpas Unit of 418,887-acre Comanche National Grassland. The area, a patchwork of public and private lands, encompasses a diversity of habitats within the grassland ecosystem. The grassland, managed by the USDA Forest Service, spreads across southeastern Colorado. The area, originally Comanche Indian territory, was overgrazed by early cattle barons and later divided by homesteaders into forty-acre tracts. But dry soil and bad farming and conservation practices created the Dust Bowl here and in surrounding states in the 1930s. In 1938 the federal government began reacquiring the homesteads and retiring them from cultivation. Today the Forest Service has reclaimed much of the grassland. Plentiful animals roam the high plains—including both mule and whitetail deer, pronghorn, black bear, opossum, mountain lion, black-tailed prairie dog, jackrabbit, snapping turtle, Texas short-horned lizard, and prairie, massasauga, and pygmy rattlesnakes. The area offers excellent bird habitats, with more than 235 bird species recorded. Common birds seen on the drive include turkey vulture, red-tailed hawk, American kestrel, western meadowlark, and raven.

The highway passes the ghost town of Timpas, an old stage station and railroad stop established in 1868. Clusters of elms and cottonwoods surround its abandoned school, houses, and weather-beaten stock yard. The road runs up the valley flank, cresting a low hill north of the Three Buttes. Soft, rolling hills broken by arroyos and shallow canyons surround a roadside overlook. A sandstone rim fringes distant bluffs, and junipers scatter across their talus slopes. The Southern Overland Mail Company stagecoach route threaded through the Three Buttes, leaving eroded ruts below the gap. Another DAR trail marker sits a couple miles down the road near mile post 51.

Following the valley floor, the highway dips across Lone Tree Arroyo, Hoe Ranch Arroyo, and Sheep Canyon Arroyo. Eleven miles from Timpas the drive intersects Iron Springs Road. The Santa Fe Trail crosses this gravel sideroad a half mile south. Iron Springs Stage Station Historic Site sits a little farther south by two stock tanks. Iron Springs, capped by a concrete box, supplies water to the tanks. Nearby lies the foundation of the station barn, a low mound marking the adobe remains of the station itself, and the stubby outline of the stage corral. The station, built in 1862 by Henry C. Withers, was burned by Cheyenne Indians in 1864. The stage station allowed for a change of horses and a chance for passengers to stretch their legs and get a meal. One early traveler, Episcopal bishop Joseph Talbot, arrived here at four in the morning after a ten-hour night ride from Bent's Fort. He noted, after dining on a "greasy breakfast of antelope," that the station was a "miserable, dirty place."

In 1872 the Atchinson, Topeka, and Santa Fe Railroad came through, replacing the old stage route. The Iron Springs Station closed and Bloom, a new railroad stop, arose just west along today's highway and railroad. The town, a cattle shipping point, was named for Trinidad banker and son-in-law of M.D. Thatcher, a prominent Colorado cattleman. After the post office

Bent's Old Fort National Historic Site, a reconstructed adobe fort along the Arkansas River, offers a glimpse of the Santa Fe Trail's colorful past.

closed in 1938 the town's fortunes sagged. Today it's a ghost town with fallen houses surrounded by leafy trees and a roadside store with shattered windows.

Past Bloom the highway bends south, crosses Taylor Arroyo, and leaves Comanche National Grassland. The road climbs away from Timpas Creek to the almost deserted railroad town of Delhi. Cresting the hill, the road again enters the broad Timpas valley. High cuestas edged with sandstone and darkly dotted with junipers flank the highway. The Spanish Peaks and the snow-capped Culebra Range loom straight ahead.

Thatcher, the next ruined town encountered, began as a stage station called Hole-in-the-Rock and became a bustling railroad town after the A.T. & S.F. Railroad pushed through in 1872. The town flourished as a cow town and was named for M.D. Thatcher, a prominent southern Colorado rancher and banker. The town's fortunes soared in the early twentieth century after a helium plant was built near local helium wells. The gas, used to inflate cumbersome dirigibles, took orders from around the world until airplanes made them obsolete. After that, the town slowly declined. The lavish train depot closed in 1965 and shortly afterwards the post office shut its doors. Now the town basks under the hot sun, empty but for a few remaining residents. Wind sifts through open doors and broken windows, and adobe walls crumble, unprotected from years of rain. Rusted car doors, a prone refrigerator, and sagging fences are scattered across weed-filled front yards. The town high school, once full of promise, lies in ruins. The gymnasium roof caved in a few years back and the front doors sit ajar.

A short side trip turns west at the only intersection in Thatcher. Head down the gravel road past the school to a narrow wooden bridge spanning Timpas Creek. Look north up the shallow rocky canyon. Hiden there is one of the prominent Santa Fe Trail landmarks on the highway—Hole-in-the-Rock. This deep tinaja, carved by flash floods into solid bedrock, kept water through even the driest times and was a welcome sight in trail days. Susan Magoffin wrote, "This road is very badly supplied with water." Her party camped here for a couple days after their cattle ran off. She described the well as "...a large 'hole in a rock' filled with clear, cold water, and to which a bottom has never as yet been found." The hole, on private property, is now filled with sand. A ruined stone barn at the ranch just east of the bridge is the remains of the Hole-in-the-Rock Overland Stage Station's barn.

The highway runs southwest from Thatcher up a broadening valley among undulating hills. Fisher Mesa, a flat-topped landmark, rises beyond the road. The drive reaches a wide-rounded ridge above the Timpas Creek headwaters and heads down a gently tilted plain covered with shortgrass prairie. The highway sweeps through a couple more mostly abandoned towns—Tyrone and Model—before dropping down into the Purgatoire River valley. The 240,000-acre Pinon Canyon Military Reservation, lying east of Tyrone and Thatcher, is used by the U.S. Army for tank and military training.

The drive's last fifteen miles border the Purgatoire River, passing pastures and fields of pinto beans, alfalfa, and sugar beets. The Purgatoire River, running 150 miles from the Culebra Range to the Arkansas River, is a river of history and character. The river's original name *El Rio de las Animas Perdidas en Purgatorio* or the River of Lost Souls in Purgatory was shortened by Anglos to Purgatoire River and given the French spelling. Cowboys mangled it to Picketwire. The river, after passing Trinidad, hastens through its lonely redrock Pinon Canyon east of the drive.

Above the river the highway intersects U.S. Highway 160, and five miles later enters 6,025-foot-high Trinidad. The road bends through the town's old downtown before ending at I-25. The summit of Raton Pass and the New Mexico state line lies thirteen miles to the south, while Walsenburg sits thirty-seven miles to the north. The Highway of Legends Scenic Byway begins on Trinidad's west side.

Trinidad, lying at the foot of Fisher's Peak, was an important Santa Fe Trail town. Founded in 1859 at the base of rough Raton Pass, the community was named *Santisima Trinidad* or "Most Holy Trinity." Sheepherder Gabriel Gutierrez first settled here on the river's south bank and soon other settlers drifted in. Trinidad, a favorite haunt of mountain men and desperadoes, acquired a rowdy reputation that was re-enforced after the Battle of Trinidad on Christmas Day, 1867. Racial friction between Anglo and Hispanic settlers escalated from a wrestling match to an all-out riot. Soldiers, called in from Fort Lyon, quelled the violence and imposed martial law. Later the town flourished when the vast coal reserves along the river to the west were mined for Pueblo's steel plant. Much of downtown Trinidad, with its narrow, bricked streets, is preserved as El Corazon del Trinidad National Historic District. The Baca House, Bloom House, and Pioneer Museum depicts life in pioneer Trinidad and displays wagons used on the Santa Fe Trail. The Louden-Henritze Archeology Museum at Trinidad State Junior College illustrates the area's diverse archeological resources and shows Indian artifacts.

2 PAWNEE GRASSLAND SCENIC DRIVE
Ault to Sterling

General description: This 125-mile-long drive traverses the Pawnee National Grassland, passing ranch lands, abandoned homesteads, and undulating high plains.
Special attractions: Pawnee National Grassland, Pawnee Buttes, Crow Valley Recreation Area, Sterling Overland Trail Museum, wide views, photography, birdwatching, hiking, mountain biking, camping.
Location: Northeastern Colorado. The drive begins in Ault, fourteen miles east of Fort Collins and Interstate 25, and ends at Sterling and Interstate 76.
Drive route name and numbers: Pawnee Pioneer Trails Scenic Byway. Colorado Highway 14, Weld County roads 77, 120, 390, 112, 111, 110,

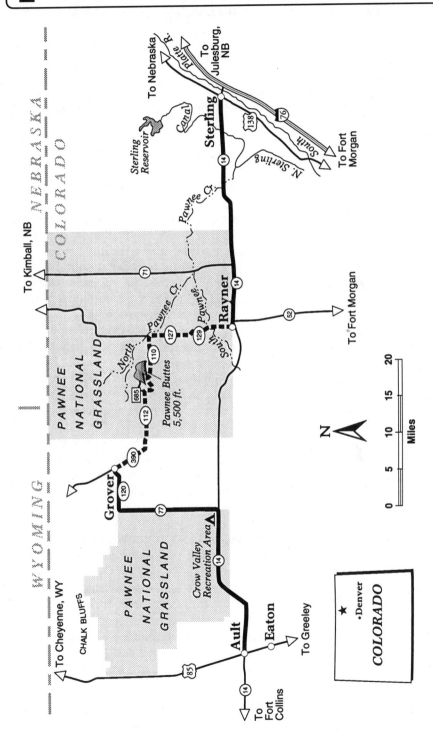

113, 110 1/2, 115, 127, and 129. Grasslands Road 685.

Camping: Crow Valley Recreation Area, 24 miles west of Ault at Briggsdale, is the only developed campground along the drive. Primitive camping is permitted elsewhere on the grassland. Watch for high winds and flash flood areas.

Services: All services in Fort Collins, Ault, and Sterling. Limited services in Raymer.

Nearby attractions: Fort Collins, Cache la Poudre National Wild and Scenic River, Lory State Park, Roosevelt National Forest, Rocky Mountain National Park, Estes Park, Trail Ridge Road, Cheyenne (Wyoming), Fort Morgan Museum, Fort Vasquez State Historic Site, Centennial Village (Greeley).

For more information: Pawnee National Grassland, 660 "O" Street, Suite A, Greeley, CO 80631, (970) 353-5004. Logan County Chamber, P.O. Box 1683, Sterling, CO 80751, (970) 522-5070 or (800) 544-8609.

The drive: Northeastern Colorado is a spare, austere landscape, a sparsely populated province of undulating hills that break into badlands, shortgrass prairie that recedes to a flat eastern horizon, and trickling streams that dwindle into sand, only to reappear later in occasional muddy pools surrounded by cottonwoods. Indians once roamed its vastness, camping along the meager creeks and hunting vast buffalo herds. Later homesteaders tilled the dry soil, but only grew loneliness and frustration. Still the prairie remains a refuge from today's urban sprawl and a place of exquisite beauty. Its buttes and mesa rims gleam white in summer's noonday sun; dancing heat waves shimmer across the plain revealing rumpled sky mirages. Evening brings smoky shadows and immense billowing thunderstorms tinged pink and rose with sunset. Out here the prairie traveler develops a new appreciation for simple forms and a devoted adoration of this elemental earth of clay, sky, and wind song.

Fickle, unpredictable weather dominates along the drive. Summer days are hot, with highs ranging into the nineties and above. Heavy thunderstorms, coupled with hail, regularly occur on summer afternoons. Rain makes the drive's dirt backroads temporarily impassable, muddy, and slippery. Watch for lightning on the exposed, higher elevations such as the Pawnee Buttes Overlook and trail parking area. Autumn days, from mid-September to early November, are pleasant and warm. Winter brings snow. Severe blizzards cause deep drifts along the backroads and melting snow closes dirt roads. Check with the grassland office in Greeley for road conditions and closures. Long warm periods in mid-winter melt the snow, dry the roads, and make for excellent traveling conditions. Spring, beginning by late March, is characterized by rain storms, heavy spring snows, high winds, and warming temperatures. Much of the prairie's twelve to fifteen inches of annual precipitation comes between April and June. May, with greening grass and carpets of wildflowers, makes an excellent travel time across the grassland.

The Pawnee National Grassland scenic drive begins in Ault, fourteen

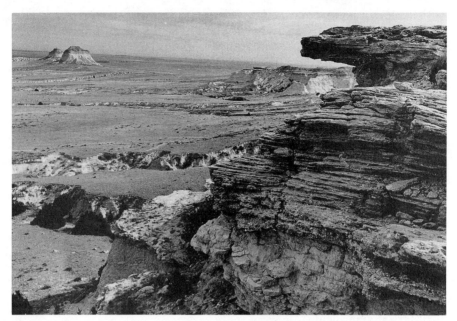

The twin Pawnee Buttes, a northern Colorado landmark, rise beyond a sandstone overlook on the Pawnee Grassland Drive.

miles west of Fort Collins and I-25 on CO 14. Take I-25 Exit 269A for CO 14 east. Ault, established in 1888 and named for Fort Collins miller Alexander Ault, has long been an agricultural town. It is a friendly, unassuming place with neat frame homes along tree-lined side-streets, and tall grain silos that line the railroad tracks on the east side of town. Ault, elevation 4,950 feet, sits at the junction of U.S. Highway 85 and CO 14. Scenic drivers head east on CO 14 from the intersection. The drive's first leg runs east twenty-four miles to Briggsdale. The first five miles run across gentle farmland seamed by the sleepy meanders of Spring, Lone Tree, and Owl creeks. Corn and wheat fields, interrupted by white farm-houses and wind breaks of cottonwoods, elms, and Russian olives, form a pastoral roadside border. After five miles the highway tilts up a long hillside and leaves the farmland behind. Ahead stretch tawny, rolling hills blanketed by shortgrass and subdivided by long fencelines. The highway bends northeast for six miles and then re-straightens eastward. At just over thirteen miles the blacktop enters Pawnee National Grassland.

Pawnee National Grassland is an immense 193,000-acre swathe of prairie managed by the USDA Forest Service. This remote land was first inhabited by prehistoric big-game hunters some eleven thousand years ago. Later nomadic plains tribes—the Pawnee, Apache, Arapaho, and Cheyenne Indians—traversed the plains while hunting bison. The first known European, Don Pedro de Villasur, visited the area in 1720, and French fur trappers regularly crossed it while trading with local Indians. Anglo homesteaders arrived here in the late 1800s, after the 1862 Homestead Act opened western lands to any able-bodied American willing to work 160-acre tracts. Early settlers plowed lands along the few perennial rivers and streams, while late-comers homesteaded the marginal dry land. The dry-land farmers, initially successful, suffered after 1920 because of low wheat prices, drought, and bad farming practices. The Dust Bowl and Great Depression of the 1930s forced the mass migration of homesteaders from their 160-acre dream parcels. The federal government began buying back the damaged lands and restoring them with a semblance of their original grass cover. The recovered lands were returned to cultivation and grazing or administered as multiple-use National Grasslands by the USDA Forest Service.

The Pawnee National Grassland, divided into two large units, is a patchwork of both public and private land. A Forest Service map, detailing the different lands, is a necessity for exploring beyond the area's gridwork of county roads. Be sure you are on public land, otherwise obtain permission from the landowner. Most of the grassland is managed for livestock grazing as well as wildlife habitat. Oil and gas deposits, tapped by over fifty producing wells, underlie the grassland particularly at the Keota Oil Field south of Grover and a small field north of Raymer. The U.S. Department of Agriculture also operates the 15,600-acre Central Plains Experimental Range for research on grassland ecology, range cattle nutrition, and the use of fertilizers and herbicides.

After entering the grassland, the straight-arrow highway rolls east, dipping through dry arroyos walled with clay. Wind-driven tumbleweeds stack against barbed wire fences, lonely windmills rise against the sky, and elms shade the occasional ranch house. The road drops into broad Crow Valley and reaches Briggsdale, an almost deserted town of a half-dozen streets south of the highway. Frank Briggs, a local real estate man and farmer, platted the townsite in 1909. The Briggsdale Museum, housed in the old school house, depicts the area's homestead history. The drive turns north here on paved County 77.

Crow Valley Recreation Area, the only developed camp and picnic ground along the drive, sits two-tenths of a mile up County 77. Shady campsites are scattered among cottonwoods and elms. The area also offers restrooms, water, a ballfield, and group picnic area. A fenced display features antique farm machinery, including various plows and a windmill. The campground makes a good base to explore the surrounding grasslands on foot and mountain bike. An auto birding tour route threads along Crow Creek in the shallow valley.

The Pawnee National Grassland, sitting on the edge of the Central Flyway, offers excellent birding opportunities, particularly in May and June when numerous migrant species nest in the varied habitats. Noted ornithologist Roger Tory Peterson calls the grassland his favorite Colorado birding area. Over 225 species, including golden eagle, horned lark, black-billed magpie, western meadowlark, American goldfinch, burrowing owl, and the lark bunting, Colorado's state bird, live on the area's grassy plains, sandstone cliffs, moist creek bottoms, and wooded draws. Grassland mammals also thrive here. Common species are pronghorn, mule deer, coyote, badger, prairie dog, and jackrabbit. Hikers should watch for rattlesnakes. They commonly inhabit dry, rocky slopes on buttes and mesas, often sunning on ledges and boulders.

The narrow road runs due north up the edge of shallow Crow Valley. Ancient cottonwoods line the creekbed and ranches and farms scatter over the rolling hills. The snow-capped Front Range rims the western horizon with sculpted peaks. Flat-topped Longs Peak, high point of Rocky Mountain National Park, looms in the southwest sky. After ten miles a low-browed escarpment of sandy cliffs fringed by green forest etches the eastern valley rim. The road passes an abandoned farm, its weather-beaten house and barn now the haunt of owls and lizards. An up-turned, rusted refrigerator lies on the ground amidst elms and tall grass. The drive turns east on paved County 120 fifteen miles north of Briggsdale and passes an empty two-story house surrounded by junked cars and a plowed field.

County 120 bends north and east past farmland in wide Crow Valley, and seven miles later rolls into Grover, "Home of the Pawnee Jackrabbit." Shady gravel streets fill this off-the-beaten-track village. A small museum in the old railroad station houses displays of local artifacts and grassland ecology. On the far eastern edge of Grover, County 120 dead ends into County 390. Turn right, or southeast, on this gravel road. The drive assumes a new character for the next forty miles to Raymer, threading eccentrically along numerous dirt roads that criss-cross the prairie. Keep a careful eye on the road signs and you'll keep on the drive route. If you blunder off, however, it's hard to get lost. Almost all the roads run north and south or east and west, eventually intersecting some major road.

County 390 runs southeast alongside the abandoned Chicago, Burlington & Quincy Railroad right-of-way. The railway, originally a branch line between Cheyenne, Wyoming and Sterling, came through in the late 1880s. During the halcyon days before World War I and the Dust Bowl, the towns and homesteaders along the track flourished with the railroad. Grover and neighboring Keota to the south offered daily passenger service, and the railroad shipped area grain to market. Locals even planned to chisel a new county called Pawnee out of eastern Weld County in 1912, but Grover and Keota argued so bitterly over who would be county seat that the entire proposal was scrapped. Oil wells, part of the Keota Oil Field, dot grass fields along the road. A wall of tumbled bluffs, the edge of an eroded upland called the High Plains Escarpment, looms to the east. Just past a low hill six miles southeast of Grover, the road intersects County 112. Turn east on County 112.

The new road, passing a ranch, twists through dry hills. After two miles it climbs onto a broad ridge studded with prickly pear cacti and yucca. Sligo Cemetery sits atop the rounded shoulder. Numerous pioneer graves dating from the early 1900s spread over this lovely hillock. Mostly young children and toddlers make up the cemetery's residents. Nameless plastic markers from Adamson Mortuary designate their remote graves. A purple cloth rose, torn and tattered by the ceaseless wind, lies half-buried in dust beside one faded plaque.

The road dips east from the cemetery ridge and enters the southern edge

Abandoned ranch buildings weather under the spacious sky on the Pawnee Grassland Scenic Drive in northern Colorado.

of a broad valley. Cliffs and deep ravines fringed with juniper stretch along it's flat-topped rim. The valley narrows as the road runs east. Five miles from the graveyard, County 112 intersects County 107. Jog south and east on County 107 over steep hills. After almost two miles the road intersects Grasslands Road 685. This marked route heads north onto a wide, rolling ridge for a mile and a half to the Pawnee Buttes Trailhead. An overlook, another half-mile further north, yields one of eastern Colorado's most dramatic views.

The monolithic Pawnee Buttes, forming distinctive landmarks, rise out of North Pawnee Creek's broad, grass-filled valley. James Michener renamed them the Rattlesnake Buttes in his Colorado-based novel *Centennial* and called them the "two sentinels of the plains." Sandstone deposited on an ancient seafloor some 125 million years ago forms the horizontal layers on the 300-foot-high twin buttes. Over the last ten million years, wind and water erosion attacked soft sediments between the overlook's rimrock pedestal and the buttes a mile to the east, chiseling these towering monuments from the soft rock. The Arikaree Formation, a layer of sandstone and conglomerate, makes an erosion-resistant cap atop the softer clay-like Brule Formation beneath. The area surrounding the buttes and overlook is a well-known fossil locale. As early as 1871 paleontologists came to dig fossil mammal skeletons dating from Miocene and Oligocene times, some thirty million years ago, in the area's deep arroyos and steep mesa slopes. The fossils here, similar to those in South Dakota's Badlands, include small hooved animals, giant megafauna such as the rhinoceros-like *Titanothere* and the clawed horse-like mammal *Chalicothere*, other ancestral horses, and turtles. The Denver

Museum of Natural History displays several mammal skeletons found here.

The Pawnee Buttes Trail, winding a mile and a half down from the trailhead to the base of the west butte, offers an excellent introduction to the grassland ecology. While much of the short grass prairie was altered by decades of overgrazing, much has returned and resembles the historic grassland that was once the hunting ground of the Pawnee Indians. Blue grama and buffalo grasses dominate the dry prairie, while taller grasses still flourish in moist ravines unreached by grazing cattle. Prickly pear cacti scatter in clumps along the trail and junipers cloak rocky hillsides. A stand of limber pines, probably a relic from wetter, glacial times, grows in Dave's Draw west of the buttes. The trail makes a good mountain bike excursion, although it's all uphill coming back.

The drive returns to County 112, which immediately bends south on County 111. The drive jogs around for the next few miles, following a single road that changes numbers almost every mile. After a mile, turn east on County 110 for another mile, north on County 113, and then east on County 110 1/2 for a mile. Turn south on County 115 and after a half-mile east again on County 110. The drive runs straight east, skirting rolling hills and dropping across dry swales. The Pawnee Buttes play hide-and-seek behind a broken bluff to the north for a few miles before the road breaks into the open on a broad valley edge. County 110 dead-ends into County 127 a few miles later. An abandoned homestead, surrounded by gangly elms, sits on the lonely corner. The drive turns south on County 127. The dirt road sweeps over the undulating landscape, dipping through Igo Creek's valley and climbing over sandstone rimrock. Scattered oil wells and windmills fringe the hillsides, and the buttes poke above the northwestern horizon. Deep grass and shallow pools of water fill South Pawnee Creek's lush valley before the track ascends a rise and reaches Raymer and CO 14.

Raymer is another one of those old homestead supply towns that prospered at the turn of the century. The town, platted by the Lincoln Land Company, named it for Burlington Railroad engineer George Raymer. The U.S. Post Office and Zip Code directory calls it New Raymer to avoid confusion with Ramah to the south, while the state highway map still calls it Raymer.

The drive turns east on paved CO 14 and traverses open grasslands and fenced farm fields. Stoneham, an 1888 railroad town, lies eleven miles from Raymer. Grain elevators, two churches, and a few houses mark this roadside hamlet. The drive leaves the Pawnee National Grassland almost five miles east of Stoneham and climbs over a low broken mesa called the Pawnee Hills. The road descends sharply through littered sandstone blocks to the broad Pawnee Valley. The sandy creekbed, lined with cottonwoods, winds southeast to the South Platte River. After gently climbing out of the valley, the highway enters farm fields irrigated by Platte water. Fields of corn and bright sunflowers border the blacktop. The road tilts downward, crosses the North Sterling Canal, and enters the 3,935-foot-high town of Sterling. This pleasant town, on the fertile South Platte River floodplain, is an agricultural hub. The town started as a post office on rancher David Leavitt's property in 1872. He named it for his Illinois home town. Sterling grew quickly a few years later after the Union Pacific Railroad pushed through to Denver. The Overland Trail Museum, just east of town by I-76, is a worthwhile stop. The museum interprets the trail's colorful history and displays artifacts including branding irons, horse-drawn farm machinery, and a stone duplicate of old Fort Sedgewick. The drive ends in Sterling. Continue east from town over the river to Exit 125 on I-76.

3 COMANCHE GRASSLAND DRIVE
Trinidad to Springfield

General description: This 192-mile-long drive explores the Comanche National Grassland and the scenic prairie and mesa country between Trinidad and Springfield.

Special attractions: Comanche National Grassland, Picture Canyon, Carrizo Picnic Ground, Mesa de Maya, short grass prairie ecosystems, birding, wildlife observation, hiking, camping, mountain biking.

Location: Southeastern Colorado. The drive begins just east of Trinidad and Interstate 25 at the junction of U.S. highways 350 and 160, and heads east on US 160 to Springfield. It turns south on U.S. 287/385 to Campo and heads west on a series of gravel county and grassland roads back to Kim and US 160.

Drive route numbers: U.S. Highway 160, U.S. Highway 287/385, Baca County roads J, 13, M, 8, P, 3, and Q, and Las Animas County roads 30.0, 211, 34.0, and 36.0.

Travel season: Year-round. The drive's gravel backroads between Campo and Kim can become impassable after heavy summer thunderstorms and when winter snow melts. Watch for thick mud and slippery roads. Inquire at the Springfield USDA Forest Service office for current road conditions.

Camping: No designated campgrounds are along the drive. Limited camping is permitted, however, at the parking areas at Carrizo Creek and Picture Canyon picnic grounds.

Services: All services are found in Trinidad and Springfield. Limited services are in Kim and Campo.

Nearby attractions: Corazon de Trinidad National Historic District, Trinidad State Recreation Area, San Isabel National Forest, Spanish Peaks, Santa Fe Trail, Purgatoire Canyon, El Capulin National Monument (New Mexico), Bents Fort National Historic Site.

For more information: Comanche National Grassland, P.O. Box 127, 27162 Hwy. 287, Springfield, CO 81073, (719) 523-6591. Springfield Town Hall, 748 Main, Springfield, CO 81073, (719) 523-4528.

The drive: The undulating plains stretch eastward across southeastern Colorado from the bold, snowy escarpment of the Culebra Range. The swelling land rolls with a lean musculature, lifting into rounded hills and low-browed mesas or breaking into sharp arroyos and sinuous hidden canyons. Out there on the tawny prairie lies the land of the flattened horizon, the land of the rising sun. It's a minimalist landscape. Everything is spare and lean, stripped of its veneer and laid bare under the blazing sun. Brittle grasses huddle in wind-swept clumps, prickly pear cacti clench together like tightly closed fists, and cottonwoods rustle along intermittent creeks. Under the yawning sprawl of sky and space, the prairie is reduced to simple forms— straight-arrow horizons, roads bordered by three strands of barbed wire that recede into the distance, and flat-topped tablelands, their sloped edges fringed in juniper, that bump against the azure sky like worn pillows. The 192-mile-long Comanche Grassland scenic drive explores this remote quarter of Colorado, crossing sun-baked prairie, dipping through shallow canyons, and finding its secret places.

Southeast Colorado is an arid land, with chilly winters and hot summers. Annual precipitation is low, bordering on desert amounts in some areas. The Springfield area receives fifteen inches of rain annually. Much of the precipitation comes in intense summer thunderstorms, with the swift runoff flooding down arroyos and canyons. Gravel backroads on the drive during or after thunderstorms can become muddy and impassable. Summers are hot. Expect daily highs in the nineties and above. Autumn and spring are more reasonable times to drive the roads. Temperatures range between sixty

A lonely windmill and homestead ruin breaks the monotony of rolling plains on the Comanche Grassland Drive.

and ninety degrees. Wind often tempers spring days. Winters are cool and dry, with occasional heavy snowstorms that quickly melt. High temperatures range from thirty to sixty degrees with cold nights. Use caution when driving the gravel backroads in winter. Blizzard conditions arise during swift-moving storms and melting snow and ice can turn gravel into impassable mud.

The drive begins five miles east of Trinidad at Beshoar Junction at the intersection of U.S. highways 350 and 160. Turn east on US 160. Springfield, the end of the drive's first leg, lies 114 miles away. The vanished town of Beshoar, named for an early Trinidad resident, sat here along the Colorado and Southern Railroad at the turn of the century. The paved highway runs east through low hills. Occasional pastures, hayfields, and ranch houses border the blacktop. Fishers Peak and Raton Mesa, dark with evergreen forest, form a broad escarpment to the south. This long, high mesa, reaching heights of 9,500 feet, is capped by eleven layers of erosion-resistant lava. After six miles the highway swings southeast past the Mooney Hills, a low, rounded mesa etched with arroyos. Three miles later the road sweeps past the hills and across a broad basin seamed with Frijole Creek, an intermittent stream arising on the mesa flank to the south. Mesa de Maya huddles darkly on the eastern horizon.

The road winds over Frijole Creek, a tamarisk-lined thread of muddy water in a brown clay arroyo, and parallels the Purgatoire River for a few miles. The 150-mile-long Purgatoire River courses across southeastern Colorado from its birthplace high on the crest of the Culebra Range west of Trinidad. The river keeps the French spelling of its name, a reminder of the itinerant fur trappers that traversed this wild country 150 years ago. The river's original name—*El Rio de Las Animas Perdidas en Purgatorio* or River of Lost Souls in Purgatory—was acquired after the members of a sixteenth century Spanish expedition, murdered by Indians on the river bank, died without the last rites of their Catholic faith. Cowboys later corrupted the Spanish to "Picketwire," a name applied to the river's forty-mile-long canyon that slices across the prairie north of the drive. The river twists through low hills, passing occasional cottonwoods on its banks, a half-mile north of the highway. After a couple miles the river bends northeast and enters Picketwire Canyon through abrupt portals of Dakota sandstone. A pinyon pine and juniper woodland fills the canyon and spills onto the rim.

The highway ascends a gradual rise onto a broad barren plain. It dips across Salt Creek's shallow valley at nineteen miles, passing black sandstone boulders mirrored in pools of clear water. Trinchera Creek, draining north to the Purgatoire like the other creeks here, lies a couple miles farther east; it's a deep canyon sharp with cliffs and coated by sparsely spaced junipers. The road climbs northeast onto a high tableland, with expansive views back west to the long ridge of the Culebra Range and the twin Spanish Peaks to the northwest. After crossing Trementina Creek, another canyon filled with cliffs, water, and thick grass, the highway ascends through a juniper forest and reaches its junction with Colorado Highway 389 at a place dubbed Walt's Corner. A store, surrounded by marvelous views and a few trees, sits at this lonely intersection on a rolling grass plain.

The dark bulk of Mesa de Maya dominates the highway view as it runs east. Cliffs of basalt deposited as lava flows cap the high flat-topped mesa and a forest of juniper and pinyon pine spills over its ragged flanks. No roads traverse this mostly wild upland, the home of mule deer, coyotes, and range cattle. Early Indians inhabited the mesa and the canyons along the drive beginning some six thousand years ago. Traces of their passage include rock art panels pecked onto smooth rock slabs, projectile points and stone tools, broken pottery shards, and manos used for grinding seeds. Meadows of tall buffalo and grama grass blanketed the mesa top and its shallow valleys over one hundred years ago, attracting cattlemen to its lush pastures in this land of little rain in the 1870s.

The highway runs over undulating plains before dropping into abrupt Chacuaco Canyon. Chacuaco Creek, rising from mesas on the New Mexico state line to the south, excavated this long cliff-lined gorge. Water trickles through the wild canyon almost all year, creating a haven for mammals and birds. The asphalt climbs out of the canyon onto another dry plain and arches northeast around Mesa de Maya. The road dips through several dry, rocky canyons that drain north from the mesa. A ghost village of abandoned stone houses sits on a canyon rim below the mesa, cattle poking through their empty rooms. Distant views unfold west from here. Rows of mountains—the Culebra Range, Spanish Peaks, Raton Mesa, Sierra Blanca, and the Wet Mountains—parade across the horizon, their snow-capped summits gleaming in the sun like white-washed castles.

The highway enters the 435,000-acre Comanche National Grassland, a sprawling spread of land managed by the USDA Forest Service and divided into the Timpas Unit south of La Junta and the Carrizo Unit along the scenic drive. The story of the national grassland began in 1884 when Baca County's first homestead patent was granted. Thousands of homestead patents in southeast Colorado were issued between 1884 and 1926 with the homesteaders required to plow forty acres of each 160-acre homestead. The homesteader's plow, along with farming marginal agricultural lands and severe overgrazing in this semi-arid region, caused the Dust Bowl of the early 1930s here and in neighboring states. The federal government began buying back damaged farms and ranches, retiring the land from cultivation, and allowing families to relocate in other areas. Over eleven million acres were acquired and rehabilitated with four million acres designated as national grassland in 1960 and assigned to the Forest Service. Crumbling stone homesteads, abandoned windmills, and empty crossroads stores are all that remain of Colorado's homestead era on today's Comanche grassland.

The highway bends straight east after entering the grassland. The ruins of Tobe sit in the field to the north. The town, established in 1910 and named for resident Tobe Benavides, was more of a post office than a town. When the filling station-post office closed doors in 1960, Tobe folded. The only remnants now are stone foundations scattered among grass and cacti.

The long, low rim of Mesa de Maya looms south of the road as it runs due east across a featureless plain coated with short grasses. Six miles from Tobe the drive passes low-browed 6,296-foot-high Fallas Mesa, a barren escarp-

The Culebra Range towers over US 160 and the Comanche Grassland Drive.

ment riddled with ravines. Dalerose Mesa, broken by canyons and cliffs, lies further south, while broad Tecolate Mesa sits to the southeast. The drive turns north at sixty-five miles and enters Kim a mile later.

Kim, named for Rudyard Kipling's orphan boy hero, was established in 1918 by Olin D. Simpson when he built a general store and post office on the corner of his homestead. The 5,690-foot-high town now serves as a ranching and agricultural center. Frame houses line neat side streets, cattle graze on the edge of town, and a cemetery makes a final resting place. The town offers an RV park, cafe, the Trail's End Bar, gas, and groceries. Picnic tables sit in a roadside park. The drive runs north and swings east after a couple miles. CO 109 intersects the drive here and continues north to La Junta.

The highway travels fifty miles from here to Springfield, passing over a mixture of federal and private land. This is flat, dry country, broken by fences and occasional irrigated fields. Pritchett, the only real town along this section, sits thirty-six miles east of Kim. The town rises out of the plain like a mirage, its skyline of trees and housetops dominated by three towering grain elevators. Boarded-up shops line the main street, a reminder of more prosperous times. The town, established in 1920, marked the western end of an Atchison, Topeka & Santa Fe Railroad branch. It was named for railway director Dr. Henry Pritchett. The highway goes east from Pritchett past farms and ranches and reaches US 287 fourteen miles later. A roadside picnic area sits at the junction. Springfield lies a mile to the north.

Springfield looms above the endless prairie like Pritchett. Grain elevators again form the highest point for miles around. Elms, maples, and cottonwoods shade the town streets. Springfield, the seat of Baca County, was established in 1887 by the Windsor Town Company and named for townsite owner Andrew Harrison's hometown of Springfield, Missouri. The town has since flourished as an agricultural hub. A National Forest office, lying just north of the highway intersection, dispenses information and directions to points of interest on the Comanche grassland.

The journey's next leg runs south twenty miles from Springfield to Campo on US 287/385. The road crosses a high plain divided into farms and ranches. A clutch of houses huddle along the highway in Campo, an old farming community aptly named with the Spanish word for "field." For the drive's last leg, turn west on Baca County J at the drugstore in Campo. The road bumps across railroad tracks, passes a grain elevator, and turns to gravel. The drive's last fifty-three miles follow numerous gravel backroads over the grassland to Kim and US 160. The dusty road courses west past farms, fields, pastures, cattle, and windmills. Baca County 18 intersects County J after ten miles. Turn south for a side trip to Picture Canyon, one of southeastern Colorado's hidden treasures.

Follow County 18 south for five miles and turn right down a marked lane into upper Picture Canyon. The road winds down the broad canyon and after a couple miles reaches the road's end. A picnic area with three covered tables spreads along the base of tall sandstone cliffs. A 2.6-mile hiking trail, following an old road, drops down the canyon. Ragged cliffs, forming abrupt canyon walls, are broken by side ravines and eroded into promontories, buttresses, and aretes. After 0.5 mile the canyon makes a sharp bend west. Pools of water surrounded by tall grass and cottonwoods spread along the creekbed. A couple panels of Indian petroglyphs, marred by modern

A ranch gate along the Comanche Grassland Drive in southeastern Colorado.

vandalism, sit along the shaded cliff base. The Picture Canyon trail continues north up a side-canyon, scales its slope onto a low mesa, and heads west to a spur of Holt Canyon and a natural arch. The trail wends east and drops through Hell's Half Acre back to Picture Canyon. Watch for rattlesnakes in the grass and on the rocky canyon sides when hiking.

Picture Canyon, along with other southeast Colorado canyons, has long attracted settlers. Early Indians found shelter in shallow caves, harvested the area's diverse plants, and hunted game. Indian campsites from the Late Archaic Period from A.D. 0 to 500 scatter under the canyon's overhanging shelters. Later inhabitants, the Apishapa culture, lived here after A.D. 1000, planting crops on the moist canyon floor and building small villages atop the canyon rims. The rock art that gave the canyon its name probably came from nomadic plains tribes like the Apaches and Comanches in historic times.

Clues to one of Colorado archeology's most puzzling mysteries sits on the canyon's west side south of the bend. Here, etched onto the soft sandstone wall, is a series of vertical lines incised into the rock. Some epigraphers or ancient language scholars say the lines are Ogam, a type of Celtic writing used as long ago as 2000 B.C. in the British Isles. This strange writing is found at over fifty sites in southeastern Colorado and the Oklahoma panhandle. Some of the translated writings include compasses, sun dials, traveler's messages and directions, and information about the area's latitude, equinoxes, and planting seasons. Irish monks traveled to Iceland, eastern Canada, and even Mexico over a thousand years ago, lending some credence to the idea that early Celtic wanderers roamed across this vastness. Most archeologists, however, are skeptical about the Celtic influence, saying not enough evidence exists to substantiate the theory. And so the Ogam remains a tantalizing unsolved mystery.

Head back north to Baca County J and continue west on it. The rest of the drive crosses undulating grassland, broken by shallow ravines, windmills, and occasional cottonwood-lined watercourses. After five miles turn north on County 13 and in three miles turn west on Baca County M. This runs west five miles to Baca County 8. At this lonely intersection sits the old Kirkwell Post Office, now used for storage by the Kirkwell Cattle Company. The post office operated from 1917 to 1921. Turn north on County 8 and after a couple miles head west on Baca County P. Carrizo Mesa, a low-slung tableland rimmed by shattered basalt cliffs, sits to the west. Canyons dark with junipers and pinyon pine slice into the mesa and Potato Butte forms a sharp summit atop the flat mesa. Baca County P dead ends against Baca County 3 above Carrizo Creek. Turn north on County 3 for a 0.5 mile and then west on Baca County Q.

County Q twists over a low ridge and dips down alongside Carrizo Creek in a wide valley. Rounded hills studded with juniper and cliff bands line the creek. Immense cottonwoods shade the trickle of water. Cottonwoods are the tree of the plains. These tall, broad-trunked trees, growing along creeks, signified water, shade, and firewood to early pioneers and Indians. Indian children made toy tepees with the wide triangular leaves and the sweet inner bark was used as winter horse feed. Cottonwood bark also yielded medicinal uses, particularly for upset stomach from bad water—an occupational hazard cowboys called the "gypwater quickstep." Nineteenth-century cattle baron Charles Goodnight, whose empire stretched into southeastern Colorado, called the bark tea "a hell of a drink, a wonderful astringent, and a bitter dose. But it is a sure shot."

The drive wends up along the creek's arroyo and passes a ranch house and barn shaded by huge cottonwood trees. The road bends northwest, edging along below Carrizo Mesa. It becomes a single-lane track for a couple miles before joining improved Las Animas County 30.0. This narrow road rolls west from the mesa over prairie toward Tecolate Mesa. This mesa, also rimmed with cliffs, stretches darkly on the west horizon. County 30.0 ends and bends north on Las Animas County 211. The drive jogs north and west for ten miles, following County 211 past Pintada Creek's bouldery valley and over broad dry ridges to Kim. The drive ends back on US 160 at Kim's cemetery. A left turn heads sixty-five miles back to Trinidad and I-25, while a right turn goes to Springfield via US 160 or La Junta on CO 109.

4	# HIGHWAY OF LEGENDS
	Walsenburg to Trinidad

General description: The Highway of Legends scenic drive forms an 82-mile-long open loop between Walsenburg and Trinidad on the eastern slope of the Culebra Range.

Special attractions: Lathrop State Park, La Veta, Fort Francisco Museum, Great Dikes of the Spanish Peaks, Spanish Peaks Wilderness Area, Cucharas Pass, Culebra Range, Cordova Pass, Monument Lake, Stonewall, Picketwire Valley, Cokedale National Historic District, Trinidad State Recreation Area, Trinidad historic sites, camping, fishing, hiking, scenic views.

Location: South-central Colorado. The drive begins in Walsenburg, off Interstate 25, runs west on U.S. Highway 160 and south on Colorado Highway 12 to La Veta. The byway continues on CO 12 to Trinidad and I-25.

Drive route name and numbers: Scenic Highway of Legends, US 160, CO 12.

Travel season: Year-round.

Camping: Four San Isabel National Forest campgrounds—Cuchara, Blue Lake, Bear Lake, and Purgatoire—lie just off the drive. Lathrop State Park has a 98-site campground, while Trinidad State Recreation Area offers a spacious 62-site campground on the lake's north shore. The Monument Lake Campground is owned and operated by the city of Trinidad.

Services: All services are found in Walsenburg, La Veta, and Trinidad. Limited services are in Stonewall and Cuchara.

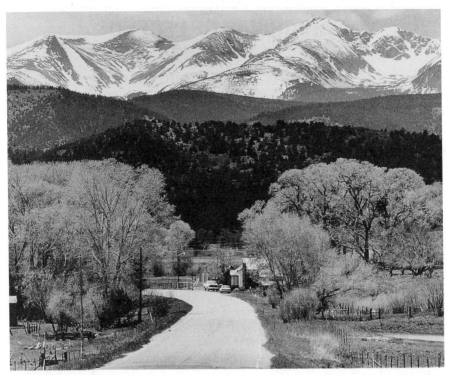

Culebra Peak, the high point of the Culebra Range, looms above cottonwoods in Stonewall Valley along the Highway of Legends.

Nearby attractions: Santa Fe Trail Scenic Drive, Wet Mountain Valley, Comanche National Grassland, Capulin National Monument, San Luis Valley, Great Sand Dunes National Monument, Wet Mountain Scenic Drive, Graneros Gorge.

For more information: San Isabel National Forest, 1920 Valley Dr., Pueblo, CO 81008, (719) 545-8737. La Veta/Cuchara Chamber, P.O. Box 32, La Veta, CO 81055, (719) 742-3676. Trinidad Chamber, 309 Nevada St., Trinidad, CO 81082, (719) 846-9285.

The drive: The eighty-two-mile-long Highway of Legends scenic drive skirts the wooded eastern flank of the Culebra Range in southern Colorado. The twisting crest of the Culebras imposes a lofty barrier between the sweep of prairie to the east and the San Luis Valley, a broad intermontane basin, to the west. The range, even still untraversed by any roads, is mostly private land, the remaining legacy of sprawling early Spanish land grants. The area's numerous Spanish place names also linger on the land. Culebra, the Spanish word for "snake," was first applied to a creek on the range's western slope, and later given to the mountain range. The scenic drive, beginning in Walsenburg, ascends the fertile Cuchara Valley to the 9,941-foot summit of Cuchara Pass before dropping south through forests and meadows on the range flank to the Purgatoire River's broad valley west of Trinidad.

•Denver

COLORADO

★

To Pueblo

To La Junta

160

Walsenburg   River

Mt. Maestas
11,569 ft.

To Alamosa

160   Cucharas

La Veta

Geommer Butte
8,043 ft.

12

SAN ISABEL
NATIONAL
FOREST

Napoleon Pk.
11,866 ft.

West Spanish
Pk. 13,626 ft.

East Spanish
Pk. 12,683 ft.

Aguilar

Cordova Pass
11,743 ft.

Bear
Lake CG

Blue
Lake
CG

Cuchara
CG

Cucharas Pass
9,941 ft.

415

25

Trinchera Pk.
13,517 ft.

12

North Lake

Monument Lake

Beaubien Pk.
13,182 ft.

Trinidad

To
La Junta

Stonewall

PICKETWIRE

Purgatoire   River

VALLEY

12

TRINIDAD STATE
RECREATION AREA

Culebra Pk.
14,069 ft.

N

0   2   4   6   8   10
Miles

To Raton

The highway is open year-round, with each season lending a distinctive flavor to the drive experience. Summers are pleasant, with high temperatures ranging from seventy to ninety degrees along the drive. Afternoon thunderstorms regularly build above the mountains, dousing the road with heavy rain and hail. September and October, the autumn months, bring warm days and cool nights. Expect golden aspen groves in late September and occasional rain showers through October. Temperatures can be hot on the drive's lower elevations. Winter days are chilly, with highs in the thirties and forties. Snow falls heavily in the upper Cuchara valley and on the pass. The lesser amounts in the low valleys quickly melt under the warm winter sun. Spring begins in April with warming days and melting snow. Look for breezy afternoons and rain or sleet storms.

The Highway of Legends, a national forest scenic byway, begins in Walsenburg just off I-25. The town is nestled in the Cucharas River's broad valley amid dusty, pinyon pine-covered hills. Walsenburg began in 1859 as an early Mexican hamlet named *La Plaza de los Leones* or Square of the Lions for prominent early settler Don Miguel Antonio Leon. When the pueblo incorporated in 1873, citizens renamed it for local shopkeeper Fred Walsen. After the Denver & Rio Grande Railroad pushed through in 1876, Walsenburg boomed as one of Colorado's largest coal producers. The remains of over fifty mines still litter the area. Town points of interest include the historic Huerfano County Courthouse built with limestone blocks in 1904, and the nearby Walsenburg Mining Museum with exhibits detailing the coal miner's life and the replica of a mine shaft.

The drive begins in downtown Walsenburg. Head west on US 160, the Navajo Trail. After passing houses, and the town park and swimming pool, the highway swings past slag heaps and abandoned mining ruins. The road crosses the Cucharas River, climbs a steep hill, and after three miles reaches Lathrop State Park. This small state park, with 1,050 land acres and 320 water acres in Martin and Horseshoe lakes, offers ninety-eight sites in Pinon and Yucca campgrounds, picnic facilities, a nine-hole golf course leased to Walsenburg, boating, swimming, and fishing. The lakes yield trout, crappie, bass, channel catfish, and perch to anglers. A hiking trail loops north from Martin Lake for almost two miles, climbing onto a scrubby volcanic hogback. Gnarled junipers spring from the bedrock amid barrel cacti, yucca, and rabbitbrush. Distant views unfold along the ridgeline—Pikes Peak, almost one hundred miles to the north, lifts its broad shoulders beyond the Wet Mountains; the barren prairie sweeps eastward to a Kansas horizon; and to the south looms the Spanish Peaks.

The highway runs west from Lathrop along the northern edge of the broad Cuchara Valley. Low hills, coated with a pygmy forest of pinyon pine and juniper, flank the road on the north, while the wide valley stretches south to forested foothills below the Spanish Peaks. Open rangelands, broken only by fence lines and a twisting grove of cottonwoods along the river banks, fill the valley floor. Perennial blue grama and needle-and-thread grasses sod the spacious pastures, while shrubby saltbush, snakeweed, and rabbitbrush cover the drier slopes. A small roadside Catholic shrine, with a statue of the

Virgin Mary and many votive candles, tucks into a sandstone alcove at six miles. The drive turns southwest onto CO 12 a few miles further west. US 160 continues over La Veta Pass to the San Luis Valley.

CO 12 follows an undulating grassy bench sprinkled with ranches and grazing cattle above the Cucharas River. The Spanish Peaks continue to dominate the southern skyline. The higher west peak reaches 13,626 feet while the east peak tops 12,683 feet. These jutting twin peaks were conspicuous landmarks to travelers on the great plains. Early explorers often confused the Spanish Peaks with Pikes Peak far to the north. Jacob Fowler noted them in 1821, "We Head a full view of the mountains, this must be the place Whare Pike first discovered the mountains Heare I took the bareing of two that ware the Highest." Indians, Spaniards, French trappers, and Santa Fe Trail traders called them a host of names—Pikes Peak, Las Cumbres Espanoles, Las Dos Hermanas, The Two Sisters, Les Tetons, Les Mamelles, and Wahatoyeh or Huajatolla. *Wahatoyeh*, a Pueblo Indian word still used, loosely translates as "Breasts of the World." Mr. Sporleder, a turn-of-the-century La Veta writer, sang the praises of the peaks: "The physical beauty of these two peaks is perfect when seen from the plains, glorious and sublime when East Huajatolla alone is viewed from the head of Sunrise Valley. Other Peaks in the Rocky Mountains may be higher, but most of them lose in magnificence and grandeur...."

After four miles the blacktop drops down to the river bottomlands and a mile later enters the town of La Veta. This lovely village spreads among ranch land at the foot of the Spanish Peaks. The town was originally established as a trading post and fort by Colonel John Francisco and Henry Daigre in 1862. A post office opened at the site, known as Francisco Plaza, in 1871 and when the Denver & Rio Grande Railroad came through in 1876 the town of La Veta arose. The name means "the vein" in Spanish and probably refers to the numerous volcanic dikes slicing across the Spanish Peaks. The Fort Francisco Museum, now operated by the Huerfano County Historical Society at the original site, makes an informative stop in downtown La Veta. The museum displays coal mining equipment, an old saloon, barbershop with poker-playing dummies, medical office, blacksmith shop, as well as an excellent collection of historical documents and letters including an 1853 letter by practicing attorney Abraham Lincoln and Kit Carson's will. La Veta offers a variety of visitor accommodations and a couple restaurants.

The drive leaves La Veta on the south and runs along the Cucharas River. Goemmer Butte, an 8,043-foot-high volcanic plug or conduit of a long-extinct volcano, rears to the west. Its cliffed summit rises five hundred feet above the valley floor. The road descends into the grassy valley, crosses the river at Three Bridges, and swings southwest below scrub oak-covered slopes. Six miles from La Veta the highway passes under Devil's Stairsteps, an abrupt volcanic rock dike that stairsteps south from the highway. This dike, as well as prominent Profile Rock to the east and other rock walls, are part of the Spanish Peaks' great dike system. The buff-colored igneous rock dikes formed, along with the Spanish Peaks, some 35 million years ago. During that period of geologic unrest when the Rocky Mountains began to rise, two blisters of molten rock pushed their way upward, buckling the sedimentary surface layers. As the strata bulged, long cracks radiated out from the molten blisters like spokes on a bicycle wheel. Liquid magma filled the cracks before the entire mass slowly cooled into classic volcanic rocks like the granite and granodorite that compose the Spanish Peaks. Erosion later attacked the old sedimentary layers and exposed the harder, more erosion-resistant igneous rocks, leaving the page of geologic history seen today. Photographs of these long dikes, considered by geologists to be one of the world's best examples of this unique earth feature, are found in geology textbooks worldwide. Over four hundred separate dikes fan out from the peaks, with the longest stretching fourteen miles. The dikes range up to one hundred feet high and vary in width from one foot to one hundred feet.

As the highway runs west the valley slowly narrows with high ridges looming overhead. The snow-capped Culebra Range towers to the west. After a few miles the road passes through a gap cut through the Dakota Wall, a sandstone hogback that stretches along the Front Range from Wyoming to New Mexico. The highway roughly follows the hogback from here to Stonewall. New Mexican locust trees, Colorado's only native locust, line the asphalt and offer colorful pink blossoms in early summer. The road enters San Isabel National Forest and a couple miles later rolls into 8,650-foot Cuchara.

Cuchara, established in 1916, is something of a ghost town today. The village sits near the head of a spectacular valley, surrounded by thick forests of spruce, pine, and fir. This spoon-shaped valley gave the Spanish name *Cuchara* or "spoon" to the town, river, and valley. Cuchara thrived in the 1980s until the savings-and-loan scandal, and the local ski resort closed. Much of the town folded up with the resort, leaving only a few cafes and lodges. Vacation cabins sprinkle through the valley around Cuchara. Spring Creek Picnic Area lies on the south side of Cuchara.

The drive steadily climbs the valley south of Cuchara and after a couple miles reaches Forest Road 413. This short dirt road climbs west along the Cucharas River to a pair of forest-lined lakes cupped in a basin beneath the Culebra Range crest. Cuchara Campground sits a quarter-mile up the road, and fifteen-site Blue Lake and fourteen-site Bear Lake campgrounds lie at road's end beside their respective lakes. An excellent two-mile trail climbs south from the spruce and fir forest at 10,500-foot Blue Lake to the alpine tundra atop the rounded summit of 13,517-foot Trinchera Peak.

The highway twists up steep aspen-blanketed slopes above the South Fork of the Cucharas River and reaches 9,941-foot Cucharas Pass. The dense forest along this drive section yields a great example of plant succession. The thick transitional aspen woodland is slowly being replaced by a climax spruce-fir forest. Autumn is gorgeous along here, with dark spruce sprinkled among golden groves of quaking aspen. Meadows, surrounded by dark woods, surround the highway and a stock corral on the broad pass summit. Henry Daigre, one of La Veta's founders, built a road from La Veta to Stonewall along an old Indian path in 1865. Today's highway follows his old track over the pass, but it wasn't paved until the 1960s.

The west Spanish Peak looms over the Devil's Backbone, a volcanic dike along the Highway of Legends.

Forest Road 415 threads six miles east from here to 11,743-foot Cordova Pass and then drops twenty-nine miles down the Apishapa River to Aguilar and I-25. A scenic trail leaves Cordova Pass's summit and meanders through grassy meadows and woods of lodgepole pine and Englemann spruce on a subalpine ridge to a timberline lookout below West Spanish Peak. Intrepid hikers can continue up the west ridge another mile to the peak's summit and its grandiose view.

The wild Spanish Peaks host an improbable fable of a lost gold mine. The legend originates with Coronado's 1541 trek across southeastern Colorado in search of mythical Quivara. Three priests were left behind to convert the natives, and two died at their hands as martyrs. The third, Fray Juan de la Cruz, journeyed to Huajatolla after hearing of wealthy Indian mines there. He found the gold, enslaved Indians to remove it from the hidden passages, and journeyed south to Mexico with gold-laden mules. The priest and his treasure, however, disappeared, never to be seen again. Persistent rumors of the lost Spanish gold echoed across southern Colorado for the next three centuries, but no trace of the gold or the fabulous mine was ever uncovered. Indeed, no geologic evidence suggests that the Spanish Peaks or its immediate neighbors ever yielded any precious metals.

The highway runs south from the pass along the Culebra Range's eastern flank, traversing rolling hills and dipping through shallow valleys. A variety of ecosystems cover the hillsides, with mixed fir and spruce forest blanketing the moist, north-facing slopes and ponderosa and limber pines and Gambel oak covering the drier south-facing hills. Open aspen-lined meadows break the woodland mosaic. The road horseshoes around North Lake, a state wildlife area and reservoir, seven miles from the pass. Peaks of the Culebra Range—13,488-foot Cuatro Peak, 13,406-foot Mariquita Peak, and 13,350-foot De Anza Peak—lift snowy ridges to the west. The Dakota Hogback forms an abrupt wall above the lake and highway. North Lake, with a boat ramp at its north end, offers fishing and boating.

Just past the lake, Forest Road 411 heads 4.5 miles west up the North Fork of the Purgatoire River to twenty-three-site Purgatoire Campground. This pleasant camping area tucks into a valley filled with spruce, corkbark fir, and quaking aspen at the foot of the Culebras. Monument Lake lies in a shallow valley a mile farther south. A turn at the southern end of the narrow mile-long reservoir leads to Monument Lake Campground, operated by the city of Trinidad. This popular recreation area offers camping, an adobe lodge, a restaurant, trout fishing, boating, and hiking. The drive continues south, crossing Whiskey and Romain creeks before dropping down Wilkins Creek to Stonewall and the upper Purgatoire River canyon.

Stonewall, at 7,460 feet, is a quiet ranching and vacation village settled in 1867 by early rancher Juan Guitterez. The town is, of course, named for an immense stone wall of Dakota sandstone. This tilted hogback, part of the Dakota Hogback seen near La Veta, was deposited along ancient beaches some seventy-million years ago during the Cretaceous Period. The formation, widespread over much of Colorado, was later uplifted during the rise of the Rocky Mountains. Culebra Peak, the range high point at 14,037-feet, forms Stonewall's western skyline. The highway, upon entering Stonewall, swings past a cliff and passes through a gap that breaches the sandstone escarpment.

The drive turns east at Stonewall and enters Stonewall Valley and then Picketwire Valley, a broad swale carved by the Purgatoire River. The term Picketwire is a bastardized version of the river's French name Purgatoire. Spanish first named the muddy river *El Rio de las Animas Perdidas en Purgatorio* or "River of the Lost Souls in Purgatory." The 150-mile-long Purgatoire, originating on the Culebra divide west of Stonewall, twists east and northeast onto the prairie before merging with the Arkansas River near Las Animas. The drive's thirty-mile leg from Stonewall to Trinidad crosses dusty plateau country. Low rock-rimmed mesas, creased with shallow canyons and dry arroyos, loom above the valley.

The highway quickly leaves Stonewall, passing clumps of towering cottonwoods and flat grassy pastures, and enters Stonewall Canyon. Pete Hills flanks the canyon on the north while Ute Hills lift rounded humps to the south. The river loops in broad meanders across the flat valley floor. Narrow-leaf cottonwood, box elder, chokecherry, and willow crowd the river banks. The highway runs east along the river's north shore. New Elk and Golden Eagle mines, originally owned by CF & I steel, now dig coal for Wyoming Fuels Corp. The hills become drier as the road heads east, with pinyon pine and juniper forest and small shrubs including mountain mahogany, skunkbush, rabbitbrush, and Gambel oak, and blue grama grass scattered across the boulder-strewn slopes.

The drive passes through a succession of old Hispanic villages and homesteads. Vigil Plaza lies five miles east of Stonewall. Weston, first called Los Sisneros, started as an 1880s ranch and was later renamed for pioneer farmer Sam Weston. An adobe structure on the town's east side is part of the original Sisneros Ranch. Farther east are the ruins of Cordova, Medina, and Valasquez plazas and San Juan, all old family communities. Segundo, a mostly abandoned town of old stone buildings and low-slung adobe houses, sits along the river. Valdez sits a mile east. It headquartered the Frederick Mine, which, with over thirty miles of tunnels, was one of Colorado's largest underground mines until it closed in 1960. Huge piles of red mine tailings are heaped alongside the road.

A few miles east of Valdez, the highway turns north from Picketwire Valley and climbs through low hills to Reilly Canyon and Cokedale National Historic District. Cokedale, spread over hillsides amid colored tailings, was established in 1906 as a company town by the Carbon Coal and Coke Company. Numerous historic homes and buildings scatter through the hamlet, and lines of coke ovens lie south of the highway. Coke, a refined form of coal that burns hotter, was shipped from the town ovens to Leadville and other smelters.

The drive climbs through low hills and drops past Trinidad State Recreation Area. The park's centerpiece is a nine hundred-acre, three-mile-long reservoir built for irrigation and flood control. A wealth of archeological sites scatter through the recreation area and Picketwire Canyon. A tepee ring, a circle of stones that once surrounded a nomad's tent, sit at Carpios Ridge Picnic Area. Forty-eight archeological sites lie beneath the lake and on surrounding ridges, while six mining towns lie submerged under the lake's green waters. The reservoir offers great fishing, as well as boating, water-skiing, board-sailing, and camping.

Trinidad, the drive's end, lies three miles east of the reservoir. The highway drops back into the Purgatoire's valley, and passes through Jansen, a town that was the eastern terminus of the Colorado & Wyoming Railroad during the area's mining heyday. Trinidad, one of Colorado's oldest and most historic communities, sits at the foot of Raton Pass. The town sprang up as a stop on the Mountain Branch of the old Santa Fe Trail. Wagon trains could rest here before climbing over the steep, rough pass into New Mexico. Gabriel Gutierrez, the town's first settler, built a cabin on the river's south bank in 1859. The town later flourished as a ranching and transportation center fueled by years of prosperous coal mining. The town, protected as El Corazon del Trinidad National Historic District, boasts several excellent historic sites including the Baca and Bloom houses and Pioneer Museum. Trinidad offers all visitor services and is the gateway to the Comanche National Grassland to the east.

5

SANGRE DE CRISTO DRIVE
Canon City to Walsenburg

General description: This 86-mile-long highway runs south along Texas Creek from the Arkansas River into the Wet Mountain Valley and the historic town of Westcliffe. The drive, bordering the rugged Sangre de Cristo Mountains, continues south into the broad sagebrush-covered Huerfano River valley before ending at Walsenburg.

Special attractions: Arkansas River, McIntyre Hills Wilderness Study Area, Wet Mountain Valley, Westcliffe, Silver Cliff, Sangre de Cristo Mountains, ghost towns, Huerfano River Valley, Walsenburg, scenic views, fishing, hiking, wildlife.

Location: South-central Colorado. The highway runs from U.S. Highway 50 and the Arkansas River 26 miles west of Canon City southeast to Walsenburg and Interstate 25.

Drive route number: Colorado Highway 69.

Travel season: Year-round. Severe winter storms and blizzards can temporarily close the highway. It's advisable to carry chains and a shovel if the weather is threatening.

Camping: No public campgrounds lie along the highway itself. Numerous campgrounds are found in the surrounding San Isabel National Forest, including Lake Creek Campground west of Hillside and Alvarado Campground southwest of Westcliffe. Other forest campgrounds are found in the Wet Mountains. Public camping is at Lake de Weese and primitive camp areas are found in the national forest.

Services: All services are found in Westcliffe and Walsenburg. Limited services in Texas Creek, Hillside, and Gardner.

Nearby attractions: South Colony Lakes, Crestone Peak and Needle, Hermit Pass, Arkansas River State Recreation Area, Grape Creek Wilderness Study Area, Canon City, Temple Canon, Hardscrabble Pass, Marble Cave, Sierra Blanca, Medano Pass, Highway of Legends Scenic Drive, Great Sand Dunes National Monument.

For more information: Custer County Chamber of Commerce, P.O. Box 81, Westcliffe, CO 81252, (719) 783-9163. San Isabel National Forest, 1920 Valley Drive, Pueblo, CO 81008, (719) 545-8737.

The drive: CO 69 rolls down the broad Wet Mountain and Huerfano River valleys for eighty-six miles from the Arkansas River to Walsenburg on the western rim of the Great Plains. The excellent route, flanked by the lofty Sangre de Cristo Mountains on the west and the swelling Wet Mountains on the east, travels an unpopulated land rich in spectacular views, lush with verdant grasslands and pastures, and alive with early Spanish and mining history. The highway is a friendly backroad, used mostly by locals who salute on-coming traffic with a wave.

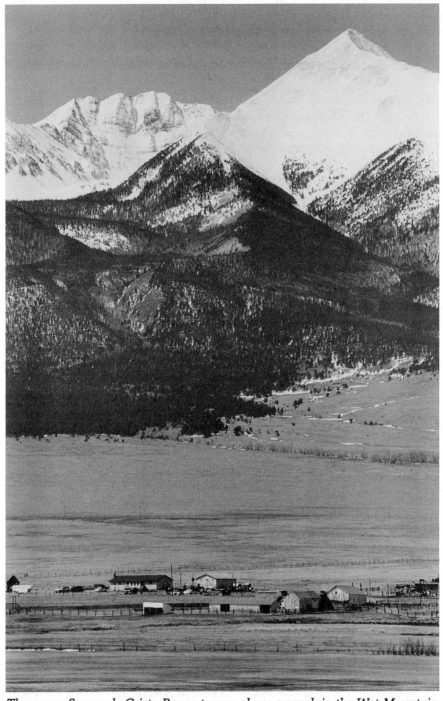

The snowy Sangre de Cristo Range towers above a ranch in the Wet Mountain Valley.

The Sangre de Cristo Mountains, one of the longest ranges in the Rocky Mountains, stretches over 150 miles from Salida to Santa Fe in New Mexico. The sierra's mid-section in southern Colorado is called the Culebra Range. Above the scenic drive and the Wet Mountain Valley, the Sangre de Cristos form an awesome escarpment of sawtoothed peaks that soar into the azure sky. Four 14,000-foot peaks—Crestone Needle, Crestone Peak, Humboldt Peak, and Kit Carson Peak—cluster along the skyline southwest of Westcliffe. Sierra Blanca, an abrupt massif containing another four fourteeners, sits further south. Although the Sangres are only twenty miles wide, no highways cross its rugged crest. The few passable gaps, including Medano, Mosca, and Hermit passes, have been well-traveled routes for centuries. The range supposedly recieved its Spanish name Sangre de Cristo or "Blood of Christ" from the Spanish explorer Valverde, who upon sighting the peaks bathed in morning alpenglow fervently exclaimed, *Sangre de Cristo.*"

Summer and fall are ideal times to drive the route. Summer days are warm, with temperatures ranging from ninety degrees near Walsenburg to the seventies at Westcliffe. Heavy thunderstorms regularly build up over the mountains and douse the valleys on summer afternoons. September and October bring a succession of clear, crisp days. Warm temperatures are occasionally broken by rain and low clouds. Winters are long and cold, with snow lasting from November to April. Expect chilly temperatures and wind. Bad road conditions, including ice and white-outs, occur during severe winter storms. The highway is a glorious drive after a winter storm. The sun glimmers in the clear sky, fresh snow blankets the undulating valley floor, and wind sweeps gossamers of snow off the high mountain ridges. Spring is cool and breezy. Daily high temperatures range from thirty to sixty degrees. Unsettled weather brings frequent storms.

The drive begins twenty-six miles west of Canon City at Texas Creek, the junction of US 50 and CO 69. Turn south on CO 69. The highway climbs south alongside Texas Creek in a steep-walled canyon broken by jumbled boulders and a scattered pinyon pine and juniper woodland. The abandoned railbed of the Westcliffe Branch of the Denver and Rio Grande Railroad parallels the highway in the canyon. The line, built in 1900, served Westcliffe and its prospering ranches. A previous narrow gauge line that hauled silver ore down Grape Creek was torn up by the Denver and Rio Grande in 1890 after a series of disasters and a downturn in the area's silver boom.

The road steadily climbs up the canyon, passing placid beaver dams. The first view of the Sangre de Cristo Range is two miles up the drive. The rough McIntyre Hills rise east of the highway forming a rugged maze of deep canyons and sharp peaks. This remote region, traversed only by a few trails, was studied for possible wilderness designation by the Bureau of Land Management but finally rejected. The hills offer excellent hiking adventures with abrupt stair-stepped canyons and plentiful wildlife including mule deer, bighorn sheep, and mountain lion.

By six miles, ponderosa pine begin mixing in the pinyon forest, lifting their rounded crowns above the low pinyons. A mile later the highway climbs away from the creek onto the northern Wet Mountain Valley, a high

To Canon City

Texas Creek

To Salida

McIntyre Hills

Arkansas River

Cotopaxi

Gem Mtn.

DE WEESE PLATEAU

Hillside

Lake Cr. CG

De Weese Res.

S A N

Westcliffe Silver Cliff

To Florence

WET MOUNTAIN VALLEY

Alvarado CG

Rosita Ghost Town

ISABEL

Kit Carson Mtn. 14,165 ft.

Crestone Pk. 14,294 ft.

Crestone Needle 14,191 ft.

SAN ISABEL NATIONAL FOREST

PROMONTORY DIVIDE

WET MOUNTAINS NATL.

FOREST

Greenhorn Mtn. 12,349 ft.

To Pueblo

S A N

L U I S

Medano Pass

RIO GRANDE NATIONAL FOREST

Malachite

Gardner

Bandits Cone

V A L L E Y

SANGRE DE CRISTO MOUNTAINS

Huerfano River

North La Veta Pass 9,413 ft.

Walsenburg

Lathrop CG

To La Junta

Mt. Lindsey 14,042 ft.

Blanca Pk. 14,345 ft.

Mt. Maestas 11,569 ft.

To Trinidad

To Fort Garland

•Denver
COLORADO
★

0   5   10
Miles

N

sagebrush plain dotted with ponderosa and pinyon pines below the looming mountain escarpment. At ten miles the drive reaches green pastures filled with grazing cattle and wide hay fields.

The Wet Mountain Valley, considered one of Colorado's prime ranch lands, flanks the Sangre de Cristos for over thirty miles from here to Promontory Divide. The broad valley, reaching fifteen miles in width, is drained by Grape and Texas creeks. The valley is rich in history. The Ute Indians frequented the valley, drawn by plentiful game and a salubrious summer climate. One early prospector remembered that "many a howling war dance has disturbed the midnight air of this pleasant valley." Spanish explorers and miners scouted the region, leaving legends of mysterious lost gold mines and treasure troves hidden in mountain caverns. In 1806 Lieutenant Zebulon Pike, on his quest to explore the southern Louisiana Purchase, traversed the valley en route to the Rio Grande and his capture by the Spanish. The first Anglo settlers were a group of 397 German immigrants who colonized the valley on a communal basis. These farmers and artisans failed due to inexperience at irrigation and at high-altitude farming. Most left for Denver and Pueblo, but those who hung on to their land eventually prospered. Descendants of these early immigrants still live and ranch in the valley.

After entering the northern Wet Mountain Valley, the highway passes Hillside, now a one-store town with gas and a post office, and swings back along Texas Creek on the valley's east edge. Just past Hillside, County Road 198 climbs west to eleven-site Lake Creek Campground in San Isabel National Forest. The drive runs south through a shallow canyon lined with volcanic cliff bands and ranches. Dense willow thickets border the tumbling creek and pines coat low surrounding hills. After five miles the highway emerges onto the valley floor. A spectacular panorama opens to the south—the Wet Mountains rim the valley on the southeast; the landmark Spanish Peaks poke their snowy heads above the southern horizon; and the Sangre de Cristo Mountains march across the western skyline. The high peaks of the southern Sawatch Range on the Continental Divide glimmer to the north. The highway runs past 8,549-foot Beckwith Mountain, an abrupt hogback broken by cliffs east of the asphalt, and after a few miles crosses meandering Grape Creek, the valley's main drainage. Westcliffe, at 7,888 feet, sits three miles south on a rounded bluff above the creek.

Westcliffe was founded in 1885 by local landowner Dr. J.W. Bell who named the picturesque community for Westcliffe-on-the-Sea, his English birthplace. The town, seat of Custer County, has long outlived its neighbors Silver Cliff, Querida, and Rosita. All three were mining boom towns in the late nineteenth century. Westcliffe, however, grew and thrived as a supply center for area ranchers and as a railhead. After the great Silver Crash of 1893 Westcliffe still prospered while its neighbors faded away. The Denver and Rio Grande Railroad came to town in 1900 but was abandoned in 1937. Westcliffe today is the county's center of commerce and offers all services to travelers.

The drive runs south from Westcliffe past verdant ranches. After three miles the highway intersects Schoolfield Road. A turn west leads six miles straight across the valley into the Sangre de Cristo Mountains and forty-four-site Alvarado Campground. This 9,000-foot-high campground makes a cool summer basecamp for exploring the valley and mountains. Trails lead west up forested valleys to alpine lakes and high peaks.

A turn east heads to the ghost town of Rosita nestled among summer cabins and ranchettes in the scrubby hills east of the valley. Silver was found here in 1870 and by 1872, when rich claims that yielded as much as 145 ounces of silver to the ton were found, the silver rush was on. Rosita, along with nearby Querida and Silver Cliff, arose around rich mines and lived and died by their earthen fortunes.

Rosita epitomizes the boom and bust mining cycle. Founded after a rich find in the winter of 1872-73, Rosita quickly became one of the Colorado Territory's largest towns. Rosita swelled with miners that dug the ore and teamsters that hauled the silver through deep canyons to Pueblo and the nearest railhead. The Pocahontas and Humboldt lodes, discovered in 1870, yielded more than nine million dollars. By 1875 the town boasted a population of fifteen hundred, a two-story school, Townsend's Brewery, three churches, a bank, the Pennsylvania Reduction Works for ore milling, the *Rosita Index* newspaper, a post office, hotels, as well as doctor and real estate offices. The mines began a slow decline in 1876 and Rosita was usurped by a new boom town, Querida, a few miles north. The decline furthered in 1878 when horn silver was discovered in Silver Cliff. Much of Rosita was destroyed in an 1881 fire and never recovered. The town lingered on as a well-preserved ghost of its former self well into the 1960s when the post office was finally closed down. Rosita, used as a film set for a few movies including *Saddle the Wind, Cat Ballou,* and *Continental Divide,* is now a forgotten, windswept corner of Colorado's colorful history. Only a few crumbling buildings remain of this faded rose along the dusty backroad. The Rosita Cemetery tells the poignant story of the town's rise and fall with quiet tombstones sheltered by pines.

The seventeen-mile-long highway section through the upper Wet Mountain Valley from Westcliffe to the crest of the Promontory Divide is simply spectacular. The broad valley, criss-crossed by arrow-straight sideroads, is divided by barbed wire fences into ranches dotted with grazing cattle. The Sangre de Cristo range pierces the western skyline, its abrupt escarpment of ragged peaks broken by plunging glacier-carved cirques and thickly wooded canyons. Four 14,000-foot peaks dominate the range here—14,294-foot Crestone Peak, 14,191-foot Crestone Needle, 14,165-foot Kit Carson Peak, and 14,064-foot Humboldt Peak. The Crestones loom overhead like flaked arrowheads, small snowfields clinging to their cliffed flanks. The peaks, named for their resemblance to a cock's comb, were the last of Colorado's fifty-four "fourteeners" to be ascended when Albert Ellingwood and Eleanor Davis climbed them in 1916. Kit Carson Peak is named for the famed western scout, and Humbolt Peak for Alexander von Humboldt, a renowned nineteenth century geographer. The peaks are usually approached from the Wet Mountain Valley via South Colony Road and Forest Road 313 up South

CO 69 runs down the Huerfano Valley beneath the snow-capped Sangre de Cristo Mountains on the Sangre de Cristo Drive.

Colony Creek. Uplifted 270-million-year-old Paleozoic sediments including sandstone, shale, conglomerate, and limestone compose the bulk of the range, although ancient granite forms the Sierra Blanca section. The sawtoothed Sangre de Cristos lie in a 265,000-acre wilderness area, the only Colorado range wholly protected.

The Sangre de Cristo Mountains, besides being an enclave of wildlife and wilderness, is rife with legends. One of the best concerns Marble Cave, called by the Spanish *El Caverna del Oro* or The Cavern of Gold, a deep cave high above timberline on the windswept flanks of Marble Mountain south of the Crestones. Myth relates that Spanish conquistadores used the cave as a stash for ill-gotten gold mined by Indian slaves. An old Maltese cross, painted on a rock wall, marks the cave's entrance. The cave makes an unpleasant exploration, reaching a depth of three hundred feet including a vertical eighty-foot pit, an year-round average temperature of thirty-four degrees, ninety-five percent humidity, and snowdrifts that reach far into the cave. The first explorers in 1929 found a crude ladder and hand-forged hammer thought to be at least two hundred years old. The gold, if it was there at all, vanished long before.

The road runs south on gravel benches above meandering Grape Creek and gently climbs toward 8,500-foot Promontory Divide, a low ridge that separates the Wet Mountain Valley from the Huerfano River drainage. As the road climbs the surrounding country dries, with undulating sagebrush hills replacing the fertile valley floor. Wild country stretches in every direction from atop the divide. The highway drops south from the divide along Muddy

Creek, a shallow trickle lined with willows and cottonwoods in a shallow valley. Rolling pinyon pine-covered hills flank the valley. Eight miles from the divide summit the drive passes Medano Road, a four-wheel-drive track that climbs over 9,950-foot Medano Pass and drops down to the Great Sand Dunes and the San Luis Valley. Past the turn the highway bends southeast down Muddy Creek's broad valley. The creek meanders through deep flash flood-carved arroyos on the valley floor. Low mesas studded with pinyon pine and juniper flank the drive.

At fifty-nine miles the highway reaches Gardner, an old southwestern settlement perched at the confluence of Muddy Creek and the Huerfano River. The town, named for pioneer farmer Herbert Gardner, retains a frontier spirit with old adobe houses shaded by towering cottonwoods. A spur road, County Road 550, heads southwest up the river through Malachite and Redwing and climbs up a four-wheel trail to the San Isabel National Forest boundary and 14,338-foot Blanca Peak. Another sideroad ascends to the summit of 9,750-foot Mosca Pass. An old Ute Indian trail drops west to the Great Sand Dunes.

Gardner Butte, a rough volcanic plug broken by cliff bands, looms just east of Gardner. The Wet Mountains, topped by 12,347-foot Greenhorn Mountain, tower to the north. Long outwash plains, cloaked with sagebrush and pinyon, sweep up to the ranges's steep forested slopes. Greenhorn Mountain is named for Cuerno Verde or Greenhorn, a Comanche chief killed in a violent 1779 battle between the Comanches and the Spanish. The mountain's southern flank is a wilderness area of remote, rugged canyons and ridges.

The drive follows benches above the Huerfano River, passing through the old Mexican town of Farista. The town, originally called Fort Talpa, was established in 1820. A few miles east the highway runs through the abandoned town Badito at the far southern edge of the Wet Mountains. The range terminus is topped by distinctive Badito Cone, a volcanic vent. The road twists through a narrow gap carved through uplifted sandstone layers by the muddy Huerfano River below the cone. The old Taos Trail, a path used by American traders and Spanish soldiers, cuts through Badito en route to Sangre de Cristo Pass and Taos. A Spanish fort was built a few miles south of here in 1819 to protect the pass from American invasion. Past the gap the highway climbs away from the river and onto the edge of the treeless Great Plains. The drive's last fifteen miles roll across shortgrass prairie, over pinyon-dotted mesas, past an old bituminous coal mine, and drop down to I-25 just north of Walsenburg.

6 LOS CAMINOS ANTIGUOS SCENIC DRIVE
Fort Garland to Cumbres Pass

General description: A 96-mile-long state scenic byway that traverses the immense San Luis Valley between Fort Garland and Cumbres Pass. The drive passes historic sites, the Rio Grande, desert hills, valley farms, and aspen forests.

Special attractions: Fort Garland State Museum, San Luis Museum and Cultural Center, Stations of the Cross, Jack Dempsey Museum, Rio Grande, Cumbres and Toltec Scenic Railroad, Cumbres Pass, Rio Grande National Forest, autumn colors, fishing, hiking, scenic views, camping.

Location: Southern Colorado. The drive begins in Fort Garland, 47 miles west of Walsenburg via U.S. Highway 160, heads south on Colorado 159 to San Luis, then west on Colorado 142 to Romeo. Turn south on U.S. Highway 285 for 7 miles to Antonito, and again west on Colorado Highway 17 to Cumbres Pass and the New Mexico border.

Drive route name and numbers: Los Caminos Antiguos Scenic Byway, Colorado highways 159, 142, and 17, US 285.

Travel season: Year-round. Heavy snow can temporarily close the highway over La Manga and Cumbres passes.

Camping: Mogote, Aspen Glade, Elk Creek, and Trujillo Meadows campgrounds lie along CO 17 west of Antonito in Rio Grande National Forest.

Services: All services are found in Fort Garland, San Luis, and Antonito. Limited services are in Manassa and Romeo.

Nearby attractions: Sierra Blanca, Great Sand Dunes National Monument, Penitente Canyon climbing area, San Isabel National Forest, Spanish Peaks, South San Juan Wilderness Area, Monte Vista National Wildlife Refuge, Alamosa National Wildlife Refuge, Silver Thread Scenic Byway, Pike's Stockade, Taos, Chama, Rio Grande Gorge, Carson National Forest.

For more information: Rio Grande National Forest, 1803 W. Highway 160, Monte Vista, CO 81144, (719) 852-5941. Antonito Chamber of Commerce, P.O. Box 636, Antonito, CO 81120, (719) 376-5443. San Luis Visitor Center, P.O. Box 9, San Luis, CO 81152, (719) 672-3355.

The drive: The ninety-six-mile Los Caminos Antiguos drive, a Colorado scenic byway, traverses the San Luis Valley between Fort Garland and Cumbres Pass in southern Colorado. The immense San Luis Valley, an intermontane basin roughly one hundred miles long and sixty miles wide, reaches from Poncha Pass to the New Mexico border. The valley, three times the size of Delaware, rolls out to the mountain horizon like a giant carpet patterned with fields, pastures, and sagebrush flats. The Sangre de Cristo and Culebra ranges wall in the valley on the east. The jagged escarpment, including nine 14,000-foot peaks, makes a formidable barrier that is crossed

by only one paved road and two four-wheel-drive tracks. The San Juan Mountains form a lower, but equally impassable barrier to the west. The Rio Grande, southern Colorado's river of history and character, breaks from the San Juans at Del Norte and meanders across the San Luis Valley between banks thick with cottonwoods and willows, before plunging down its wild gorge into New Mexico. The valley drive passes old towns and historic sites, threads over volcanic hills, follows the sparkling Conejos River, and climbs through fir and spruce forests to the summit of 10,022-foot Cumbres Pass, a stone's throw from New Mexico.

The San Luis Valley, lying at elevations above 7,500 feet, is classified as desert with an average precipitation of only ten inches. The valley, the driest part of Colorado, lies in the rain shadow of the San Juan Mountains. Storms laden with Pacific moisture unload on the San Juans, but by the time the clouds reach the valley most rain has already been wrung out. The bulk of the year's meager moisture generally falls in torrential thunderstorms on July and August afternoons. The San Juans west of the valley are Colorado's wettest region. Heavy snows fall on the mountains, including an average 267 inches atop Cumbres Pass. On the other hand, Manassa along the drive, receives only eighteen inches of snow each winter. Summer and fall are the best times to travel the highways. Summer days are warm and sunny, with highs generally in the seventies and eighties. Autumn brings cooler days and bright skies. Winters are frigid, with temperatures often falling below zero and snow lingering on the valley floor. Spring months are cool and windy, with occasional rain showers.

The drive begins at Fort Garland, forty-seven miles west of Walsenburg and Interstate 25, at the intersection of US 160 and CO 159. Turn south on CO 159 toward San Luis. Fort Garland, now a sleepy little crossroads, started out in 1858 as an army fort to protect settlers from marauding bands of Ute Indians. Colorado's first permanent settlements, established in the early 1850s in the San Luis Valley, lay on newly acquired territory ceded by Mexico after the Mexican-American War. The military built Fort Massachusetts, Colorado's first military post, in 1852 northeast of Fort Garland. The poor location and stagnant water, however, prompted the army to relocate the garrison to Fort Garland a few years later. The new fort, named for Brigadier General John Garland, maintained order in the valley until the Utes were moved westward in 1880. The unneeded post was abandoned in 1883. Famed scout, Indian fighter, and soldier Kit Carson commanded the fort in 1866-67, before his death two years later at Fort Lyon. Soldiers considered a post at remote Fort Garland to be a type of involuntary exile. One visitor wrote that he was "struck with commiseration for all the unfortunate officers and men condemned to live in so desolate a place." The old fort, a grassy parade ground surrounded by low adobe buildings, is now open year-round as a state historic site that preserves a slice of Colorado's colorful past. Exhibits include a re-creation of the commandant's quarters during Carson's tenure and displays of military life and Hispanic folk art from the San Luis Valley.

The highway runs straight south from Fort Garland, passing farmland watered by deep artesian wells and wide sagebrush-covered flats. Scrubby,

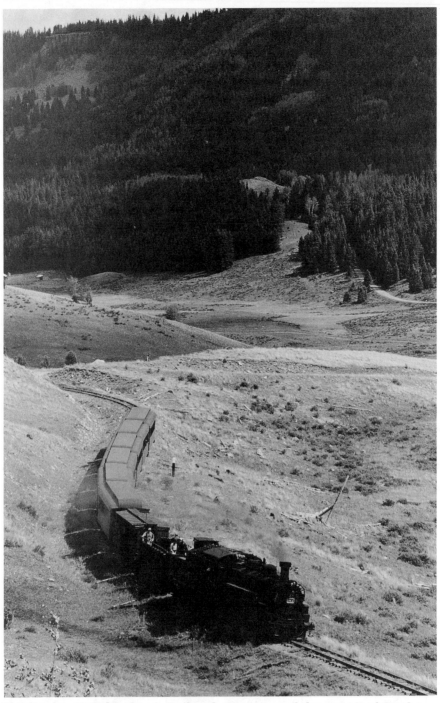

The Cumbres & Toltec Scenic Railroad steams toward the summit of Cumbres Pass on Los Caminos Antiguos Scenic Drive.

broken mesas rimmed by ancient lava flows border the drive to the east, forming low foothills below the lofty crest of the Culebra Range. Most of these hills are subdivided as part of the Forbes Trinchera Ranch, but they were originally part of the million-acre Sangre de Cristo Land Grant given by the Mexican government to Stephen Lee and thirteen-year-old Narcisco Beaubien for eventual colonization in 1843. The land passed, after the two were murdered during a Taos Indian uprising two years later, to Beaubien's father, Charles, owner of the Maxwell Land Grant near Trinidad. Much of the grant was acquired in 1863 by William Gilpin, Colorado's first territorial governor and a land speculator, and used for grazing.

The Spanish presence in southern Colorado began in the 1500s when gold-hungry conquistadors explored the northern part of the New Mexico province. They criss-crossed the valley, traveled over the mountain passes on old Indian trails, built forts, discovered mines, and fought with the Indians. Little is actually know of Spanish incursions into southern Colorado, most of those records have disappeared, but their legacy continues in numerous Spanish place names.

The Culebra Range (*Culebra* is the Spanish word for snake) forms a ragged wall east of the highway. This thirty-mile-long range twists south from La Veta Pass into New Mexico. Much of the range, topped by 14,069-foot Culebra Peak, remains wild, uninhabited country where visitors are unwelcome. The Maxwell and Sangre de Cristo land grants kept the mountains out of the public domain and even today most of the Culebra Range is private property. Hikers pay for the privilege of crossing private land to climb Culebra Peak, one of Colorado's fifty-four 14,000-foot peaks. The range, like the Sangre de Cristos to the north, is an uplifted fault-block range shaped by glaciation.

After fifteen miles the highway drops down into Culebra Creek's broad, shallow valley and 7,965-foot San Luis, Colorado's oldest town. Historians acknowledge the community is the first continuously occupied town in today's Colorado, although Taos resident George Gould established a nearby settlement in 1842. The original San Luis, called San Luis de Culebra, was built three-quarters of a mile south of today's town on the Sangre de Cristo land grant in 1851 by six Spanish families. The town, a collection of low-slung adobe buildings, is huddled around a central plaza for protection from Indians and the surrounding arable land is divided into ranches and farms. A canal diverted water from Culebra Creek and Colorado's first water right was established. Today the town, a national historic district, boasts strong civic pride and a sense of community. Many local ranchers and farmers here are descendants of the original settlers. The excellent San Luis Museum, Cultural, and Commercial Center displays southern Colorado's classic Hispanic culture in *La Cultura Constante de San Luis* exhibit and includes a brilliant collection of *santos* or carved religious icons. The Stations of the Cross shrine, following a 1.4-mile round-trip trail up a dark mesa just northwest of town, depicts the last hours of Christ's life in a series of dramatic bronze sculptures by sculptor Huberto Maestas. The shrine attracts numerous pilgrims who walk the path and ruminate on their faith.

53

The scenic drive turns west onto CO 142 at the Stations of the Cross trailhead. The road runs alongside a low mesa, rimmed with basalt blocks and coated with sagebrush. Verdant hay fields, watered by meandering Culebra Creek, fill the wide valley south of the blacktop. After eight miles the highway passes through San Acacio. Only a few houses and abandoned buildings remain in this town founded in 1853. Early settlers battled the Utes here in the name of San Acacio, a Spanish soldier canonized as Saint Acacius. A mile past the town the drive bends south and runs across a flat, creek flood plain for two miles before turning west again on an almost arrow-straight road. The San Luis Hills, rough volcanic knobs, hills, and mesas, rear up to the north and west, forming a wall gray with sagebrush and mottled with pinyon pines and junipers. The highway heads across brushy flats toward the hills for nine miles and reaches the Rio Grande tucked in a shallow cliffed canyon.

The Rio Grande, the second longest river in the United States at 1,887 miles long, arises on the Continental Divide west of the San Luis Valley. The river placidly winds across the valley to this crossing where it begins cutting into basalt layers. Farther south it enters a deep gorge and plunges into New Mexico. This upper section offers good canoeing through quiet, steep-sided canyons. The cliffs and open spaces attract numerous raptors including bald eagles, common winter residents.

The highway crosses the Rio Grande on a long bridge and begins climbing over rolling benchlands to a wide saddle between the Pinon Hills on the south and Flat Top, an abrupt mesa to the north. Several connected groups of low, barren mountains—South Pinon Hills, Pinon Hills, Flat Top, and Brownie Hills—compose the San Luis Hills. The hills, rising as much as 1,000 feet over the surrounding valley, are the eroded remnants of the huge volcanic deposits that form the San Juan Mountains. The hills, rejected for inclusion in the wilderness system by the Bureau of Land Management (BLM), are nonetheless wild country. The steep slopes, blanketed in sagebrush, salt-bush, and rabbit-brush, and dotted with pinyon pine and juniper, house numerous wildlife species, including mule deer, pronghorns, coyotes, bob-cats, and eagles. Pristine grasslands thrive on the upper elevations. Hikers can park anywhere along the highway here or take one of the side roads to access the backcountry. A good hike climbs to Flat Top's broad summit and yields marvelous views of the valley and surrounding ranges.

The highway crests the saddle after four miles and begins a gradual descent to the Conejos River valley. After four miles the road reaches the valley floor and crosses Rio San Antonio, a small stream densely lined with narrow-leaf cottonwoods and willows. The highway swings around a low hill and crosses the Conejos River a mile later. Farms and hayfields cover the moist flood plain, with cattails and bright sunflowers lining marshland along the highway. After two miles the drive enters Manassa, a well-kept rural community with wide streets and orderly clapboard houses. The town, established in 1878 by Mormon colonists, is famed as the 1895 birthplace and childhood home of heavyweight boxing champion Jack Dempsey. Dempsey, who fought as a teenager in surrounding mining camps as "Kid Blackie," won the crown at age 24. Nicknamed "The Manassa Mauler," Dempsey is considered the best heavyweight in the first half of the twentieth century. The Jack Dempsey Museum, a one-room cabin where he grew up on Main Street, displays boxing memorabilia and family photos. Two miles west of Manassa, the drive enters Romeo and intersects US 285. Turn south on US 285.

The highway runs south over farmland, crosses the Conejos River again, passes the turn-off to Conejos, and reaches Antonito after six miles. Conejos is well worth a visit. The town, first settled by Major Lafayette Head and eighty-four Hispanic families in 1854, soon rivaled their cross-valley cousins at San Luis with numerous settlers, productive farms, and Colorado's first church, dedicated by Bishop Lamy of Santa Fe in 1863. The beautiful Guadalupe Church dominates the town with its twin domed towers.

Conejos thrived as a commercial center until 1881 when the Denver and Rio Grande Railroad bypassed the town and founded Antonito just down the road. Conejos became a footnote in Colorado history when the state's last hanging took place on July 16, 1889. Abran Ortiz was hung for murder.

Antonito began in 1881 as a railroad stop. The line originally planned on stopping at Conejos but high land prices and difficulty in obtaining a right-of-way prompted the Denver and Rio Grande to build a new town. The narrow gauge railroad, now known as the Cumbres and Toltec Scenic Railroad, ran from Alamosa through Antonito and west over Cumbres Pass to Durango. A branch, the "Chile Line," went south from Antonito to Espanola. The town quickly became the south valley's business hub, with warehouses, hotels, saloons, bordellos, and banks. Antonito retains its old

Blanca and Little Bear peaks tower over Los Caminos Antiguos Scenic Drive near San Luis.

55

charm and remains a ranching and farming community. It's most popular attraction is the sixty-four-mile railroad between Antonito and Chama. The Cumbres and Toltec Railroad, America's longest narrow gauge line, twists along the Colorado and New Mexico border and passes through scenic Toltec Gorge. The train runs daily from early summer to late fall.

At the train station on Antonito's south side, US 285 turns south toward New Mexico. The scenic drive continues west on CO 17. Past Antonito, the road runs through a succession of small, old towns—Paisaje, Mogote, and Las Mesitas. All began in the 1850s as settlers spread out from Conejos across the fertile bottomlands along the Conejos River.

Paisaje is best remembered as the home of the Espinosa brothers. The duo, Felipe and Julian, claimed that a vision told them to kill "gringos." In the spring of 1863 they went on a brutal rampage, murdering numerous Anglos in the South Park area. A posse surprised the pair near Cripple Creek and Felipe was killed in a shootout. In his diary they found an entry that the brothers had sworn to kill six hundred men. A $2,500 bounty was put on the escaped Julian and soldiers at Fort Garland mobilized to find him, dead or alive. In September, army scout Thomas Tobin tracked Espinosa and his nephew to Cucharas Pass, where he shot them at their evening campfire. Tobin collected his reward after bringing the outlaw's head to the fort commandant.

After crossing the Conejos River, the highway swings through Las Mesitas. Adobe houses and small ranches mark the town today, along with the gutted roadside ruins of San Isadore church. The church burned down in 1975, leaving its massive walls open to the sun and rain. The canyon narrows and the road runs west beneath a high mesa. Scattered pinyon pine and juniper mix with sagebrush on its steep slopes. The highway passes through Fox Creek and a mile later enters Rio Grande National Forest. Mogote Campground, with nine sites at 8,300 feet, nestles among ponderosa pines and tall cottonwoods along the Conejos River.

The highway runs alongside the river for the next ten miles, passing into a deep canyon lined with volcanic cliffs and dense forests. The Conejos River, draining from 13,172-foot Conejos Peak, is one of Colorado's least known yet wildest rivers. Excellent trout fishing, great wildlife habitat, and its undammed flow provide recreation for fishermen, kayakers, and naturalists. Aspen Glade Campground, with twenty-seven sites, sits just past the first roadside aspen grove. Numerous stands of golden aspens gild the hillsides along the drive in late September. The canyon widens into a broad, glaciated valley twenty miles from Antonito. Forest Road 250 continues up the valley, passing several campgrounds and lakes to Platoro, an old 1880s mining ghost town. The scenic drives crosses the river, passes the turnoff to thirty-one-site Elk Creek Campground and begins the final climb.

Today's highway follows an old Indian trail over La Manga and Cumbres passes. Highway construction began in 1920 and the road to Chama was finished in 1928. The road switchbacks up through aspen and spruce forest on the western flank of 10,561-foot McIntyre Mountain and after a few miles follows La Manga Creek to the grassy 10,230-foot summit of La Manga Pass.

The highway drops south along a creek to the meandering Rio de Los Pinos in a broad valley, swings around forested Neff Mountain above the railroad tracks, and climbs to the summit of 10,022-foot Cumbres Pass. Just before the summit, a road heads northwest to Trujillo Meadows Reservoir and Campground. A small railroad station sits among the spruce forest atop the pass. The low mountains between La Manga and Cumbres passes offer excellent cross-country skiing in winter with plentiful snow and gorgeous scenery. The drive continues southwest, dropping over rolling hills studded with crags and covered with meadows and forest before quietly ending on the Colorado and New Mexico border. Chama, a picturesque New Mexico town, sits eight miles south of the border.

7 WET MOUNTAINS SCENIC DRIVE
Florence to Colorado City

General description: A 58-mile drive that traverses the Wet Mountains between Florence and Colorado City, passing historic sites, ragged canyons, and recreational areas.

Special attractions: Florence, San Isabel National Forest, Hardscrabble Canyon, Bishop Castle, Lake Isabel, Greenhorn Mountain, camping, hiking, fishing, aspen colors, rock climbing.

Location: South-central Colorado. The drive begins in Florence 5 miles south of U.S. Highway 50 at the junction of Colorado highways 115 and 67. The highway runs south, joins Colorado 96 in Wetmore, and intersects Colorado 165 at McKenzie Junction. The drive ends in Colorado City at Exit 74 on Interstate 25 south of Pueblo.

Drive route name and numbers: Colorado Highways 67, 96, and 165. The Greenhorn Highway.

Travel season: Year-round.

Camping: Three national forest campgrounds—Ophir, Davenport, and Lake Isabel—lie along the drive. Primitive camping is also permitted on forest land. Greenhorn Meadows Park in Colorado City offers camping.

Services: All services are found in Florence and Colorado City. Limited services are in Wetmore, San Isabel, and Rye.

Nearby attractions: Sangre de Cristo Wilderness Area, Westcliffe, Canon City attractions, Gold Belt Tour Back Country Byway, Royal Gorge, Pueblo area attractions, Lake Pueblo State Recreation Area, Lathrop State Park, La Veta, Spanish Peaks, Highway of Legends Scenic Byway.

For more information: San Isabel National Forest, 1920 Valley Dr., Pueblo, CO 81008, (719) 545-8737. Canon City Chamber, P.O. Bin 749, Canon City, CO 81215-0749, (719) 275-2331. Greenhorn Valley Chamber, P.O. Box 426, Rye, CO 81069, (719) 676-3000.

Colorado Highway 67 slashes across a dry arroyo on the Wet Mountain Drive south of Florence.

The drive: Far away, across the dusty prairie, the Wet Mountains lift above the western horizon like a hump-backed, blue cloud. Early pioneers, inching across the Great Plains in wagon caravans, saw a promise in those dreamlike mountains. Up there, beyond the dry land of short grass, yucca, and rattlesnakes, lay a cool oasis lush with wind-ruffled pine forests, wildflower-dotted meadows, and sparkling streams of clear water. A party of early Mormon emigrants, on reaching this mountain outpost, reveled in the wooded slopes and rain-laden clouds after their months-long trek over what was then called "The Great American Desert." They named them the Wet Mountains; oddly enough, a name also given by the Spanish and Indians.

The Wet Mountains, the southern vestige of the Front Range, makes a broad arc from the Arkansas River west of Canon City to the Huerfano River at Badito. The range, composed of Precambrian granite and metamorphic rocks, formed when a fault uplifted those old rocks and thrust them onto younger sedimentary layers. The range summits lie between 9,000 and 12,000 feet, with 12,349-foot Greenhorn Mountain the highest point. Creeks slice into the ancient bedrock creating abrupt, cliff-lined canyons and shallow, grassy valleys. The Wet Mountain scenic drive, beginning in Florence in the Arkansas River Valley, wends through the canyons and valleys for fifty-eight miles before emptying onto the prairie at Colorado City.

Weather along the drive is generally pleasant year-round. Summer temperatures range from the nineties at the lower elevations at Florence and Colorado City to the seventies in the mountains. Immense thunderstorms build over the Wet Mountains and the neighboring Sangre de Cristo Range on summer afternoons. Expect localized heavy rain. Autumn days are warm and clear, with golden aspens sprinkled on the hillsides. Winter sets in by early November and snow locks the upper reaches until April. Spring is short and unpredictable with periods of rain, snow, and sun.

The scenic drive begins in Florence, five miles southwest of US 50 and Penrose and ten miles east of Canon City at the intersection of CO 115 and 67. Turn south on CO 67 just east of downtown Florence. Florence lies on the south bank of the Arkansas River in a broad, arid valley hemmed in by the Pikes Peak massif to the north and the Wet Mountains to the south. The river, after bursting from the mountains and the Royal Gorge at Canon City, gently braids across a wide channel lined with towering cottonwoods. Florence, founded in 1860, was first named Frazerville for early miner Joe Frazer who developed coal mines south of town and planted the first apple orchards here. The town was renamed for the daughter of local oilman James McCandless in the 1870s. Besides seams of coal, oil deposits underlie the Florence area. A.M. Cassiday drilled the first well in 1862 in nearby Oil Canyon where an oil spring bubbled to the surface. The oil field, called the "Florence Pool," is the second oldest in the United States. Well No. 42, considered the oldest continuously operating oil well in the world, has pumped out over a million gallons of crude since it was drilled in 1889.

The drive bumps across the railroad tracks and heads south on CO 67 leaving the fertile river bottom behind. The straight road runs across a gently tilting plain seamed with shallow valleys and scarred by deep arroyos.

To Canon City

To Colorado Springs

To Canon City

Penrose

N

115

50

Florence

Arkansas

67

To Pueblo

River

96

To Pueblo

SAN

Hardscrabble
Mtn.

Wetmore

Smith Creek
Picnic Area

To Westcliffe

96

WET

ISABEL

To I-25

165

Round Top Mtn.
10,180 ft.

Gobblers Knob
10,781 ft.

NATL.

78

Ophir CG

PUEBLO
MTN. PARK

Bishop Castle

St. Charles
Pk. 11,784 ft.

Charles River

St.

To Pueblo

Lake Isabel CG

**Colorado
City**

Greenhorn
Valley CG

FOREST

MOUNTAINS

North Peak
12,220 ft.

Rye

To Pueblo

25

•Denver

COLORADO
★

Greenhorn Mtn.
12,349 ft.

To Walsenburg

0   5   10
Miles

60

Shortgrass prairie studded with cholla cactus and yucca covers the dry plain. The highway crosses a succession of dry creekbeds—Cocklebur, Newlin, and Mineral creeks.

Cottonwoods, indicating underground water, border the creekbeds and low scrubby mesas, fringed with tawny rimrock and scattered junipers, form low ramparts. Round-shouldered Pikes Peak looms to the north above the wide Arkansas Valley. After seven miles the road climbs onto a flat, barren bench surrounded by low-browed hills. The Wet Mountains, a high escarpment of green forested peaks and canyons, towers to the west and south.

A state historic marker at nine-and-a-half miles commemorates the area's earliest settlements. The first was *El Cuervo* or The Raven, an Indian trading post built by Maurice LeDuc a mile west of the marker near the mountain base at the junction of Adobe and Mineral creeks. Colonel Henry Dodge of the First Regiment of United States Dragoons noted a camp of sixty Arapaho tepees at the post in 1835. The pueblo of Hardscrabble was established in 1844 at the confluence of Adobe and Hardscrabble creeks a few miles north of the marker and used as a trading post for Indians and trappers. The village, low-slung adobe buildings erected in a protective square, was visited by explorer John C. Fremont in 1845. Twenty-five trappers with Indian wives and children lived there. Fremont stopped by again in late November, 1848 during his disastrous fourth expedition in search of a transcontinental railroad route along the 38th parallel. Few people inhabited the village, most having moved to Pueblo after Indian attacks. Richard Kern, an expedition member, described Hardscrabble in his journal as the "summer resort of hunters." The expedition lingered only two days, buying and shelling 130 bushels of corn and dining on chicken and pumpkin before heading west to the San Juan Mountains.

The highway continues due south, passing a lone ponderosa pine and running two miles to Wetmore on Hardscrabble Creek's gravel banks. Frances and William Wetmore bought an old homestead here and surveyed, named, and established the town around 1880. It served as a stagecoach station on the line between Pueblo and the Wet Mountain Valley. CO 67 deadends here against CO 96. Turn west on CO 96.

The new highway bends south onto a bench above Hardscrabble Creek in a broad valley. The valley edge gently rises west toward the mountains where tilted sandstone layers form rocky hogbacks against a soaring mountain wall. Rounded hills cloaked in oak and pine flank the valley's east side. As the road runs south the valley narrows and deep forests of scrub oak and ponderosa pine mix with open meadows. Tall cottonwoods shelter the creek below the road. At fifteen miles the drive enters San Isabel National Forest. A half-mile later the road swings west into North Hardscrabble Canyon's abrupt defile. Forest Road 306 begins here and runs south and west up South Hardscrabble Creek. Near this road junction sits a rock face inscribed with famed frontiersman Kit Carson's name and his wife Josefa Jaramillo's initials.

The highway heads west up the canyon, cutting through sandstone hogbacks and passing steep side-canyons. Bighorn sheep and mule deer graze in open meadows along the drive. As the road climbs, the canyon steepens and narrows. Ponderosa pine, pinyon pine, and juniper scatter over the warm north slopes, while deep forests of spruce and fir darken the south side. A picnic area sits part-way up the canyon along the creek. Towering peaks, including rough Hardscrabble Mountain, tower above the canyon floor. Tilted layers of metamorphic rock form bands of cliffs and break into sharp buttresses, pointed pyramids, and blocky castles. The definite origins of the name Hardscrabble are lost, but local legend says the name came after Ute Indians massacred settlers in Pueblo on Christmas Day, 1855. The Indians, pursued by soldiers, fled up the creek and had a "hard scrabble" to elude capture.

At nineteen miles the canyon narrows and the highway twists through roadcuts. The creek below tumbles over boulders forming frothy cascades. A pulloff at Rattlesnake Gulch is a good picnic stop. A trail climbs the steep gulch, passing numerous climbing crags and boulders. The canyon widens above the gulch, the road grade abates, and narrowleaf cottonwoods densely line the creek. McKenzie Junction, the intersection of CO 96 and 165, sits in the widening, grassy valley. The drive turns south on CO 165, while CO 96 heads west sixteen miles to Westcliffe.

CO 165, the Greenhorn Highway, runs thirty-five miles from the junction to Colorado City. The road climbs south up Hardscrabble Creek's South Fork, a shallow valley fringed with pine and fir forest, aspen groves, and bald meadows. The road steadily ascends and reaches 9,379-foot Wixson Divide after five miles. This broad saddle, surrounded by grassland and open forests, lies below pointed Wixson Mountain. The drive drops down another valley, crosses South Hardscrabble Creek, and begins climbing another shallow valley to the summit of Bigelow Divide. Edging south above Bigelow Creek, the drive passes old ranch buildings and bends west up Middle Creek. Ophir Creek Campground, with twenty-seven sites, tucks into a wooded valley along the creek where the highway makes a hairpin turn. Forest Road 400 heads west up Ophir Creek here and reaches the Wet Mountain range crest. Forest Road 403 winds along the crest to a point just west of Greenhorn Mountain's lofty summit.

The drive climbs out of the valley, slices through several roadcuts, and reaches Bishop Castle. The castle, a marvelous stone building rising out of the forest above the highway, is testimony to the ingenuity and labor of Jim Bishop. Bishop, starting in 1969, began building the castle from his imagination. Today, without blueprints, he slowly crafts arches, turrets, towers, and huge rooms from local cobbles and mortar. The main tower when completed will soar 150 feet into the sky. This marvelous structure, looking less like a traditional medieval castle and more like a storybook fantasy, attracts over sixty thousand travelers a year. Jim, a wiry man with strong hands, calls the castle "the largest one man project in the world," and says it's "a tourist attraction without being a tourist trap." The castle, owned by the nonprofit Bishop Castle Foundation, donates money raised from donations for newborn heart surgery. Admission is free and the castle and a gift shop are open year-round.

Past Bishop Castle the highway runs south, dipping across Davenport

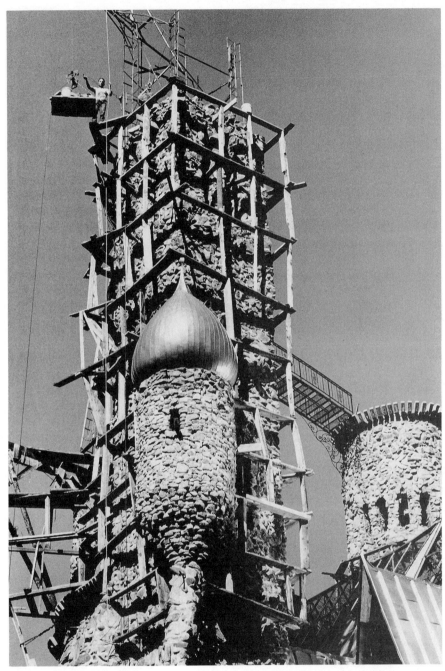

Mason Jim Bishop lays stone atop Bishop Castle's tower along the Wet Mountain Drive.

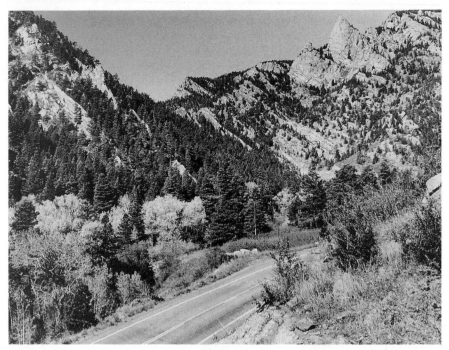

Hardscrabble Mountain lifts steep cliff-strewn slopes above the Wet Mountain Drive.

Creek, climbing over Greenhill Divide, and dropping down brushy Willow Creek valley. At the valley base sits San Isabel, a small resort with lodging, restaurants, and supplies. Lake Isabel nestles in the broad valley beyond the town, its deep blue water attracting anglers. The lake, formed by St. Charles Dam, impounds the infant St. Charles River. High forested ridges and rounded peaks studded with granite crags loom above the aspen-fringed lake. A parking area on the highway allows angler and hiker access. A turn south of the lake leads to the national forest's Lake Isabel Recreation Area with a forty-eight unit campground and a large picnic area.

The drive intersects the twisting Old San Isabel Road a mile past the lake. Here the highway begins winding downward, dipping through shallow canyons and passing groves of quaking aspen. Greenhorn Mountain, its south summit reaching 12,349 feet, towers above the drive. Steep ridges and slopes, scaled with dense conifer forest, rise above. This wild land of woods and canyons is part of the 22,040-acre Greenhorn Mountain Wilderness Area, one of Colorado's newest wilderness additions. The name Greenhorn, *Cuerno Verde* in Spanish, commemorates a Comanche chief killed in a fierce battle with Spanish soldiers led by Governor Juan Bautista de Anza in 1779 on the plains below the peak.

As the road descends the mountain flank the vegetation changes from spruce, fir, and aspen forest to a drier woodland of ponderosa pine and scrub oak. The highway leaves the national forest six miles from San Isabel and traverses high, rolling foothills coated with scrub oak and open grassland.

Sandstone-rimmed cuestas or upturned mesas seamed with abrupt canyons break from the hills and drop eastward. After a few miles the road passes grazing cattle and pastures and bends into Rye. This quiet, pastoral town, established in 1882, was named for surrounding grain fields. It serves today as a ranching center.

The drive runs east from Rye along the north side of Greenhorn Creek's broad valley. Fields scattered with hay bales and cattle lie along the creek. Higher mesas rimmed with Dakota sandstone and covered with pine and oak rise north of the asphalt. The road and creek continue descending eastward and the climate and hills steadily dry. By the time the road reaches the valley floor, short grass, yucca, and cactus dominate this Upper Sonoran life zone. Greenhorn Meadows Park, with a cottonwood-shaded campground, sits along the creek. The nearby Cuerno Verde monument memorializes the Indian chief killed here. Passing over low, scrubby hills the highway climbs up to Colorado City, one of the state's newest communities. The town, called Crow Junction in the 1880s, was founded in 1963 as a resort and commercial enterprise and named for the Colorado City Development Company. Now it's a placid crossroads with visitor services, a golf course, and Beckwith Reservoir, offering fishing and boating. The drive ends at I-25's exit 74. Pueblo lies almost twenty-five miles to the north, while Walsenburg sits twenty-four miles to the south. Graneros Gorge, just south of the interchange, is a spectacular canyon sliced into grassy hills.

8 PHANTOM CANYON AND SHELF ROAD
Canon City to Cripple Creek

General description: A 64-mile-long open loop drive that follows Phantom Canyon and Shelf roads through precipitous canyons on the south slope of Pikes Peak.

Special attractions: Indian Springs Trace Fossil Site, Beaver Creek Wilderness Study Area, Cripple Creek and Victor National Historic Districts, Cripple Creek & Victor Narrow Gauge Railroad, Window Rock, The Shelf, Shelf Road Climbing Area, Garden Park Fossil Area, Red Canon Park, Canon City attractions, hiking, rock climbing, camping, fishing, wildlife, mine ruins, photography.

Location: Central Colorado. The drive follows Shelf Road north from Canon City to Cripple Creek, then turns south on Colorado 67 to Victor and down Phantom Canyon to U.S. Highway 50 near Florence.

Drive route names and numbers: Shelf Road, Phantom Canyon Road, Colorado Highway 67, Fremont County 9, Teller County 88.

Travel season: Year-round. Snow and mud may temporarily close the roads during winter. Watch for slick roads after heavy summer thunderstorms. Both roads are very narrow, often only one lane wide with tight turns. **Vehicles over twenty-five-feet wide including motor homes, large campers, and travel trailers, should not attempt the drive.**

Camping: Private campgrounds are in the Cripple Creek and Canon City areas and at Indian Springs. Primitive camping is allowed at the Shelf Road Climbing Area in designated sites. National Forest campgrounds are in nearby Pike National Forest.

Services: All services in Canon City, Cripple Creek, Victor, and Florence.

Nearby attractions: Royal Gorge Park, Temple Canyon Park, Arkansas Headwaters State Recreation Area, Mueller State Park, Florissant Fossil Beds National Monument, Pikes Peak, Beaver Creek State Wildlife Area, Eleven Mile Canyon, Colorado Springs attractions, Lake Pueblo State Recreation Area.

For more information: BLM, Canon City District Office, 3170 E. Main Street, P.O. Box 2200, Canon City, CO 81212, (719) 275-0631). Canon City Chamber, P.O. Bin 749, Canon City, CO 81215-0749, (719) 275-2331. Cripple Creek Chamber, P.O. Box 650, Cripple Creek, CO 80813, (719) 689-2169.

The drive: Pikes Peak, towering to 14,110 feet, anchors the southern Front Range and forms a distinctive landmark for travelers. Abrupt canyons slice into its bedrock southern slopes, forming deep defiles separated by high, forested ridges. This rugged country remains one of the Front Range's wildest and least-accessible landscapes. It's a bold, sculpted land overlooked by pink granite bastions and inhabited by bighorn sheep, mountain lions, falcons, and rattlesalong the creek nakes. This sixty-four-mile-long scenic drive makes an open loop between Canon City and Cripple Creek on two narrow gravel roads—Shelf Road and Phantom Canyon Road—that thread through precipitous canyons on Pikes Peak's southern slope.

The roads, part of the Bureau of Land Management's Gold Belt Tour Back Country Byway, offer an out-of-the-ordinary scenic driving experience. Both are winding dirt and gravel tracks that often narrow to a single lane for miles at a time in deep canyons or on exposed slopes. Frequent pullouts allow passing on narrow sections. Neither road is well maintained and each is often rough and corrugated, particularly after heavy rain. The Shelf Road's shelf section should not be driven after rain or during snowmelt; its clay surface becomes extremely slippery and there is no guardrail to stop a slip to oblivion. **Trailers, motor homes, or vehicles over twenty-five feet in length should not attempt to travel either road.** Drive defensively on the roads. Always expect another car on blind corners, don't speed, and remember that uphill traffic has the right-of-way.

The drive is open year-round with each season offering its own flavor. Summers tend to be hot in the lower elevations, with highs regularly climbing into the nineties near the Arkansas Valley. The pleasant upper elevation temperatures range from sixty to eighty degrees. Expect thunderstorms on summer afternoons. Autumn days are warm and clear, with occasional showers. Winter brings variable weather. Mild winter weather rules in the

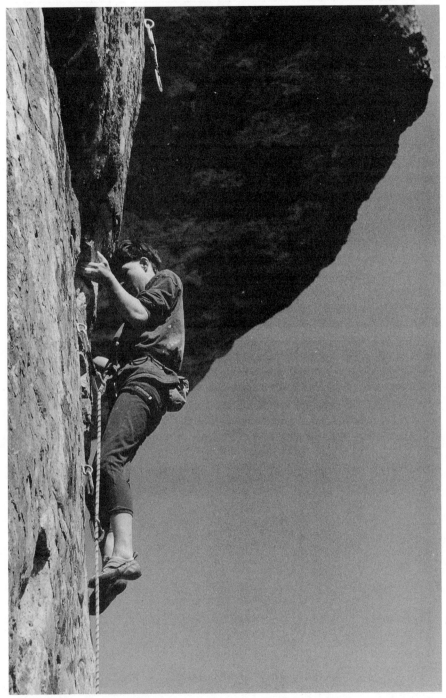

A climber scales The Example, *one of the most difficult climbing routes at the* Shelf Road Climbing Area.

To Divide

MUELLER
STATE PARK

PIKE

•Denver

★

COLORADO

67

Pikes Peak
14,110 ft.

Rhyolite Mtn.
10,780 ft.

NATIONAL

Fourmile

Mt. Pisgah

Cripple Creek

Victor

FOREST

Creek

Phantom

Skaguay
Reservoir

Shelf

Shelf Road
Rock Climbing
Area

RED CANYON
PARK

Canyon

To Colorado
Springs

Cooper Mtn.

Road

Garden Park
Paleontology
Area

Road

115

To
Salida

50

To
Canon
City

Arkansas

Penrose

N

Florence

50

River

To Pueblo

0   2   4   6   8   10
Miles

To Wetmore

lower elevations, with days as warm as fifty degrees and light snowfall. Snowpack and ice slicken shaded road sections near Cripple Creek and Victor between November and February. Spring brings warm, breezy weather to the area along with rain and snow showers.

The Shelf Road drive segment begins in east Canon City. Turn north on Raynolds Avenue from US 50. A Colorado state scenic drive sign with a columbine marks the turn. Head north on Raynolds for 0.7-mile through a residential neighborhood. The street dead ends. Bend left on Pear for 0.1-mile and then north of Fields through fenced pastures and scattered houses. The street, turning into Shelf Road, quickly leaves Canon City behind and climbs a low hill. It crests the flat hill topped with homes and drops through shale hills into Fourmile Creek's canyon.

The roughly paved road swings past a small ranch and tall cottonwoods, and at four-and-a-half-miles enters a cliffed portal carved through tilted Dakota sandstone cliffs by the creek. The canyon quickly deepens with the sandstone layer capping the canyon rim. Slopes below the rim cascade down to the road with a veneer of fallen boulders and scattered pinyon pine, juniper, and rabbit-brush. The first oil well west of the Mississippi River was drilled in this canyon in 1862. The drive winds along benches on the creek's western margin. Indian petroglyphs decorate one roadside boulder. A BLM picnic area with an information kiosk sits part-way up the canyon. The road, turning to gravel past the picnic tables, continues up the shallow canyon. Steep slopes of colored shale and mudstone stairstep back to the higher sandstone rim from the creek. These unassuming soft rock layers, called the Morrison Formation, house one of Colorado's most astounding natural wonders—a dinosaur graveyard.

The Morrison Formation, a thick widespread layer of sandstone, mudstone, siltstone, and shale, was deposited on a vast, swampy floodplain along the edge of a retreating sea during Jurassic times almost 150 million years ago. Wide rivers and streams, flowing from distant mountains and volcanic peaks, sluggishly meandered across a broad basin. Trees lined the river banks and backwater ponds and life flourished on the fertile, sub-tropical landscape. The most prominent residents of this ancient land were giant dinosaurs. The rivers and swamps swallowed their bones after death, slowly entombing, petrifying, and preserving the remains until small Fourmile Creek exhumed the bones in another age.

Dinosaur bones hide in the Morrison Formation all over Colorado and Utah, including Riggs Hill near Grand Junction, the famous quarry in Dinosaur National Monument, near Morrison outside Denver, and at the Garden Park Quarry along Shelf Road. The area's first finds came to local school superintendent O.W. Lucas in March, 1877. Lucas, an amateur botanist studying local plants, found several fossil fragments including a five-foot-long leg bone weathering out of the strata. He sent off samples to eminent Philadelphia paleontologist Edward D. Cope who promptly dispatched excavators to the Garden Park site. Over the next few years Cope and rival Yale scientist Othniel C. Marsh dug into the soft shale and mudstone slopes and found a staggering number of gigantic, almost complete dinosaur

Shelf Road clings to abrupt canyon slopes below limestone cliffs.

skeletons. The first stegasaurus, the official Colorado state fossil, came from the Garden Park quarries, as well as camarasaurus, diplodocus, allosaurus, and ceretosaurus remains. The area also yielded bones from numerous small dinosaurs, plants, and trees. The Denver Museum of Natural History continues to probe the Garden Park Quarry, excavating dinosaur remains in 1992. A state historic marker, sitting near the canyon's northern end, commemorates the Garden Park Quarry and its buried treasures.

The drive swings across Fourmile Creek beneath low bluffs and climbs into Garden Park, a long broad valley flanked by rolling hills and steep mountains. The dusty road traverses the valley for almost five miles, passing hayfields, fenced paddocks with grazing cattle and horses, and the cotton-wood-lined creek. Mule deer and wild turkeys often congregate in the open fields along the creek in early evening. The drive passes the entrance to Red Canyon Park, a six hundred-acre Canon City parkland, just after crossing the creek half-way up the valley. The park, a maze of upturned sandstone layers, fringes the base of Rice Mountain on Garden Park's western edge. This primitive, off-the-beaten-track park offers eroded hoodoos and spires, long sweeping escarpments chiseled from red sandstone, a maze of hiking trails that thread among the formations, and picnic tables.

The road continues north past a couple ranches into dry hills studded with pinyons and junipers. At twelve miles the University Wall looms to the east, lifting its leaning limestone rampart above Fourmile Creek's shallow gorge. The road passes a stylish ranch house and climbs onto an almost level plain coated with shortgrass and surrounded by low woods. Just east of here inside the canyon rim lie two small caves—Marble and Fly caves. Wilson Cave hides further up Helena Canyon.

Prominent limestone cliff bands rim the low hills and canyons north of the road. These short, sharp cliffs comprise Shelf Road Climbing Area, one of Colorado's best sport climbing areas with hundreds of established routes. Two turns lead to the best crags. The first goes through a gate and bumps northwest across a pasture to a primitive campground and parking area for The Gallery and Sand Gulch. A tenth of a mile north is a marked BLM road that climbs north to The Bank and The Dark Side, two long cliff bands in Trail Gulch. Some of the area's best routes, including Thunder Tactics, Heavy Weather, and Back to the Future, ascend The Bank's blond limestone walls. Almost all of the area's routes are protected with permanent bolts and anchors. A primitive campground sits at the parking area above The Bank.

Shelf Road twists down a slight canyon with pinyon pines, junipers, and boulders tacked to the hillside. After a stone's throw the track emerges onto a four-mile-long shelf hacked from a steep slope between cliff bands in Helena Canyon. This spectacular road section offers stunning scenery, dramatic dropoffs below the passenger windows, and a white-knuckle grip for inexperienced mountain drivers. Most of the shelf is single-lane, with only the occasional outside pullout for passing. The road edges sinuously along the shelf, only leaving the main canyon to dip into Trail Gulch. Fourmile Creek, dashing over worn boulders and bedrock, riffles far below the road in a somber granite gorge. Above, the shelf stretches a band of limestone broken into varnished black faces and tawny overhangs and aretes. Steep slopes littered with boulders and cholla cacti cascade below the cliffs to the roadside. The Ordovician period sandstone deposited atop the ancient Precambrian granite below the road preserves traces of some of the world's oldest known vertebrate life. Small blue dots are revealed through the microscope as fossilized platelets of *Agnathid* fish that swam in an ancient ocean over five hundred million years ago here.

The road follows the track of an 1892 toll stage road that ran from Canon City to the new gold camp at Cripple Creek. The uphill ride took six hours and required eighteen horses in teams of six. Stages paid tolls on each rig's number of horses at both ends of the shelf itself. The lower tollkeeper's cabin ruin lies on a spacious bend on the canyon floor just after the shelf road begins.

After three miles the road begins a gentle descent through a mixed conifer forest and a mile later reaches the canyon floor and crosses the creek. The drive winds up the east side of the creek in a broadening canyon for a couple miles before reaching a long stack of tailings excavated from the Carlton Drainage Tunnel. The six-mile-long tunnel, bored in 1941, drained water from gold mines north of Victor. Past the tailings the drive turns away from Fourmile Creek and enters a steep canyon carved by Cripple Creek.

Shelf Road follows Cripple Creek for the next eight miles. The road corkscrews up a deep canyon flanked by towering granite cliffs and steep talus and scrub oak-covered slopes. The creek trickles over boulders and past small quaking aspen groves. Window Rock, an unusual granite arch, towers over the road a couple miles up-canyon. Bighorn sheep often graze along these boulder-strewn slopes. Higher up the canyon becomes a shallow grassy valley and passes several old mines before intersecting paved CO 67 just south of the town of Cripple Creek.

Cripple Creek and its sister city, Victor, lie in the fabulously wealthy Cripple Creek Mining District, a collapsed volcanic caldera rimmed with gold. Local cowboy Bob Womack first found gold in nearby Poverty Gulch in 1890. His claim, the El Paso Lode, sparked a gold rush to the Pikes Peak region. Almost overnight a town sprang up and by 1900 more than fifty thousand people lived in Cripple Creek, Colorado's fourth-largest city. During the boom years the district's 500 mines yielded over 340 million dollars in gold at the prevailing price of $20.67 per ounce. The area mines eventually yielded more ore than the California and Alaska gold rushes combined. Today active mining continues and geologists say a fortune in gold still lies underground. Cripple Creek, now preserved in a national historic district, offers numerous attractions including the Cripple Creek District Museum, the Cripple Creek & Victor Narrow Gauge Railroad, the Old Homestead brothel, and gambling houses.

The drive turns south on CO 67, winding five miles south to Victor through aspen, spruce, and pine forests. Dramatic views unfold along this lofty highway stretch of the snow-capped Sangre de Cristo Range and the broad Arkansas River Valley. The highway passes the Carlton Mill, part of the Cripple Creek and Victor Gold Mining Company. The road bends through a roadcut and enters 9,729-foot Victor, nicknamed the "city of mines." The slopes of Battle Mountain, looming north of town, are studded with colored mine tailings from famous mines like the Ajax, Portland, and Independence. The Gold Coin Mine operated within Victor itself. Victor, a national historic district, remains a mining town at heart, with old brick buildings, frame houses, and working-class ethic. The drive meanders through downtown Victor before bending onto the Phantom Canyon Road at the town's far southeast corner.

The dirt Phantom Canyon Road runs thirty-one miles south to US 50. The road initially loops across high benches and rolling hills covered with meadows, aspen groves, and spruce and pine forests. A turn, just outside Victor, leads east six miles to eighty-four-acre Skagway Reservoir, a popular state wildlife area with fishing and camping. The road traverses the abandoned railbed of the old Florence and Cripple Creek Railroad, "The Gold Belt Line." The railroad carried raw ore from Cripple Creek's mines to nine reduction mills in Florence. At Alta Vista the road begins a slow descent for a few miles before dropping steeply into Phantom Canyon. The train originally climbed the Wilbur Loop on four percent grades out of the canyon with helper engines.

After reaching upper Phantom Canyon the road bends south and follows the canyon floor past granite crags, aspens, and pine-covered hills. The road gently winds down, the canyon alternately widening and narrowing. Fifteen miles down, the canyon pinches off to a narrow slot, with Eightmile Creek and the road twisting below tall cliffs. Beyond the canyon widens and drops steeply below the road as it edges across dry mountain slopes. After crossing a steel bridge built in 1897, the road reaches a BLM information booth and the parking area for access to the adjoining Beaver Creek BLM Wilderness Study Area. This proposed 20,750-acre wilderness area, accessible via a trail by the bridge, encompasses the rugged canyons of East and West Beaver creeks and a renowned cutthroat trout fishery.

The narrow road continues down-canyon past the abandoned townsite of

The Teressa Mine, one of the Cripple Creek Mining District's largest gold producers, sits above Victor and the Phantom Canyon Road.

Adelaide, a train watering stop. As the road descends the canyon deepens and becomes drier. Pinyon pine, juniper, cactus, and yucca replace the spruce, fir, and pine forests of higher elevations, and the creek slows to a trickle among cottonwoods. The road runs through two tunnels built in 1895 after floods destroyed the original track alignment. A mile past Tunnel #1 the canyon walls slacken, the mountains become rounded, and the drive runs through a narrow gate hemmed in by tall rock walls. The canyon widens and the road bends west along a sandstone hogback and then south into a broad valley flanked by the mountain uplift and the sawtoothed Dakota hogback. The road becomes paved and swings past the turn to Indian Springs Trace Fossil Natural Area.

This national natural landmark, on private land, exhibits surface trails on sandstone of 460-million-year-old arthropods. The area, once a mudflat in a tidal lagoon, preserves some twenty-five different kinds of markings left by diverse animals including a brachiopod; the walking, foraging, and borrowing of an ancestral horseshoe crab; walking and swimming tracks from a giant trilobite; and evidence of a jawless armor-plated fish, one of the world's first known vertebrates. The site's owners conduct tours and offer a private campground.

The drive passes through a deep notch chiseled into the hogback, twists through a shallow canyon, and climbs onto a broad bench above Sixmile Creek. The road runs south through a typical Upper Sonoran ecosystem with short grass and cholla cacti, and stops a few miles later at US 50. Canon City sits four miles to the west, while Florence lies three miles straight south on CO 67 along the Arkansas River.

9 PIKES PEAK HIGHWAY
Cascade to the summit of Pikes Peak

General description: A 20-mile-long paved and gravel toll road that climbs to the windswept summit of 14,110-foot Pikes Peak, Colorado's 31st highest peak.

Special attractions: Scenic views, hiking, rock climbing, Bottomless Pit, Glen Cove, tundra plants and above-timberline ecosystem, Barr Trail, Pikes Peak Cog Railroad, fishing.

Location: East-central Colorado. Pikes Peak towers over Colorado Springs and the surrounding Front Range 70 miles south of Denver. The scenic highway begins in Cascade off U.S. Highway 24 about 5 miles west of Manitou Springs.

Drive route name and number: Pikes Peak Highway, Forest Road 58.

Travel season: The road is usually open from May through October depending on the weather and snow conditions. Call the tollgate for more information.

To Woodland Park

Denver

UTE PASS

24 **Green Mountain Falls**

Catamount Reservoirs

Crow Gulch Picnic Area

Halfway Picnic Area

Crystal Creek Reservoir

Cascade

PIKE

Glen Cove Picnic Area

24 To Colorado Springs

Mt. Manitou

Bottomless Pit

Barr Trail

Railroad

Manitou Springs

Sentinel Point 12,526 ft.

Pikes Peak 14,110 ft.

Pikes Peak

Cog

Cameron Cone 10,707 ft.

NATIONAL

Lake Moraine

FOREST

N

Almagre Mtn. 12,226 ft.

0 2 4 6 8 10
Miles

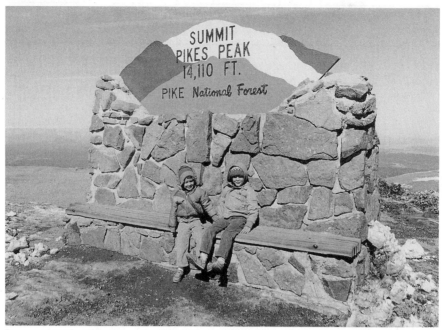

Boys enjoy the thin air atop Pikes Peak's lofty 14,110-foot-high summit.

Camping: No camping is allowed along the highway. Many campgrounds are found in the surrounding Pike National Forest at the Crags, Eleven Mile Canyon, north of Woodland Park on Colorado Highway 67, and along the Rampart Range Road. Private campgrounds are in Colorado Springs.

Services: There are no services on the drive, except for food at Glen Cove and the Summit House. Limited services are available at Cascade and Green Mountain Falls at the highway's base. Complete visitor services are found in Colorado Springs, Manitou Springs, and Woodland Park.

Nearby attractions: Colorado Springs attractions, Air Force Academy, Garden of the Gods, North Cheyenne Canyon, Cripple Creek, Florissant Fossil Beds National Monument, Eleven Mile Canyon, Pike National Forest, Lost Creek Wilderness Area, Mueller State Park, Royal Gorge, Gold Belt Tour Back Country Byway.

For more information: Pikes Peak Highway Tollgate, (719) 684-9383. Colorado Springs Dept. of Public Works, P.O. Box 1575, Colorado Springs, CO 80901, (719) 684-9383. Colorado Springs Convention and Visitors Bureau, 104 S. Cascade, Suite 104, Colorado Springs, CO 80903, (719) 635-7506 and (800) 888-4748.

The drive: Pikes Peak stands high above the tawny Colorado prairie like a strong, silent sentinel. From far out on the undulating plains it appears against the western horizon like a gleaming white cloud. From its base, the peak lifts bulky shoulders over its low, forested neighbors, rising almost 8,000 feet from Colorado Springs to its snow-capped 14,110-foot summit.

The great peak has long been a beacon for travelers. Its distinctive outline, seen from over one hundred miles away, was a landmark to the Ute Indians, early explorers and trappers, traders on the Santa Fe Trail, and prospectors and settlers heading west during the 1850s "Pikes Peak or Bust" rush to northern Colorado's gold fields. The peak, Colorado's thirty-first highest summit, is perhaps America's most famous mountain. More people reach its sixty-acre summit—via Barr Trail, the Pikes Peak Cog Railroad, and the Pikes Peak Highway—than any other high peak in the United States. The highway, ascending twenty miles to the peak's summit, is one of Colorado's highest and best drives. The paved and gravel road offers expansive views and dramatic scenery.

The Pikes Peak Highway is one of the most expensive roads to maintain in the United States. Deep snow, as much as seven million cubic feet, is removed from the highway every spring. Melting snow also damages and erodes the road surface. Because of costly maintenance, the City of Colorado Springs, which operates the highway under permit from Pike National Forest, charges a toll for all travelers.

Allow at least two hours for the forty-mile round trip. Drivers should make sure their vehicles are in excellent operating condition. Use lower gears when ascending and descending the peak to avoid overheating and riding the brakes. The Pikes Peak Patrol checks brakes at Glen Cove for excessive brake heat on busy days and weekends. Use the numerous highway pullouts for sightseeing and allowing faster traffic to pass. The highway is very narrow in places, clinging to steep slopes. Stay on your side of the road, do not cut corners, avoid passing on blind corners, and stay within the speed limit. Up-hill traffic has the right-of-way. The Pikes Peak Patrol regularly traverses the highway and provides road assistance. **Travelers with cardiac and respiratory problems should not make the ascent.**

The Pikes Peak Highway is generally open from May through October, although, depending on weather conditions and snowfall it may open earlier and close later. Highway travelers should be prepared for all weather conditions. Snow often falls on the highway leaving a muddy and slick surface. The weather atop the peak is usually cool and breezy. While summer temperatures in Cascade at the drive's start are often in the eighties, it can be as cold as thirty degrees on Pikes Peak's summit. Be prepared by bringing warm clothes and a raincoat. Autumn days are generally brisk and clear.

The Pikes Peak Highway begins off US 24 in 7,400-foot-high Cascade five miles west of Manitou Springs. Exit west off US 24 and follow the signs to the highway tollgate almost a mile from Cascade. The road begins climbing immediately up steep mountain slopes thickly clad in ponderosa pine, Douglas-fir, and Engelmann spruce. The highway reaches Camera Point, the first overlook, just under a mile from the tollgate. This lofty point yields a spectacular view down Ute Pass to Colorado Springs and the distant prairie.

Ute Pass is not a pass at all, but rather an abrupt canyon sliced into the Front Range escarpment that separates the Pikes Peak massif from the

Rampart Range. The canyon, carved by Fountain Creek, follows the weakened line of the almost sixty-mile-long Ute Pass Fault. Ute Pass has long offered an easy passage from the plains into the mountains. The Ute Indians regularly followed a trail down the pass from their mountain strongholds to the mineral springs at Manitou Springs and the rich hunting grounds east of the Front Range. A freight road was built up the pass in 1872 to better serve the South Park mining camps, and the Colorado Midland Railroad, a standard gauge line between Colorado Springs and Aspen, was completed in 1887. The railroad, with tunnels and railbed still existing in Ute Pass, climbed four percent grades up the pass to Divide. The pass was a dangerous place in the 1860s with numerous robberies and murders.

The road swings west from the viewpoint and quickly enters Cascade Creek's hanging valley. The highway twists up a shallow canyon. Immense granite boulders, scattered hillsides of pine and fir, and groves of quaking aspen line the highway. A picnic ground with restrooms sits at Crow Gulch on the road's north side at three miles. Beyond, the highway climbs up and away from Cascade Creek, reaches nine thousand feet, and drops north above Crystal Creek Reservoir. Most of Pikes Peak is part of the Colorado Springs watershed. Numerous dams plug the mountain's creeks forming sparkling reservoirs. Trout fishing is allowed at Crystal Creek Reservoir. After crossing the reservoir spillway, the highway climbs rounded gravel ridges and at seven miles the road surface becomes graded gravel.

Pikes Peak towers south of the highway, an abrupt wall of ragged cliffs, buttresses, cirques, and ridges. Steep gullies coated with snow and ice plunge down the peak's north face. Pikes Peak, composed of billion-year-old Pikes Peak granite, is a huge batholith or mass of once-molten rock that cooled under the earth's crust as the core of a mountain range. The granite later lifted as part of the ancestral Rocky Mountains eroded, and then rose again as today's peak. Glaciers chiseled and sculpted Pikes Peak's distinctive features over the last million years. Thick glaciers perched on the mountainside, carving out huge cirques on the peak's east flank including the Crater, North Pit, and Bottomless Pit. The last of the glaciers disappeared about eleven thousand years ago.

Pikes Peak and the surrounding granite region is renowned for its exquisite minerals and gemstones, some that have been found include smoky quartz, topaz, amethyst, amazonstone, fluorite, and zircon crystals. Delicate blue topaz crystals are found on the steep cliffs above Glen Cove on the highway. Pikes Peak, while not a volcano, has suffered volcanic episodes on its western slopes. Rich gold deposits hide in the Cripple Creek mining district southwest of the peak in the caldera of a collapsed volcano.

The highway climbs southward over humpbacked ridges broken by shallow canyons toward the looming peak. At almost ten miles the road reaches 10,000 feet and passes Halfway Picnic Ground. Past here the highway begins switchbacking across steep forested slopes and three miles later reaches Glen Cove at 11,425 feet. Glen Cove, with limited services for travelers, lies in a north-facing alpine cirque carved by a hanging glacier. Granite crags and boulders litter the steep mountainsides above the cirque

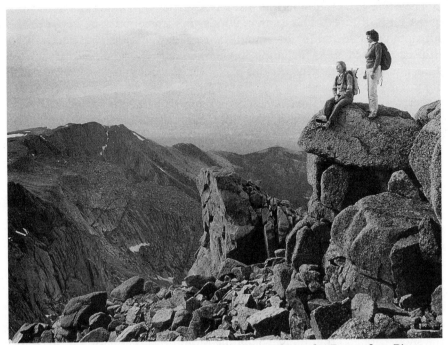

Hikers pause on Pikes Peak's abrupt north face above the Bottomless Pit.

floor. Steep snow-filled couloirs attract extreme skiers in May and early June.

Pikes Peak began attracting tourists in the 1870s who trekked on foot or mule to its lofty summit above the new resort community of Colorado Springs. The first road, a seventeen-mile carriage road, reached the summit in 1889 allowing visitors to ride in comfort to the top. But the completion and popularity of the nearby cog railway in 1891 forced the wagon route to close by 1905. In 1913 Cripple Creek mining magnate Spencer Penrose joined with Charles Noble, a retired railroad man, and petitioned the Department of Agriculture to build a new road for automobiles to the peak's summit. Naysayers said no automobile had enough power to climb the peak, but on July 17, 1913 two Denver men drove a Buick Bear Cat up the carriage road to the summit in four hours. The first auto to reach the summit was a Locomobile Steamer in 1901. In 1914 the federal govenment gave Penrose a permit to build the road, warning him it would cost as much as $25,000. The highway, completed in 1915, climbed 6,746 feet on an average six percent grade to the peak's apex and ended up costing over $250,000. Penrose started the Pikes Peak Hill Climb auto race, the world's highest auto race, in 1916 to give needed publicity to his expensive road. The race tradition continues every July on the highway's gravel section. The highway operated as a toll road until 1936, but Penrose never recognized a profit on his investment due to the road's expensive maintenance. The deteriorating road was free until 1948 when Colorado Springs recieved a permit from the National Forest Service to operate the highway.

The drive reaches timberline just past Glen Cove. Timberline marks the upper limit of forest. This snowy, windswept transition zone between the subalpine spruce and fir forest and the treeless tundra is characterized by stunted, twisted trees including Englemann spruce, subalpine fir, limber pine, and bristlecone pine. At this elevation, the trees grow slowly because of extreme temperatures and the short growing season.

Past timberline the highway climbs steeply up a flattened ridge. Elk Park, a grassy knoll with a parking area, lies a mile past Glen Cove. A marvelous view of the peak's rugged north face and surrounding mountains and valleys spreads out below this timberline viewpoint. A trail, following an old road, heads southeast from here and drops into North Pit, an abrupt glacier-carved cirque.

The road edges up the mountain flank for the next two miles, gaining almost one thousand feet of elevation on eight twisting switchbacks. This airy road section is particularly treacherous on both cars and drivers. Remember to keep to your side of the highway on the sharp turns. Use lower gears when ascending to keep a constant speed and avoid overheating, and when descending to keep brakes from overheating. Pump the brakes to reduce speed rather than applying continuous pressure. At the top of the switchbacks sits 16-Mile Turnout. This overlook offers spacious views to the north across the broad rolling South Platte River country. Beyond the river basin stretches the snow-capped Front Range including Mount Evans and Mount Bierstadt. The Tarryall Range lifts its jagged brow of broken rock and rough summits to the northwest.

Devils Playground lies immediately south of the pullout. A good hike

The Pikes Peak Highway snakes up the peak's boulder-strewn north flank.

heads west along a rounded ridge to a couple good viewpoints. This area is a good place to explore the delicate alpine tundra ecosystem. The climate and growing season on this lonely, windswept ridge are the same as that in northern Canada and Alaska. Despite the climatic rigors, including a below-freezing mean annual temperature, a frost-free season that is at most two months long, and winds exceeding one hundred miles per hour, numerous plants and shrubs thrive at this elevation. July and August bring a carpet of colorful wildflowers to these mountain heights—greenish-white Arctic gentians, yellow paintbrush, spiked elephant flowers, brilliant alpine sunflowers, and many others. Over 250 plant species grow above timberline in the Colorado Rockies. Most are small perennials that not only endure but thrive in this stark land of never summer.

From the Devil's Playground parking area the highway uncoils across Pikes Peak's long northern ridge. The road slowly climbs past 13,000 feet and passes a couple great viewpoints. The first overlooks the deep chasm of North Pit, its steep walls littered with soaring granite crags and buttresses. Past the North Pit view the highway swings around a rocky knob and reaches the Bottomless Pit overlook at 13,200 feet. The cirque falls away below the viewpoint. Long rock ribs plunge north from the peak's summit to the distant cirque floor. Vertical cliffs, stained with snowmelt and cracked by ice, line the precipitous abyss far below.

The highway's final two miles slowly scale the boulder-strewn western slope of the peak's final rock pyramid, edging across precipitous slopes. After the last switchback and the last incline the road ends on the peak's level sixty-acre summit. This lofty sky-island sits more than two and a half miles above sea level at 14,110 feet.

Pikes Peak is, of course, America's most famous mountain. The peak, well known to the Indians, was called "Long Mountain" by the Arapahoes. Black Elk, an Oglala Sioux medicine man, had a vision of the sacred peak at the age of nine as the cloud home of the six Grandfathers that represented *Wakantanka*, the Great Spirit of the Sioux religion. Lieutenant Zebulon Pike first spotted the peak that bears his name from far out on the Colorado plains on November 15, 1806. He recorded the occasion in his journal: "At two o'clock I thought I could distinguish a mountain to our right, which appeared like a small blue cloud." Pike dubbed it Grand Peak and calculated its elevation at 18,851 feet. Pike and a small party of soldiers were dispatched by President Thomas Jefferson in 1806 to explore and determine the southern boundary of the newly acquired Louisiana Purchase, a vast swath of pristine land that swept from the Mississippi River to the Pacific coast.

Pike and three of his ill-equipped men later left their Arkansas River camp in today's Pueblo and attempted to scale Grand Peak. Freezing temperatures and a blizzard conspired to defeat the feeble effort. Pike noted in his journal that "the summit of the Grand Peak, which was entirely bare of vegetation and covered with snow, now appeared at the distance of fifteen to sixteen miles from us, and as high again as what we had ascended, and would have taken a whole days march to have arrived at its base, when I believe no human being could have ascended to its pinnacle."

The peak was first ascended by Anglo-Americans on July 14, 1820 when botanist Dr. Edwin James and two companions from Major Stephen Long's "Expedition from Pittsburgh to the Rocky Mountains" ascended its east flank. In the process the trio started a major forest fire after leaving a smoldering campfire. In 1858 twenty-year-old Julia Archibald Holmes became the first white woman to ascend Pikes Peak. On the summit she penned a letter to her mother, saying: "In all probability I am the first woman who has ever stood upon the summit of this mountain and gazed upon this wondrous scene, which my eyes now behold...all, and everything, on which the eye can rest, fills the mind with infinitude, and sends the soul to God."

Not much has changed over the last 150 years, magnificent panoramas still spread out below the rocky summit in every direction. To the east, the peak's escarpment sweeps down to low forested mountains, jewel-like reservoirs and lakes nestled among ridges, and the urban sprawl of Colorado Springs. Beyond stretches the brown prairie, its grasslands reaching the Kansas horizon. The Spanish Peaks, twin landmarks on the Santa Fe Trail, and the serrated crest of the Sangre de Cristo Mountains glisten in the sunlight like alabaster towers in the south. The Continental Divide, Colorado's mountainous spine, marches across the western rim. Its distant peaks and ridges painted in smoky blue and shaded with pastels. Clear days yield marvelous views northward to Longs Peak in Rocky Mountain National Park over one hundred miles away, while Denver's skyscrapers huddle in a broad basin below the mountain uplift.

The breathtaking views from Pikes Peak's summit inspired "America the Beautiful," the nation's unofficial anthem. Katherine Lee Bates, a visiting eastern English professor at Colorado College, rode to the summit in a wagon in the summer of 1893. The view inspired her to write: "Oh beautiful for spacious skies, for amber waves of grain, for purple mountain majesties above the fruited plain...." She later recalled, "The opening lines of the hymn floated into my mind as I was looking out over the sealike expanse of fertile country spreading away so far under those ample skies."

The Pikes Peak Summit House sits on the eastern edge of the summit, with a snack bar and gift shop. The Barr Trail, a thirteen-mile National Recreation Trail, drops east from the summit house, swinging down a broad face and over forested mountains to Manitou Springs almost 8,000 feet below. The strenuous Pikes Peak Marathon follows the trail every August. The Pikes Peak Cog Railway, the highest in the world, also ends at the Summit House. The 8.9-mile railway climbs to the acme on grades as steep as twenty-five percent. Follow the highway back down the peak to Cascade twenty miles away. Remember to let the auto's gears do the work, and don't ride the brakes.

General description: This 72-mile drive runs north from Woodland Park to Deckers where the road divides and forms a loop that follows the South Platte River and the river's North Fork to the historic town of Buffalo Creek and the drive's end at Pine Junction.

Special attractions: Pike National Forest, Manitou Lake, South Platte River, Buffalo Creek, Pine, North Fork National Historic District, hiking, fishing, camping, picnicking, rock climbing, hiking, Colorado Trail, mountain biking, scenic views.

Location: Central Colorado. The drive's southern terminus begins in Woodland Park off U.S. Highway 24 20 miles west of Colorado Springs. The northern access is via U.S. Highway 285 at Pine Junction some 25 miles west of Denver.

Drive route numbers: Colorado Highway 67, Jefferson County Roads 126, 96, and 97, Douglas County roads 40 and 67.

Travel season: Year-round. The drive is open all winter, although snow and ice accumulate in shaded areas.

Camping: Ten national forest campgrounds—Redrocks, South Meadows, Colorado, Painted Rocks, Lone Rock, Wigwam, Kelsey, Top of the World, Platte River, and Bridge Crossing—are found along the drive.

Services: All services are found in Woodland Park. Limited services are at Pine Junction, Pine, Buffalo Creek, and Deckers.

Nearby attractions: Lost Creek Wilderness Area, Mount Evans Wilderness Area, Rampart Range Road, Devils Head, Mount Evans scenic drive, Guanella Pass scenic drive, Chatfield State Recreation Area, Denver area attractions, Colorado Springs area attractions, Cripple Creek, Florissant Fossil Beds, Pikes Peak Highway, Mueller State Park, Rampart Reservoir Recreation Area.

For more information: Pike National Forest, Pikes Peak Ranger District, 601 S. Weber St., Colorado Springs, CO 80903, (719) 636-1602. South Platte Ranger District, 19316 Doddard Ranch Crt, Morrison, CO 80465, (303) 275-5610.

The drive: The South Platte River, arising on the Continental Divide's snowy peaks above Fairplay, twists 360 miles across Colorado to the Nebraska border. The river, draining over 28,000 square miles, is Colorado's workhorse. The South Platte and its mountain tributaries irrigate the state's fertile northeastern corner and yield tap water for over sixty percent of Colorado's population including Denver, Boulder, and Fort Collins. From the air, this working river looks like a string of watery pearls, with numerous reservoirs that impound its tumbling waters. Still, despite the dams and irrigation projects, the river retains a wild character through much of its

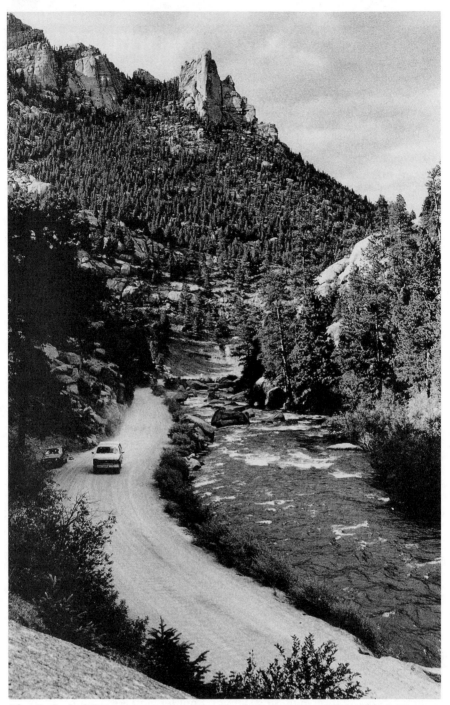

The Cathedral Spires tower above the North Fork River and the South Platte River Roads Drive.

To Denver

Pine Junction

To Fairplay

To Denver

Sedalia

To Castle Rock

Cathedral Spires

Pine

North   Fork

Buffalo Creek

Top of the World CG

River

Long Scraggy Pk. 8,812 ft.

Kelsey CG

LOST

Green Mtn. 10,421 ft.

PIKE

COLORADO

•Denver

CREEK

Buffalo Pk. 11,588 ft.

WILDERNESS

Lone Rock CG

Bridge Crossing CG

AREA

Wigwam CG

Deckers

Devils Head 9,748 ft.

Cheesman Lake

Platte

NATIONAL

Thunder Butte 9,836 ft.

Turkey Rock

South

Manitou Lake

Painted Rocks CG

Colorado CG

FOREST

South Meadows CG

Red Rocks CG

To Hartsel

Lake George

Woodland Park

N

Divide

UTE PASS

0   5   10

Miles

Pikes Peak 14,110 ft.

To Colorado Springs

rugged mountain course. Some of the river's best scenery remains in deep, wooded canyons in the low mountains southwest of Denver, an area the Denver Water Board wants to change someday with its proposed Two Forks Dam. The seventy-two-mile South Platte River scenic drive, following CO 67 and several county roads, explores these canyons and the surrounding piney mountains between Woodland Park and Pine Junction. The area, close to both Colorado Springs and Denver, is a popular destination for weekend campers and fishermen.

Weather along the drive is generally pleasant year-round, although spring, summer, and fall are the preferred travel seasons. Spring days are mild and windy, with highs reaching sixty degrees with occasional rain. Summer highs range between sixty and eighty degrees, with afternoon thunderstorms usually falling somewhere along the drive. Summer at the drive's higher elevations gives welcome relief from flatland heat. Fall brings cooler but dry days until the first snow falls in November. Winter days can be very mild, with highs reaching into the fifties. Snow generally clings to cold north-facing slopes, but the roads are usually dry with ice only in shaded spots.

The scenic drive begins at the intersection of US 24 and CO 67 on the west side of Woodland Park twenty miles northwest of Colorado Springs. Woodland Park, a mountain bedroom community at 8,500 feet, spreads across a broad, wooded valley west of the Rampart Range. The town offers all traveler services. The drive's first twenty-three miles, following CO 67, traverse lovely countryside with rolling hills, forested mountains, grassy valleys, and shallow canyons to Deckers on the South Platte River. This slice of landscape is more representative of Colorado's Front Range than the usual image of immense snow-capped peaks. It's a land of intimate views—a sweep of wind-rippled grass; cloud reflections in a serene beaver pond; aspen groves strewn with sky-blue columbines; the dusty smell of dry ponderosa pine needles clotting the forest floor.

The drive heads north on CO 67 and leaves most of Woodland Park's suburban development behind after two miles and enters Pike National Forest at four miles. Pike National Forest sprawls across 1.1-million acres of central Colorado's mountains and includes not only the South Platte's canyons but the historic landmark Pikes Peak, Lost Creek Wilderness Area, and the lofty Mosquito Range. Sixty-four-site South Meadows Campground, the first in a succession of national forest campgrounds scattered along the highway, is reached at five miles. Past the campground the road leaves the pine forest and skirts the east side of willow-lined Trout Creek in a broad valley. The highway passes Colorado Campground, with eighty-one sites, at almost seven miles, crosses the creek, and reaches the turn to Painted Rocks Campground, a pleasant eighteen-site area just west of the drive. The Painted Rocks are small eroded pinnacles nestled in the pine forest, the remains of downfaulted Paleozoic sandstone rocks that floor the valley north of Woodland Park. Both the highway and Trout Creek follow the Ute Pass Fault, a major Front Range fault that runs over sixty miles from south of Colorado Springs to north of Woodland Park.

Manitou Lake Picnic Area, with forty-two sites, sits alongside Manitou

Pikes Peak reflects in Manitou Lake along the South Platte River Roads Drive.

Lake, a small reservoir on Trout Creek. This popular recreation area offers fishing, canoeing, and hiking as well as picnicking. A paved two-mile-long bike/hike trail, bordering the highway, links the lake area with Colorado and South Meadows campgrounds to the south.

The highway dips and rolls past Manitou Lake, running through open ponderosa pine woods and green meadows west of Trout Creek before turning away from the broad valley onto rounded ridges clad in spruce, fir, and aspen. At thirteen miles the road crosses a divide, passes a pioneer cemetery, and drops down to West Creek's canyon. Thunder Butte, a ragged 9,836-foot mountain, dominates northwest of the drive, while domed Sheep's Nose, a premier rock climbing crag, and Bell Rock sit to the west. The drive turns north and follows West Creek through a shallow, winding canyon, lined with pine, spruce, and fir, that alternately wides and narrows for nine miles to Deckers on the South Platte River.

Deckers, a small fishing resort with a restaurant and supplies, sits at a crossroads on the river. The townsite, founded about 1885 as Daffodil, was renamed in 1912 for Steve Decker who operated a store and saloon here. The scenic drive makes a loop from here, heading north on Jefferson County 126 to Pine Junction on US 285 before backtracking to Buffalo Creek and following county roads along the North Fork and the South Platte River back to Deckers. The drive crosses the river at Deckers and heads west up County 126 along the north bank. This river section offers excellent fishing with flies and lures only. Nineteen-site Lone Rock Campground sits alongside the river just upstream from Deckers. The drive continues above the river, crossing gravel slopes studded with ponderosa pines.

Two-and-a-half miles from Deckers the road turns away from the river up Wigwam Creek and shortly afterwards swings northward up Sixmile Creek. A side road turns off the main drive along Wigwam Creek and heads southwest past Cheeseman Lake and Lost Creek Wilderness Area toward Lake George and US 24. Wigwam Campground, with ten walk-in sites, sits alongside the drive where it turns north. The paved road climbs steeply up Sixmile Creek's valley, widening to three lanes, and reaches a broad ridge crest after three miles. Green Mountain, its 10,421-foot summit wreathed in broken granite and forest green, looms to the west.

Kelsey Campground, with seventeen sites nestled in pine and aspen woods, sits a mile farther up the drive. The road bends around Little Scraggy Peak onto its abrupt east flank and reaches a scenic overlook. This lofty point offers spectacular views eastward across the South Platte drainage—Long Scraggy Peak lifts its craggy ridge to the east while the river canyon hides in a maze of forest below. The Rampart Range, dominated by Devil's Head, rims the eastern horizon. The drive continues north along Little Scraggy's east slope onto a broad ridge. A roadside parking area here offers access to popular sections of the Colorado Trail, a 469-mile-long footpath that winds from Denver to Durango. A mile past the trailhead, Forest Road 538 turns east and runs 1.75 miles to Top of the World Campground, a seven-site campground that straddles a high ridge.

The road drops abruptly through pine forest and after two miles reaches the broad valley of the North Fork of the South Platte River and the picturesque community of Buffalo Creek. The town, mostly vacation cabins, is anchored by the Green Mercantile, an immense granite building perched on the riverbank alongside the drive. This old-fashioned country store, run by the same family since 1883, offers groceries and local chat. Buffalo Creek began as a railroad stop for area mines and lumber in 1880 on the now-abandoned Denver, South Park, and Pacific Railway.

The scenic drive forks at Buffalo Creek. A ten-mile spur continues north up County 126 to Pine Junction on US 285 west of Denver. This short road section, allowing drive access from Denver, is not to be missed. From Buffalo Creek the road twists through a granite-walled gorge. The river, in early summer, roars with mountain snowmelt alongside the drive. After a mile the road enters a wide, placid valley with the North Fork gently meandering between grassy banks. Grazing cattle and horses dot the meadows and complete the pastoral scene. Two miles later the road enters 6,738-foot-high Pine and the North Fork National Historic District. Pine, like its downstream neighbor, was established in the early 1880s as a railroad stop called Pine Grove. This charming, historic community sits amid spectacular granite monoliths and bucolic meadows at Sphinx Park. Sphinx Rock, bearing a fanciful resemblance to its Egyptian counterpart, looms east of town. Past Pine the drive twists up Pine Gulch through dry hills covered with ponderosa pine, mountain mahogany, and yucca and reaches Pine Junction and US 285 six miles from Pine. To complete the scenic drive, backtrack to Buffalo Creek.

The last leg of the scenic drive follows the South Platte River's North Fork and the South Platte River for twenty-four miles to Deckers. Most of this drive section is unpaved and is intensively managed by Pike National Forest as the South Platte River Corridor. This river segment, lying close to Colorado's major metropolitan areas, is both used and abused. The forest's management plan addresses and alleviates use problems to create a positive recreational experience for visitors. The fifteen-mile road section from Buffalo Creek to Nighthawk is a day-use only area. Parking is permitted only in designated parking areas. Camping is allowed on the Nighthawk to Deckers section only in designated campgrounds.

The drive's first ten miles, following Jefferson County 96, heads northeast then southeast from Buffalo Creek to the confluence of the river's two forks at South Platte, following the abandoned railbed of the Denver, South Park, and Pacific Railway, a narrow gauge line that ran from Denver to the rich mining district of Fairplay and on to Buena Vista and Gunnison in the 1880s. In 1885 George Crofutt described the railside scenery through the Platte Canyon in his *Grip-Sack Guide of Colorado*: "The road...crosses and recrosses the river many times while ascending the narrow gorge between towering mountains...In places these mountains are sloping and covered with pine, spruce and cedar trees; in the summer the shrubs, moss, ferns and countless flowers clinging to and growing from every nook and crevice, present a scene of gorgeous beauty, a scene where the God of nature has displayed his handiwork far beyond the comprehension of mortal beings."

A couple miles from Buffalo Creek, the drive passes under the Cathedral Spires, a collection of soaring granite pinnacles and slabs perched high above the road. The spires, including Cynical Pinnacle and The Dome, offer some of Colorado's best granite rock climbing. Downriver, the drive passes through Foxton, now a group of vacation cabins but once a railroad stop, and reaches Jefferson County 97, the Foxton Road, after another mile. Just up the road lies Reynolds Ranch County Park, part of Jefferson County's huge open space system, with hiking and picnicking among the pines. The drive winds southeast from here, bordering the river and offering secluded fishing holes and picnic sites. A granite grave stone, inscribed "Tell my wife I died thinking of her," sits alongside the road among willows. After ten snaking miles the road reaches the quiet confluence of the North Fork and the South Platte rivers at the old railroad stop of South Platte.

This confluence, called Two Forks, has long been a battleground between the Denver Water Board and Coloradans concerned with losing some of the Front Range's best recreational lands and one of the nation's prime trout fisheries. The water interests have long proposed putting a large dam here that would bury these scenic canyons under five hundred feet of lake water. It would ostensibly provide boating recreation as well as both lawn and tap water to burgeoning Front Range cities. Below the forks, the South Platte tumbles down through wild Waterton Canyon before emptying into Chatfield Reservoir, a flood-control impoundment in the hills south of Denver.

At South Platte the drive crosses the river and bends southwest on Jefferson County 97. This river canyon is more gentle than its North Fork cousin, with bulging granite domes and rounded hills veneered with fir and pine trees. The river itself is also calmer, riffling over cobbled shoals and gliding past immense boulders. Designated parking areas allow anglers access to the river and hikers and mountain bikers access to canyon trails. Five miles from the forks the road intersects the Pine Creek Road, Douglas County 40. This road climbs over the flattened northern end of the Rampart Range and ends at Sedalia seventeen miles to the east.

Nighthawk spreads across the broad valley just south of the road junction. Today it's a group of spread-out cabins, but one hundred years ago it was a teeming gold mining settlement and lumber camp. The town, platted in 1896 included a hotel, post office, general store, livery stable, blacksmith, and two newspapers, the *Mountain Echo* and the *West Creek Mining News*. A narrow gauge railroad ran through the canyon between 1904 and 1916.

The drive parallels the river for the next ten miles to Deckers, passing a succession of picnic areas and campgrounds. Willow Bend and Scraggy View picnic grounds sit below the castellated ramparts of 8,812-foot Long Scraggy Peak that towers to the west. Fishing along this river section is by flies and lures only with a two trout, sixteen-inch minimum. The road then passes Ouzel camping area and Platte River Campground with walk-in sites. Past Bridge Crossing Picnic Area the canyon broadens with grass meadows and open ponderosa pine woodlands. A couple miles later the canyon again narrows and the road twists alongside the river to an end at Deckers and CO 67.

11 RAMPART RANGE ROAD
Garden of the Gods to Sedalia

General description: A 60-mile-long gravel road that travels the forested crest of the Rampart Range from the Garden of the Gods near Colorado Springs to Colorado Highway 67 10 miles west of Sedalia.

Special attractions: Garden of the Gods, Queens Canyon, Rampart Reservoir Recreation Area, Devils Head National Recreation Trail, Devils Head Lookout, scenic views, fishing, camping, hiking, picnicking, rock climbing, mountain bike trails, motorized vehicle trails, cross-country skiing.

Location: East-central Colorado. The drive runs along the Rampart Range between Colorado Springs and southwest Denver. Access from the south is via Garden of the Gods park and U.S. Highway 24. The drive's northern terminus is reached from south Denver and Interstate 25 via U.S. Highway 85. Turn west on CO 67 at Sedalia.

Drive route name and number: Rampart Range Road, Forest Road 300.

Travel season: Year-round. The lower section of the road from Rampart Reservoir to Garden of the Gods is unmaintained in winter. Snow blankets the upper reaches here. The northern section of the road from fourteen miles north of the Mount Herman Road to north of Devils Head is closed in winter. Travel at your own risk and carry chains and a shovel. Watch for icy spots in winter and slick sections after summer thunderstorms. Check with Pike National Forest for road closure information.

Camping: 7 forest campgrounds lie on or just off the drive. Thunder Ridge and Meadow Ridge at Rampart Reservoir Recreation Area offer 40 sites on the lake's south shore. The campgrounds heading north from here are 30-site Springdale, nine-site Jackson Creek, 21-site Devil's Head, 19-site Flat Rocks, and 11-site Indian Creek. Primitive camping is allowed on the numerous side roads off the Rampart Range Road. Practice low-impact camping techniques, pick up your trash, and put all campfires out completely.

Services: No services are found along the drive. Complete services are found in Colorado Springs, Woodland Park, and south Denver. Limited services in Sedalia, including gasoline.

Nearby attractions: Pikes Peak Highway, Colorado Springs attractions, Cave of the Winds, Florissant Fossil Beds National Monument, Mueller State Park, Lost Creek Wilderness Area, South Platte River roads, Roxborough State Park, Chatfield State Recreation Area, Colorado Trail, Denver area attractions.

For more information: Pikes Peak Ranger District, Pike National Forest, 601 S. Weber, Colorado Springs, CO 80903, (719) 636-1602.

To Denver △ **Sedalia**

To Castle Rock

85

67

Indian Creek CG

To Deckers

300

To Sedalia

P I K E

Flat Rocks CG

507

Cabin Ridge Picnic Area

Devil's Head CG

Topaz Point Picnic Area

Devil's Head 9,748 ft.

Jackson Creek CG

N A T I O N A L

Storm Peak 9,199 ft.

To Deckers

Mt. Deception

Chimney Peak 9,185 ft.

To Denver

25

Monument

Mt. Herman 9,063 ft.

•Denver ★

COLORADO

0 1 2 3 4 5
Miles

N

Painted Rocks CG

Colorado CG

South Meadows CG

320

To Colorado Springs

Red Rocks CG

67

393

Springdale CG

Rampart Reservoir

Meadow Ridge CG

Woodland Park

24

Thunder Ridge CG

To Divide

Ormes Peak 9,727 ft.

24

F O R E S T

Cascade

Cave of the Winds

Garden of the Gods Park

Manitou Springs △ To Colorado Springs

92

The drive: The Rampart Range Road, one of Colorado's best off-the-beaten track drives, traverses the undulating crest of the Rampart Range for sixty miles between Colorado Springs and Sedalia. The scenic gravel road yields spectacular views of Pikes Peak, the prairie, and the rugged Front Range and Tarryall Mountains, and offers quiet camping, diverse mountain biking and camping opportunities, and one of Colorado's last fire lookouts atop Devils Head.

Spring, summer, and fall are the best times to drive the road. Expect cool, breezy days in spring, with occasional showers and snow storms. Summer days are pleasant and mild, with highs in the seventies and eighties. Severe thunderstorms occur almost daily somewhere along the drive on July and August afternoons. Mornings, however, are generally clear. Autumn offers colorful aspen foliage and a succession of bright, clear days with only occasional storms. Winter brings cold temperatures and deep snows that blanket the drive.

The road is plowed and maintained in winter from Rampart Reservoir Recreation Area to fourteen miles north of the Mt. Herman Road. Drive with caution and watch for icy corners. The lower road section from the reservoir to Colorado Springs is unmaintained in winter. Drive at your own risk and carry chains and a shovel. By late March the lower road is generally passable to passenger cars. Inquire at the forest office for current road conditions. The lower road, running over corrugated sandstone bedrock, is rough year-round. The upper road section gets washboarded in summer after heavy rainstorms. Drive slowly to avoid vehicle damage.

The Rampart Range Road begins at the western end of the Garden of the Gods, a 1,368-acre Colorado Springs city park, just off US 24. The Garden of the Gods is a dramatic landscape, a place of soaring sandstone hogbacks nestled against the Rampart Range's southern flank in an outdoor sculpture garden. The strangely eroded rock formations have long attracted visitors. The Ute Indians often camped among the rocks and later nineteenth-century travelers bestowed fanciful names on them—Montezuma's Tower, The Three Graces, Kissing Camels, and Weeping Indian. After Colorado Springs was established in 1871, the Garden became a tourist attraction. *New York Tribune* writer Ernest Ingersoll described the place in 1886 as "the mouldering ruins of some half-buried city of the desert," while *Collier's Weekly* correspondent Julian Street deemed it "a pale, pink joke." Writer and poet Helen Hunt Jackson wrote, "You wind among rocks of every conceivable and inconceivable shape and size...all bright red, all motionless and silent, with a strange look of having been just stopped and held back in the very climax of some supernatural catastrophe."

The Rampart Range Road begins on the west edge of the Garden at three hundred-ton Balanced Rock. The rocks here are the gently tilting strata of the four thousand-foot-thick Fountain Formation. This 300-million-year-old maroon formation, comprising alternating layers of sandstone, mudstone, and conglomerate, was deposited as an alluvial apron by rushing streams and rivers below Frontrangia, an ancestral mountain range. The dirt road turns north just east of Balanced Rock and begins climbing. Another balanced rock

Pikes Peak towers above grassy meadows and aspen glades along the Rampart Range Road.

sits below the road past Balanced Rock, and after 0.3 mile the road swings north and bumps up a shallow canyon. A pygmy forest of pinyon pine, juniper, and scrub oak lines the roadside.

The road's first couple miles travel up rounded ridges west of the Garden of the Gods and after four miles reaches a good viewpoint above Queens Canyon. This abrupt canyon, draining southeast out of the Rampart Range, is lined with sharp granite precipices and buttresses. Glen Eyrie, Scottish for "Valley of the Eagle's Nest," sits at the canyon's entrance below the overlook. This Tudor-styled castle, built among soaring sandstone towers, was the home of General William Jackson Palmer, the founder of Colorado Springs. Queens Canyon is named for his wife, Queen Palmer. An abandoned gravel strip mine sits atop the ridge above Queens Canyon east of the overlook.

The road begins corkscrewing upwards here, passing scrub oak copses and scattered ponderosa pines. The first eight miles of road, passing over sandstone bedrock, has a rough, corrugated surface. Magnificent views of Pikes Peak and Colorado Springs unfold from the road as it slowly climbs the southern flank of the Rampart Range. At mile six the road traverses a ridge west of Williams Canyon and passes the South Rampart Shooting Range. A mile and a half later the drive passes a lofty viewpoint above upper Queens Canyon and then swings west above Williams Canyon. Upper Williams Canyon is a shallow gorge studded with granite crags. The lower canyon to the south is lined with white limestone cliffs and numerous caves including the Cave of the Winds. By eight miles the road encounters its first aspen grove tucked into a moist side-canyon.

The drive climbs onto another lofty ridge and after twelve miles reaches the range crest and a spectacular fenced overlook perched atop granite crags. Pikes Peak, the 14,110-foot pioneer landmark of the Rockies, towers to the west. Over the last few million years during the Pleistocene Ice Ages, glaciers excavated the peak's deep alpine cirques. Pikes Peak, climbed annually by millions via the Pikes Peak Highway, cog railway, and Barr Trail, was first attempted by an ill-equipped party led by explorer Zebulon Pike in snowy November, 1806. Pike dubbed the mountain Grand Peak and estimated its height as 18,581 feet. Far below the overlook stretches Ute Pass. The pass is not really a pass at all but an abrupt canyon that follows the Ute Pass Fault, a major fault eroded by Fountain Creek that separates the Rampart Range from the Pikes Peak massif. The canyon, offering relatively easy passage from the Great Plains into the mountains, was first used by the Ute Indians. Wagon roads and the Midland Railroad to the South Park and Cripple Creek mining areas later traversed the pass. US 24 now ascends Ute Pass from Manitou Springs to Woodland Park.

Another scenic viewpoint perches on the rim of Ute Pass another 0.3-mile further north. A roadside monument here remembers the Rampart Range Road's dedication on June 19, 1938, and the USDA Forest Service and Civilian Conservation Corps workers that built the scenic drive.

The road twists north at an elevation of 9,000 feet along the western edge of the Rampart Range, dipping through shallow canyons densely lined with pine, fir, and spruce. Forest Road 303 is reached after fifteen miles. This road allows access to 9,727-foot Ormes Peak, the range high point. The Rampart Range is laced with numerous abandoned roads and trails, a legacy left by early lumbermen. Timber crews fanned out across the range in the late nineteenth century, cutting trees for railroad ties. Trees were funneled down the range's eastern slope for the Denver and Rio Grande Railroad and into

Bighorn sheep roam remote mountainsides along the Rampart Range Road.

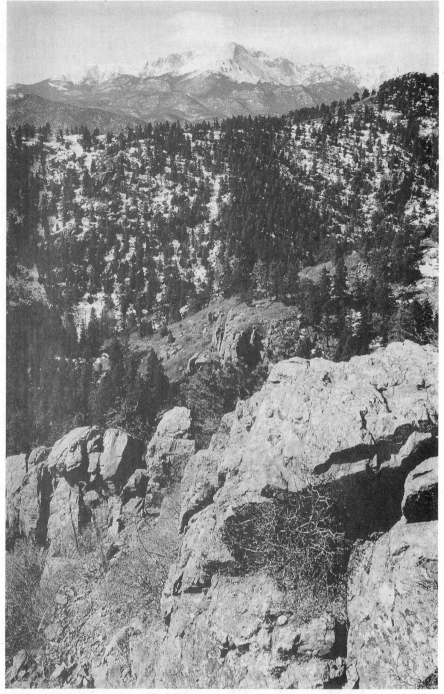

Pikes Peak looms above upper Williams Canyon along the Rampart Range Road.

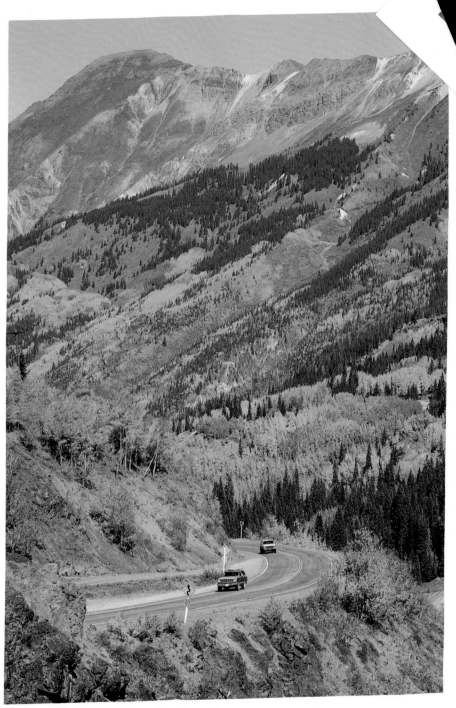

Red Mountain Pass on the San Juan Skyway.

The ghost town of Independence, along the Independence Pass drive, bustled with mining fever more than 100 years ago.

Top: *Silverton, a National Historic District, lies in the heart of the San Juan Mountains on the Million Dollar Highway.*

Bottom: *The Sangre de Cristo Range looms beyond the Teressa Mine above the Phantom Canyon Road.*

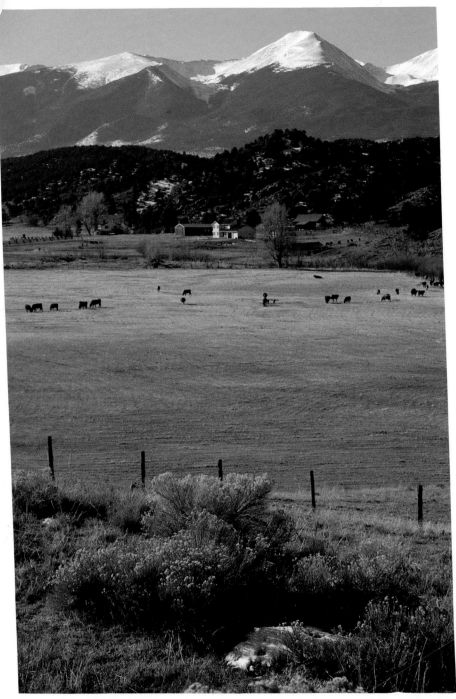

The Sangre de Cristo Range lifts a snowy crest high above a ranch on the Sangre de Cristo Scenic Drive.

Top: *Silverton, a National Historic District, lies in the heart of the San Juan Mountains on the Million Dollar Highway.*

Bottom: *The Sangre de Cristo Range looms beyond the Teressa Mine above the Phantom Canyon Road.*

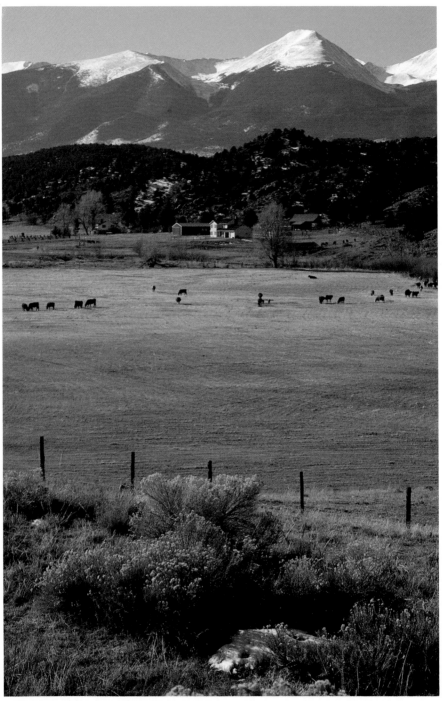

The Sangre de Cristo Range lifts a snowy crest high above a ranch on the Sangre de Cristo Scenic Drive.

Top: *A Wet Mountain Valley rancher checks his horse along the Sangre de Cristo Scenic Drive.*

Bottom: *A rocky overlook views the twin Pawnee Buttes along the Pawnee Pioneer Trails Scenic Drive in northeastern Colorado.*

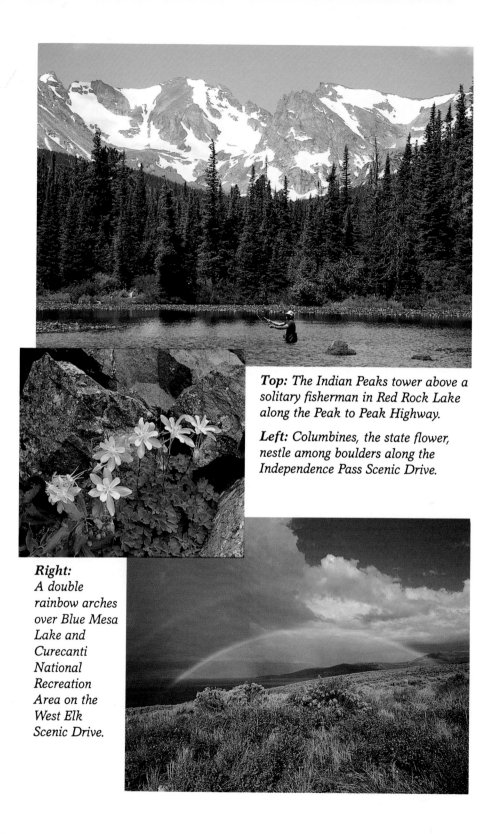

Top: *The Indian Peaks tower above a solitary fisherman in Red Rock Lake along the Peak to Peak Highway.*

Left: *Columbines, the state flower, nestle among boulders along the Independence Pass Scenic Drive.*

Right: *A double rainbow arches over Blue Mesa Lake and Curecanti National Recreation Area on the West Elk Scenic Drive.*

Top: *A Wet Mountain Valley rancher checks his horse along the Sangre de Cristo Scenic Drive.*

Bottom: *A rocky overlook views the twin Pawnee Buttes along the Pawnee Pioneer Trails Scenic Drive in northeastern Colorado.*

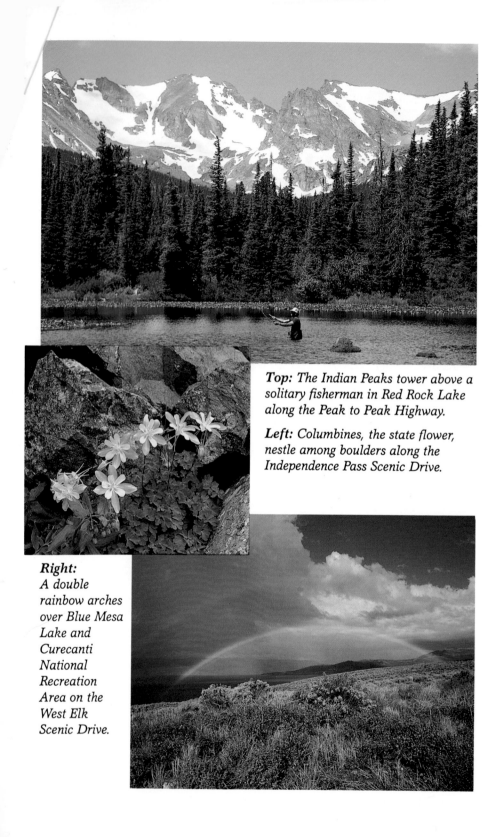

Top: *The Indian Peaks tower above a solitary fisherman in Red Rock Lake along the Peak to Peak Highway.*

Left: *Columbines, the state flower, nestle among boulders along the Independence Pass Scenic Drive.*

Right:
A double rainbow arches over Blue Mesa Lake and Curecanti National Recreation Area on the West Elk Scenic Drive.

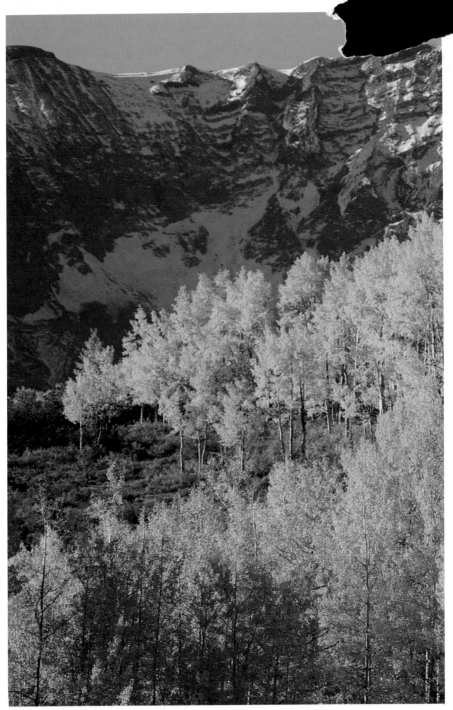

Snowy ridges form a wintery counterpoint to changing aspens on Dallas Divide along the Lizard Head Pass Scenic Drive.

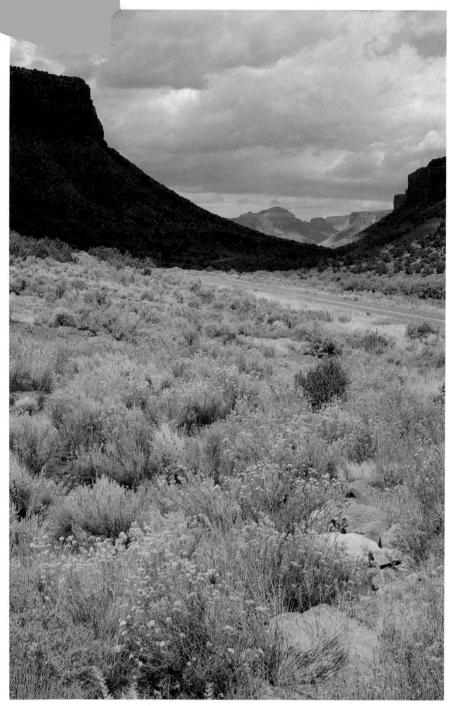

The Unaweep-Tabeguache Scenic Drive follows the Dolores River through cliffed palisades of Wingate sandstone in the Dolores Canyon.

Ute Pass for the Midland Railroad. Scars from the steep drags remain mountainsides. Timber is still harvested in the range's central section.

Past FR 303 the Rampart Range Road improves dramatically with smooth gravel surface maintained by the city of Colorado Springs for access to its reservoirs. At almost eighteen miles a turnoff leads east three miles to Rampart Reservoir Recreation Area. The four hundred-acre reservoir, part of the Colorado Springs watershed, is a popular recreation site managed by the Forest Service. Facilities include nineteen-site Meadow Ridge and twenty-one-site Thunder Ridge campgrounds, Promontory Picnic Area, the barrier-free BPW Interpretative Trail, and a boat ramp. Lake Shore Trail, a popular twelve-mile-long mountain bike and hiking path, circles the reservoir. Another popular trail, 1.2-mile Rainbow Gulch Trail, begins on the Rampart Range Road a mile and a half north of the reservoir turnoff. The trail drops down to the reservoir through a stately ponderosa pine forest broken by open meadows.

Past Rainbow Gulch, the road climbs onto a high rolling grassland studded with pine groves. Great views unfold along this road section. The Sawatch Range and the Continental Divide poke above the far western horizon. The snow-capped summits of Mount Evans and Longs Peak are far to the north. Alert drivers can spot elk, mule deer, and wild turkey browsing in the broad meadows. Springdale Campground, with thirty sites, sits at 9,200 feet in an evergreen copse on the northern meadow edge. Past the grassland the drive intersects with Loy Creek Road, a short paved road that drops a couple miles down to Woodland Park and US 24. Another spur road to Woodland Park sits 1.6 miles to the north. Woodland Park offers all services for travelers.

The road rolls north, hemmed in by thick forest. Occasional pullouts yield views across the range to distant peaks and the tawny prairie. The Rampart Range, seen from the plains and surrounding high peaks, appears almost flat with only occasional peaks rising above the level surface. Indeed, the range crest seldom climbs above 9,000 feet and only in eroded valleys does it drop below that elevation. The Rampart Range is what geologists call a pediment or old erosional surface. Its granite hills are the worn down stubs of what were once great mountains. The pediment, once continuous with the high plains and extending over much of the Front Range, was uplifted some 28 million years ago.

The Mount Herman Road, Forest Road 320, branches east four miles north of Loy Creek Road. This scenic road edges around 9,063-foot Mount Herman to Monument and I-25. The Rampart Range Road continues north, passing numerous side roads and Saylor Park, a popular cross-country ski area. At the microwave towers, some thirty-six miles from the road's start, a gate is locked in winter limiting access to the road. Past the gate the drive drops down a shallow canyon. A trickling stream lined with aspen groves and beaver ponds borders the road. Beyond the canyon it swings around a granite boulder-studded mountainside and twists northward. Forest Road 348, reached at forty-two miles, heads west through Long Hollow to CO 67.

Devil's Head, the 9,748-foot high point of the Rampart Range, dominates the northern section of the drive. The peak rears above the dusty road, its forested flanks broken by ragged granite crags and outcrops. The Forest Service's last Front Range fire lookout is stationed atop the lofty peak. Since 1910 a spotter has been stationed here looking for forest fires. The 1.5-mile Devil's Head National Recreation Trail threads up the peak's steep northern slopes to the fire lookout. The last trail section scales a series of staircases to the rocky summit. The view is astounding, taking in the entire Front Range from the Spanish Peaks almost 150 miles to the south to flat-topped Longs Peak to the north. The plains stretch eastward, while mountain range upon mountain range spread west to the setting sun. Denver's urban sprawl lies in the Denver Basin to the northwest, its glass buildings shimmering in the sun. Legend says that over $60,000 in gold coins were stashed somewhere on Devil's Head's rough sides after an 1870s train robbery. Treasure hunters still canvas the mountain for the hidden gold.

Forest Road 507, reached at forty-four miles, heads northeast down scenic Jackson Creek. Jackson Creek Campground, with nine spacious sites, sits two miles down the road. The scenic drive swings around the west side of Devil's Head. Topaz Point Picnic Area and Viewpoint sits on a rocky knoll just west of the road. A short hike to the overlook yields a wide view of the South Platte River country from a weathered granite shelf. A display identifies the surrounding mountains.

The Rampart Range Road climbs up and over the northern shoulder of Devil's Head and after two miles reaches a spur road that leads a half-mile south to twenty-one-site Devil's Head Campground and the start of the Devil's Head Trail. Cabin Ridge Picnic Area sits a mile farther north. The road begins steadily losing elevation past Cabin Ridge, passing from spruce and fir forest to a drier ponderosa pine woodland. Nineteen-site Flat Rocks Campground and Overlook sit another four miles up the road. The overlook offers views of wooded ridges and canyons, the flat-topped mesas around Castle Rock, and the plains. This upper road section is the Rampart Range Motorized Recreation Area with 120 miles of all-terrain vehicle and motorcycle trails. The area is busy in the summer, especially on weekends. The drive ends on CO 67 at a Pike National Forest work center. Indian Creek Campground, with eleven sites, lies just west of the highway junction. A right turn runs down Jarre Canyon ten miles to Sedalia and US 85, while a left turn drops down Douglas County 67 to the South Platte River and Deckers.

12 SOUTH PARK - TARRYALL LOOP DRIVE
Lake George, through South Park, and back to Lake George

General description: This 121-mile loop drive follows Tarryall Creek along the Tarryall Mountains into broad South Park, traverses the park's western edge beneath the Park and Mosquito ranges, then turns east and

COLORADO

•Denver

N

FOREST

River

Platte

South

Happy Meadows CG

Lake George

To Colorado Springs

24

To Denver

Kenosha Pass
10,001 ft.

LOST CREEK

TARRYALL WILDERNESS

AREA

NATIONAL

Bison Pk. 12,431 ft.

McCurdy Mtn. 12,165 ft.

RANGE

S. Tarryall Pk. 11,206 ft.

Tarryall

Creek

TARRYALL RESERVOIR STATE WILDLIFE AREA

Spruce Grove CG

Farnum Pk. 11,378 ft.

Tarryall

Badger Mtn. 11,294 ft.

Wilkerson Pass 9,502 ft.

ELEVEN MILE STATE REC. AREA

SPINNEY MTN. RESERVOIR STATE REC. AREA

9

To Canon City

285

Jefferson

13,082 ft.

Mt. Silverheels 13,822 ft.

33

Schoolmarm Mtn. 11,332 ft.

24

SOUTH

PARK

Fork

Hartsel

To Breckenridge

Boreas Pass 11,482 ft.

To Breckenridge

PIKE

Como

9

Middle

Fairplay

285

Antero Reservoir

9

Four Mile CG

Horseshoe CG

Buffalo Spr. CG

Trout Cr. Pass 9,487 ft.

To Buena Vista

Mt. Sherman 14,036 ft.

Horseshoe Mtn. 13,898 ft.

West Buffalo Peak

East Buffalo Peak

Miles

0 2 4 6 8 10

Pronghorn antelope roam South Park's broad expanse.

crosses the park and Wilkerson Pass back to Lake George.

Special attractions: Pike National Forest, Lost Creek Wilderness Area, Puma Hills, Tarryall Creek, Tarryall Reservoir State Wildlife Area, South Park, Fairplay, Park Range, Como, South Park City, Mosquito Range, Antero Reservoir State Wildlife Area, Buffalo Peaks, Spinney Mountain Ranch State Wildlife Area, Wilkerson Pass, hiking, backpacking, fishing, rock climbing, scenic views, picnicking.

Location: Central Colorado.

Drive route numbers: U.S. Highway 24, U.S. Highway 285, Park County Road 77.

Travel season: Year-round. The highways are plowed in winter. Be prepared, however, for blowing and drifting snow during blizzards, icy roads, and hazardous driving conditions. Park County 77 can be temporarily closed in severe weather.

Camping: Several national forest campgrounds lie on or just off the drive. 7-site Happy Meadows Campground and 28-site Spruce Grove Campground are on Park County 77. Kenosha Pass, Aspen, Lodgepole, Jefferson Creek, Michigan Creek, Selkirk, Beaver Creek, Four Mile, Horseshoe, and Buffalo Springs campgrounds all sit on forest roads west of US 285 between Kenosha Pass and Antero Junction. Eleven Mile State Recreation Area, 11 miles south of the drive in eastern South Park, offers a large state-run campground. Numerous forest campgrounds are found in Eleven Mile Canyon south of Lake George at the drive's eastern terminus. Primitive camping is permitted on national forest lands, particularly in the Puma Hills. Practice low-impact camping and make sure your fire is out.

Services: All services are found in Fairplay. Limited services, including gas, in Jefferson, Hartsel, and Lake George.

Nearby attractions: Breckenridge, Boreas Pass, Brown's Canyon, Arkansas Headwaters State Recreation Area, Sawatch Range, San Isabel National Forest, Eleven Mile Canyon, Cripple Creek, Florissant Fossil Beds National Monument, Bristlecone Scenic Area, Mosquito Pass, Guanella Pass Scenic Drive, South Platte Scenic Drive.

For more information: Pike National Forest, 1920 Valley Drive, Pueblo, CO 81108, (719) 545-8737. South Park Ranger District, P.O. Box 219, Fairplay, CO 80440, (719) 836-2031. Park County Tourism Office, P.O. Box 701, Fariplay, CO 80440, (719) 836-2771.

The drive: The 121-mile-long South Park-Tarryall scenic drive makes a spectacular open loop through some of Colorado's most spacious scenery. The drive traverses the granite-studded canyons and valleys of Tarryall Creek and crosses the open, sweeping grasslands of South Park, a high inter-montane basin that sits in the state's middle. This land of wide views and historic sites boasts a long human history from the Ute Indians who hunted buffalo on the park's broad expanse and a fierce 1844 battle between the Utes and Arapahoes witnessed by pathfinder Kit Carson to rich silver and gold diggings around Fairplay and sheep and cattle ranching. Today, this is a land of peace and quiet. Wind ruffles the surrounding pine forests, thunderstorms spread a veil of rain and lightning over the stubby mountains, and short grass broken by fencelines and roads carpets the park floor.

South Park, lying at 9,000 feet, and the higher surrounding mountains are cool in summer and cold in winter. Summer days are generally clear and warm in the morning with highs in the seventies. Thunderstorms build up in the afternoon over the high peaks to the west. Expect heavy localized rain and lightning. Avoid being in the open or under trees during lightning storms. Autumn brings clear, warm days and a frosting of snow to the above-timberline ranges. Winters are cold and windy. Heavy snow blankets South Park and the Mosquito and Park ranges. Ground blizzard conditions are common during snowstorms. Temperatures are frigid, often dropping below zero, in South Park because cold air sinks onto the valley floor from adjacent higher slopes. Spring days are cool and often windy. The snow cover slowly melts away, leaving dry grass by April.

The drive begins one mile west of Lake George and forty-five miles west of Colorado Springs along the South Platte River. Turn north off US 24 onto roughly paved Park County 77. This first leg of the byway journey ends forty-two miles ahead in Jefferson on US 285. The road turns north along the river and follows a broad, grassy valley through rolling, ponderosa pine-clad hills. After a mile the river leaves the road and bends into a deep canyon that twists northeastward through the Front Range to Denver. A spur forest road follows the river for a mile to seven-site Happy Meadows Campground, a popular summer site for anglers.

After leaving the river, the road follows broad Tappan Gulch northward past small ranches and grassy meadows grazed by horses and cattle. Low granite hills, sparsely covered with ponderosa pines, line the valley floor. After four miles the road crosses a divide below 8,954-foot Tappan Mountain and drops into Tarryall Creek's scenic drainage. Tarryall Creek slices through a wide canyon that separates the rugged Tarryall Mountains to the northeast from the Puma Hills to the west. The creek meanders through a verdant valley here, swinging past wide meadows, hay fields, and gray granite crags. A mile after reaching the creek, the drive intersects Matukat Road, Forest Road 211. This scenic dirt road sweeps around the east flank of the Tarryalls and offers views into the South Platte River drainage. After another mile, the drive turns west away from the creek up Marksbury Gulch. The gulch is named for an early homesteader, buried in the Lake George cemetery, who was killed by Ute Indians after stealing an Indian pony. The China Wall, a long granite escarpment, parallels the dry arroyo on its north side. The road passes the boulder-strewn hillsides, climbs into rounded, grassy hills, crosses a divide, and drops into the historic town of Tarryall at twelve miles.

Tarryall, formerly called Puma City, got its start in 1859 when prospectors found gold nuggets "as big as watermelon seeds" in the creek below. The new town supposedly got its name when a miner remarked, "Let us tarry all." Those who came latter, however, found the best placer sites claimed and derided the town as "Grab all" before starting the competing town of Hamilton on the opposite creek bank and heading across South Park and founding Fairplay. Hamilton quickly surpassed its neighbor and boasted a transient population of six thousand by 1860. The town offered saloons, casinos, its own newspaper, and a theater. Tarryall was officially laid out in 1861 and was the Park County seat for a short while. In the summer of 1861 miner John Parsons began his own mint, stamping out $2.50, $5, and $20 gold coins that are today worth over $30,000. Slowly the placer claims were exhausted and miners left Tarryall and Hamilton for new strikes elsewhere. By 1875 the towns were mostly deserted. Tarryall now is a small community of mostly rustic cabins. Still visible, however, is Whiskey Hole. This deep pit was set aside during the boom days for poor miners to pan enough gold to buy a shot of whiskey at local watering holes. The Tarryall School, listed on the National Historic Register, sits on the roadside entering Tarryall. The elegant white clapboard building, with a steeple and bell, was built in 1922 and now serves as a town meeting hall. Nothing remains of Hamilton save a few mining scars.

Just past Tarryall, the road becomes gravel and descends to Tarryall Creek. The drive parallels the creek through abrupt canyons and broad valleys for the next twelve miles to Tarryall Reservoir. The Puma Hills, a long ridge of timbered hills topped by 11,570-foot Farnum Peak, borders this spectacular road section on the west, while the Tarryall Range, a twenty-five-mile-long sierra studded with bold granite cliffs and deep forests of aspen and evergreen, lifts its serrated escarpment to the east.

The 105,000-acre Lost Creek Wilderness Area protects most of the Tarryall

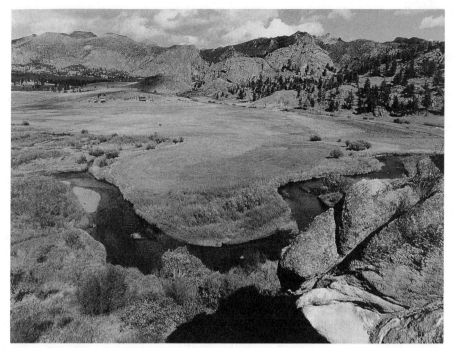

The rugged Tarryall Mountains rise beyond Tarryall Creek and hayfields on the South Park Loop Drive.

Range from encroaching civilization. Numerous trails explore this mountain fastness, wending up ponderosa pine-covered slopes, passing trickling creeks lined with columbines and aspens, and switchbacking to the summit of 12,431-foot Bison Peak, the range high point. The Tarryalls are formed by Pikes Peak granite, a billion-year-old, pink, coarse-grained rock that formed after a massive batholith or underground reservoir of molten magma slowly cooled over millions of years. Eons of erosion chipped away at the granite, sculpting today's rocky wonderland of spires, flying buttresses, domes, castles, and rounded boulders. Besides being an excellent getaway for hiking and backpacking, the wilderness area offers rock climbing, fly-fishing in cold streams, and wildlife observation. The area is one of the best spots to see Rocky Mountain bighorn sheep. Any hiker scrambling to the cobbled summit of the high peaks here has a good chance of seeing these elegant, sure-footed mammals. Other wildlife includes mule deer, black bear, mountain lion, golden eagle, elk, turkey, porcupine, and raccoon. The wilderness is easily accessed from the scenic drive at Spruce Grove Campground, Twin Eagles Picnic Ground, and at Ute Creek. The Pike National Forest office in Colorado Springs offers detailed maps and trail descriptions.

Spruce Grove Campground, with twenty-eight sites at 8,600 feet, sits just off the drive a mile north of Tarryall. This lovely campground, surrounded by jagged cliffs, nestles among tall pines along the swift creek. Twin Eagles Picnic Area and Trailhead, a popular stop for anglers, lies two miles northward along a sharp creek bend. A broad valley, carpeted with green hay fields and dotted with grazing cattle, stretches away from the road just beyond the picnic area to the lofty Tarryall Range. The road follows the meandering creek, passing grassy banks lined with dense willow thickets and dipping across dry drainages below timbered Farnum Peak. After almost twenty-two miles the drive reaches the Ute Creek Trailhead, a popular jumping-off point for backpackers trekking into Lost Creek Wilderness Area. The canyon broadens beyond Ute Creek, but steep mountain slopes clad in pine and granite continue to wall the canyon. Fishing along this section of Tarryall Creek is allowed with artificial flies and lures only. At twenty-three miles the pavement begins again and views of the snow-capped Park Range unfold to the west. Tarryall Reservoir State Wildlife Area appears two miles later.

The seven hundred-acre lake is a glistening jewel nestled among treeless, rolling hills studded with brief rock outcrops. It's a popular destination for anglers who come to troll its depths for trout and picnic on its shores. The scenery dramatically changes beyond the reservoir as the drive ventures onto the hilly northeastern fringe of South Park. The road continues following Tarryall Creek northwestward, crossing dry Schoolhouse and Graveyard gulches and passing abandoned cabins, a cemetery, and picturesque ranches. Scrubby forests scatter across the rolling hills including 10,073-foot Observatory Rock, a prominent peak to the southwest. Twelve miles from the reservoir, Michigan Creek and the drive enter South Park itself. A wide, lush grassland, watered by snowmelt from the peaks of the towering Park Range, stretches westward to the distant forest edge. The creek meanders through meadows enclosed by barbed wire fences. The drive's first leg ends five miles later in Jefferson at US 285. Jefferson was hastily erected in 1879 when the Denver, South Park & Pacific narrow gauge railroad pushed across northern South Park in a race to reach Leadville before the rival Denver & Rio Grande did from Canon City. The old railroad depot still stands alongside the highway. By 1881 the town boasted a post office and three hundred residents. Jefferson became an important shipping and ranching center for area cattle and sheep outfits, a role it continues to play.

The scenic drive's next leg runs south on US 285 along the western edge of South Park from Jefferson sixteen miles to Fairplay and another twenty-three miles to Antero Junction at the park's southwestern corner. South Park is a huge intermontane basin fifty miles long and thirty-five miles wide with an area of over nine hundred square miles, a little less than Rhode Island. Elevations range from 8,500 feet to over 10,000 feet. The park, covered with short grass, is broken by several long, forested hogbacks. The South Platte River, arising on the Continental Divide near Hoosier Pass, drains the valley and the surrounding mountains. Mountains rim South Park—the Puma Hills, bisected by Wilkerson Pass on the east; the dark rounded peaks of the old Thirty-Nine-Mile Volcanic Field to the south; and the lofty snow-capped Mosquito and Park ranges on the west and north. The Mosquito Range includes four peaks—Mounts Lincoln, Bross, Democrat, and Sherman—that top 14,000 feet. Mosquito Pass, Colorado's highest pass at 13,180 feet, crosses the range west of Fairplay en route to Leadville. South Park, one of Colorado's four mountain basins (the other ones being North Park, Middle Park, and the San Luis Valley), was originally named *Valle Salada* or *Bayou Salado* or Salt Valley for the white saline deposits left on flat, evaporated lake beds on the valley floor. One of the salts is sodium chloride or common table salt.

The drive runs southwest on US 285 from Jefferson, crossing well-watered meadows covered with summer wildflowers including sky-blue iris. West of the highway looms the snow-covered Park Range, an extension of the Front Range. The Continental Divide, separating the Pacific and Atlantic ocean drainages, meanders along the range crest over high peaks including 13,370-foot Mt. Guyot and 13,082-foot Boreas Mountain. Gravel roads climb west from the highway into Pike National Forest up Jefferson, Michigan, and Tarryall creeks to alpine valleys, beaver ponds, and several forest campgrounds. The Boreas Pass Road, ascending Tarryall Creek from Como to 11,482-foot Boreas Pass, makes an excellent back road excursion to Breckenridge. The well-maintained gravel road generally follows the old narrow gauge Denver, South Park & Pacific Railroad grade. The railroad, in use from 1881 to 1937, climbed 4.5 percent grades and 435 curves on this stretch of track. Fifteen-site Selkirk Campground sits along the road at 10,500 feet.

The drive reaches Como, an old railroad town, seven miles from Jefferson. Como, like neighboring Jefferson, was a boom town during the heady days of railroad construction with a population of more than six thousand, most of whom lived in tents. The town also prospered with coal mining in the nearby hills. The dangerous Como mines claimed numerous victims, including thirty-five Chinese miners in 1885 and twenty-five Italians in 1893. The mines closed in 1896 and Como began a quiet life as a railroad center.

The highway climbs a low, forested ridge southwest of Como, drops across Trout Creek, and steeply ascends to the summit of 9,943-foot Red Hill Pass. Red Hill is a long hogback of tilted Dakota sandstone that runs southward across South Park from here. The road falls down the summit's western slope, runs across grassy benches, and enters Fairplay three miles later. The drive intersects Colorado 9 here, which runs north to Hoosier Pass and Breckenridge.

Fairplay, South Park's largest town and the seat of Park County, sits at the lofty elevation of 9,953 feet on gravel benches above the Middle Fork of the South Platte River in the park's extreme northwestern corner. Fairplay, once a brawling, boisterous mining camp, retains a quaint historic charm with log cabins, gingerbread-adorned Victorian homes, and a friendly atmosphere. The town sprang up in 1859 at the core of a rich placer mining district by miners incensed by claim-grabbing at Tarryall across the valley. The frontier town slowly grew not only as a mining center, but as a freight, transportation, and supply hub as well. By the 1870s Fairplay boasted hotels, a post office, the Sumner Brewery that made South Park Lager Beer, a stone courthouse, the Fairplay *Sentinel* newspaper, and of course several churches to minister to the heathen miners. The Sheldon Jackson Memorial Chapel, named for the superintendent of the West's Presbyterian missions, was built in 1874. This elegant, white church is considered by some to be one of the nation's best examples of Timber Gothic architecture. Fairplay offers all services to visitors, including accommodations, dining, groceries, and gas.

Today old Fairplay lives in South Park City Museum, a living history museum that preserves buildings and artifacts from the past. Real history is found in real people. Trod the dusty streets here, peer through shop windows, examine an old cabin, and study a miner's tools. South Park City gives the traveler a moment to re-experience history, to share in its making, to take a step backward in time to a place where everyday is yesterday.

The drive continues south on US 285 twenty-three miles to Antero Junction. This highway section runs atop rolling hills and plains of stream-deposited glacial gravels on South Park's western margin beneath the rounded Mosquito Range, a high range that twists south from Hoosier Pass to Trout Creek Pass. Most of the range crest soars above timberline and includes four 14,000-foot peaks. The high peaks west of the drive—14,036-foot Mount Sherman, 13,898-foot Horseshoe Mountain, and 13,739-foot Ptarmigan Peak—are rounded bumps on the range crest. Glaciers contoured and smoothed the range's ancient sedimentary rock layers into broad valleys and steep-walled cirques. Most of the range names are of Civil War vintage, with miners naming Mount Lincoln for the president and Mounts Sherman and Sheridan for generals. Myth has it that the Mosquito Range acquired its name in 1861 when a mosquito was found pressed on the blank spot of a legal document where the name of a proposed mining district was to be written, giving the name to the district, pass, and range.

Several gravel roads head west from the drive onto the eastern flank of the Mosquitos. The Fourmile Creek Road, just south of Fairplay, twists up Fourmile Creek past nineteen-site Horseshoe and fourteen-site Fourmile campgrounds to the abandoned ghost town site of Leavick. An easy trail climbs west from here to the summit of Mount Sherman, considered the easiest of Colorado's fourteeners to scale. The Weston Pass Road ascends to 11,921-foot Weston Pass. **The west side of the pass is four-wheel-drive only.**

The Buffalo Peaks, a twin-summited mountain of lava and volcanic ash, dominates the southern Mosquito Range and the drive. The peaks, in a proposed wilderness area, are densely forested and teem with wildlife including bighorn sheep and elk. Access is via several forest roads. This drive section ends at Antero Junction at US 285's junction with US 24. US 285/24 continues west over Trout Creek Pass to Buena Vista. The scenic drive, however, turns east on US 24 onto the treeless steppe of South Park.

This last drive segment runs east thirty-nine miles across the park, over Wilkerson Pass, and on down to Lake George and the loop drive's starting point. The highway drops away from Antero Junction, crosses several dry arroyos, and reaches the old Colorado Midland Railroad grade after a couple miles. The grade parallels the highway from here to Hartsel, before heading east to Elevenmile Canyon. The Colorado Midland, built by Colorado Springs mining magnates with interests in the Leadville and Aspen mines in the 1880s, was the first standard gauge railroad into the Colorado Rockies. The

A deserted ranch sits on dry hills along the South Park Loop Drive.

railroad often ran "Wildflower Excursion" trains from Colorado Springs to South Park for passengers to collect colorful bouquets. The rail line was torn up in 1921.

The highway, running northeast, passes prominent Twin Peaks, swings down a dry, shallow valley, and reaches the turnoff to Antero Reservoir after almost nine miles. Antero Reservoir, a popular fishing lake, was built in 1913 and supplies water to Denver. Numerous Indian sites line this road section, including a large campsite and battleground near Twin Peaks. South Park, with plentiful game including buffalo and deer, was a popular summer hunting ground for the Ute, Comanche, Cheyenne, Kiowa, and Arapaho Indians. Legendary scout and trailblazer Kit Carson witnessed a three-day battle between the Comanches and Utes in eastern South Park. The Utes were defeated on the third day after forty braves were killed and over one hundred Ute horses were taken as battle spoils.

Hartsel sits on the South Platte River in the middle of the park thirteen miles from Antero Junction. The town, named for early rancher Sam Hartsel, once thrived as a mini-resort on the Colorado Midland line. A small hot spring, with 134-degree water, attracted visitors who stayed overnight at a hotel. The bathhouse, now abandoned, sits just south of town above the river bank. A more modest shack with a single bathtub now graces the hot springs and allows weary travelers a moment's respite in what has been called "Colorado's hottest hot spring"—the radon-laden water is radioactive.

US 24, after intersecting Colorado Highway 9, which runs north to Fairplay and south to Canon City, crosses the meandering South Platte River, its grassy banks lined with grazing cattle. The drive continues east, skirting several low mountains, and passes the turnoff to Elevenmile State Recreation Area after eleven miles. The 3,300-acre reservoir, built in 1932 as part of Denver's water supply, is one of Colorado's most popular mountain lakes. Trophy-sized trout, kokanee salmon, and northern pike are regularly pulled from its chilly waters. The highway climbs into the Puma Hills beneath 11,294-foot Badger Mountain and snakes up to the summit of 9,507-foot Wilkerson Pass. Imaginative eyes can spot an Indian head composed of metamorphic cliff bands on Badger Mountain's western slope.

Wilkerson Pass, with a rest area and Forest Service visitor center, offers spectacular views to the west of South Park, the Mosquito Range, and beyond to the Sawatch Range. To the east towers bulky 14,110-foot Pikes Peak surrounded by a green forest mantle. The highway winds down the Puma Hills gentle east flank, passes sixteen-site Round Mountain Campground, and twists down Pulver Gulch to the South Platte River, Lake George, and the drive's eastern terminus. Colorado Springs lies another forty-five miles to the east.

13 MOUNT EVANS SCENIC & HISTORIC BYWAY
Idaho Springs to the summit of Mount Evans

General description: The 28-mile Mount Evans Highway, the nation's highest automobile road and a national forest scenic byway, climbs from Idaho Springs to the boulder-strewn 14,264-foot summit of Mount Evans.
Special attractions: Pike National Forest, Arapaho National Forest, Mount Evans Wilderness Area, Echo Lake, Mount Goliath Natural Area, Summit Lake, camping, picnicking, fishing, rock climbing, wildlife observation, spring skiing, hiking, bristlecone pines, scenic views.
Location: Central Colorado. The drive is in the Front Range just west of Denver.
Drive route name and numbers: Mount Evans Highway, Colorado Highways 103 and 5.
Travel season: Summer only. The road to the summit, Colorado Highway 5, usually opens to Summit Lake by Memorial Day and all the way to the summit by late June depending on the winter's snowfall depth. The road closes on Labor Day. The lower elevation highway is open year-round. Expect severe driving conditions on the upper mountain in summer, with possible heavy thunderstorms and even snow. The road can become slick and icy.
Camping: 2 national forest campgrounds—11-site West Chicago Creek and 18-site Echo Lake—lie along the drive. Three picnic areas are found on the drive.

13 MOUNT EVANS SCENIC & HISTORIC BYWAY

To Georgetown

Idaho Springs

To Denver

70

103

188

Ponder Point Picnic Area

West Chicago Creek CG

Chicago Forks Picnic Area

ECHO LAKE PARK

Echo Lake

Echo Lake CG

Squaw Pass 9,607 ft.

103

To Denver

MT.

EVANS

Mt. Goliath 12,216 ft.

MT. GOLIATH NATURAL AREA

Gray Wolf Mtn. 13,602 ft.

Lincoln Lake

★ •Denver

COLORADO

Summit Lake

Mt. Evans 14,264 ft.

Mt. Bierstadt 14,060 ft.

WILDERNESS

Epaulet Mtn. 13,523 ft.

AREA

Rosalie Pk. 13,575 ft.

0   2   4   6   8   10
Miles

N

109

*The Continental Divide rises beyond the Mt. Evans Highway as it twists up
Mt. Goliath's bouldery northern slopes.*

Services: All services are found in Idaho Springs.
Nearby attractions: Guanella Pass Scenic Byway, Oh My God Road,
Central City, Georgetown National Historic District, Georgetown Loop
Railroad, Loveland Basin Ski Area, Arapaho Basin Ski Area, Golden Gate
Canyon State Park, Clear Creek Canyon, Mount Evans State Wildlife
Area, Evergreen, Buffalo Bill Grave, Red Rocks Park, Denver area
attractions.
For more information: Arapaho National Forest, 240 W. Prospect Road,
Fort Collins, CO 80526, (970) 498-1100. Clear Creek District Ranger, 101
Chicago Creek, P.O. Box 3307, Idaho Springs, CO 80452, (970) 567-2901.
Idaho Springs Visitor Center, 2200 Miner Street, P.O. Box 97, Idaho
Springs, CO 80452, (970) 567-4382.

The drive: Colorado's Front Range lifts its snow-flecked peaks high above
the parched eastern plains. The sawtoothed mountains cut across the
horizon, the old, sturdy summits etched against an azure sky. While the
procession of seasons alters the mountain garb—carpets of summer wildflowers, emerald green forests in spring, aspen leaves that flutter like newly
minted gold coins in autumn, and winter's blanket of dazzling snow—the
peaks seem unchanging, silent, and even aloof with the passage of endless
measures of time. The Front Range escarpment fronting the prairie is
dominated by three massive peaks that lift bulky shoulders above their

neighbors—Pikes Peak, Longs Peak, and Mount Evans. Mount Evans, rising to 14,264 feet, is Denver's mountain. It's always visible from the city streets—glistening in the sun like an alabaster castle or its ridges obscured by windswept clouds. Its conspicuous presence is a reminder that out there, beyond the urban gridlock, is a wild, wonderful world waiting to be explored. The twenty-eight-mile-long Mount Evans scenic drive, a National Forest Scenic Byway, explores this lofty peak. The paved highway, beginning off Interstate 70 in Idaho Springs, twists and winds up canyons and across ridges, passes ancient bristlecone pine forests and clear alpine lakes, and ends with spectacular views that encompass all of central Colorado.

The road to Mount Evans' summit, CO 5, is open only in summer from Memorial Day to Labor Day. The lower drive section above Idaho Springs is open year-round. The summer weather on Mount Evans, like any high Colorado peak, is fickle. Expect clear skies in the morning and clouds and possible thunderstorms in the afternoon. Temperatures range from the eighties at Idaho Springs to the thirties atop the mountain. Snow, below-freezing temperatures, and high winds can occur on any summer day. Be prepared by bringing warm clothes, including long pants and a rain coat. Beware of lingering on the summit or high ridges during lightning storms. The road surface can be slick with rain, snow, and ice during and after storms—drive cautiously. Many visitors will experience altitude sickness from the quick elevation gain. The rarefied air offers less oxygen than lower elevations. The best remedy is to descend from the upper heights.

The scenic drive begins at Exit 240 on I-70 in Idaho Springs thirty miles west of Denver. Idaho Springs, at 7,540 feet, stretches along narrow Clear Creek Canyon among dry, steep-walled mountains. Idaho Springs was the site of Colorado's first important gold strike. In January of 1865, George Jackson, a prospector and cousin to scout Kit Carson, descended Chicago Creek alone on a hunting trip. He camped at the confluence of Chicago Creek and Clear Creek just south of today's Exit 240 and kept warm with a campfire. The next morning he "removed the embers and panned out eight treaty cups of dirt, and found nothing but fine colors; with one cup I got a nugget of gold." Jackson marked his claim and returned later in the spring to pan out thousands of dollars worth of gold and the stampede was on. Miner Street in Idaho Springs quickly became a wall-to-wall tent city with a population of twelve thousand. Its less-populous eastern neighbor, Denver had only two thousand residents. The placer deposits were soon exhausted, but the discovery of rich ore veins in the surrounding metamorphic gneiss and schist rock kept the town alive. In 1868 the local hot springs began attracting health-seeking tourists and Idaho Springs discovered new wealth as a spa. Visitors still come to Idaho Springs to soak in the hot springs as well as to visit downtown Idaho Springs, a registered National Historic District dotted with picturesque Victorian homes and buildings. The town is also the gateway to central Colorado's ski areas. A good backroad drive heads eight miles north from town up Russell Gulch to Central City. This twisting road, nicknamed the Oh My God Road, follows the treacherous old trail between the two mining camps.

The drive begins by turning south on CO 103 from I-70. Arapaho National Forest's Clear Creek Ranger Station sits just south of the highway junction. The visitor center here, open from 8 a.m. to 8 p.m. between Memorial Day and Labor Day, dispenses forest maps, an offering of guidebooks, and free information about the national forest and surrounding communities. The highway runs southwest up Chicago Creek in a deep, broad canyon. Groves of juniper and thickets of mountain mahogany and skunkbush line the dry, south-facing slopes, while mature ponderosa pines lift stately crowns above the moister, north-facing hillsides. As the road climbs, the forest changes, with ponderosas lining the northern walls and dense fir and spruce forest shrouding the southern slopes. Willows and aspen groves line the tumbling creek. Numerous houses and abandoned mines lie along Chicago Creek.

After 6.5 miles the highway turns south from Chicago Creek and begins climbing steep, wooded slopes above the creek. Forest Road 188 continues up West Chicago Creek three miles to eleven-site West Chicago Creek Campground. The scenic drive, with steep grades and sharp curves, ascends past Chicago Forks and Ponder Point picnic areas. Ponder Point, perched above a hairpin turn, offers the first view of Mount Evans to the southwest. The road continues climbing and by thirteen miles reaches Echo Lake and the Echo Lake Picnic Area at 10,600 feet. Scenic Echo Lake, part of Denver's city park system, is a popular stopover for picnickers and anglers. The road bends southeast from the lake and a half-mile later reaches the junction of Colorado highways 103 and 5. The scenic drive turns west here on CO 5. Echo Lake Lodge, a large three-story log building, sits at the intersection. The lodge, opening in 1927, has been a hunting lodge, brothel, Army winter survival base in World War II, and is now a popular restaurant. Arapaho National Forest's eighteen-site Echo Lake Campground sits south of the lodge. This wooded campground makes an excellent overnight stopover for highway travelers.

The scenic drive turns west at the campground and lodge on CO 5. The roadway narrows and begins sharply ascending through a thick subalpine forest on the northern slopes of Goliath Peak, a 12,216-foot spur of Mount Evans. Lodgepole pine, a straight tree favored by Indians for teepee poles, dominates the forest, along with subalpine fir and Engelmann spruce. After a couple miles the highway swings onto Goliath Peak's southern slope and marvelous views begin to unfold of the surrounding lower mountains and valleys. Here at treeline, at an elevation just above 11,000 feet, grows a limber pine and bristlecone pine woodland, one of Colorado's most unique forests. These trees, unable to compete with the vigorous spruce, fir, and pine forests of lower elevations, thrive on exposed rocky slopes at timberline with high winds, long snowy winters, and fierce temperature ranges. The twisted, windswept bristlecones, among Colorado's oldest living trees, are over one thousand years old. A parking area allows hikers to explore the bristlecone forest. The bristlecone forest and the alpine tundra on Goliath Peak are protected by the Mount Goliath Natural Area, a 160-acre preserve that spreads across the rounded mountain.

The highway switchbacks and climbs north past timberline onto Goliath

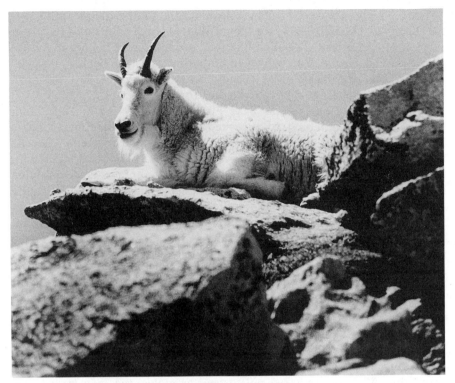

A mountain goat sits alongside the Mt. Evans Highway.

Peak's north slopes. A roadside pullout allows marvelous views northward to the snow-covered Continental Divide. Echo Lake glistens far below amid the forest. The road edges westward and after a mile-and-a-half crosses a 12,152-foot saddle just west of Goliath Peak. The Alpine Garden Trail begins at a small parking area here. This half-mile loop explores the alpine tundra and lichen-covered boulders.

This site is an outstanding example of the land above the trees, a land of punishing climatic extremes. Driving up the highway to this airy garden is like taking a compressed journey to northern Alaska beyond the Arctic Circle. Indeed, Colorado's tundra shares many of the same plants found in the Arctic as well as a similar climate with a brief growing season—few frost-free nights, fierce winds, shallow soils, and humidity so low that the land is a high-altitude desert. Primitive plants—lichens and mosses—dot the granite boulders, while dwarfed, slow-growing perennials hug the ground and avoid the desiccating wind. The alpine sunflower, the largest plant found here, is full grown at six inches high. Other flowers include alpine avens, bistorts, alpine forget-me-nots, alpine phlox, and snow buttercups. These delicate alpine plant communities are extremely sensitive to disturbance, sometimes taking centuries to recover. Stay on the trail and don't pick any flowers. The Mount Goliath Trail also begins at the parking area and drops 1.1 miles down through bristlecone pines and subalpine firs to the Mount Evans road.

The highway runs west for a few miles along the southern slopes of 13,391-foot Rogers Peak and 13,291-foot Mount Warren, high points on a long spur ridge of Mount Evans. The shelf-like road swings across the top of a huge glacier-carved cirque. Far below at timberline, nestled behind a glacial moraine, lies Lincoln Lake. Deep snow drifts and cornices line this road section in early summer. Past the lake the drive traverses gentler tundra and willow-clad slopes on Summit Lake Flats before arriving at 12,850-foot Summit Lake. This alpine lake, tucked into a lofty, cliff-rimmed basin scoured by glaciers, is the gem of Denver's mountain park system. After the ice melts off the lake in July, the Colorado Division of Wildlife stocks it with cutthroat trout for anglers. Picnickers and hikers also enjoy this scenic alpine lake. A short hike northeast from the parking area leads to a divide and a magnificent view down the glaciated, U-shaped valley of Chicago Creek.

The highway begins its final ascent of Mount Evans from Summit Lake. The road bends abruptly south and begins switchbacking up steep, bouldery slopes for five miles to the summit. This final section of highway reached Mount Evans' summit on October 10, 1930. Work began on the road at Echo Lake in 1922. Mount Evans, originally named Rosalie by pioneer painter Albert Bierstadt in 1863 for his wife, was renamed in 1895 for John Evans, Colorado's second territorial governor.

Mountain goats and bighorn sheep often graze along the drive's upper sections. The introduced goats thrive on Mount Evans, with the herd numbering about sixty. A few hunting licenses are sold each year to cull the population. Visitors are asked not to feed or molest the seemingly tame, roadside mountain goats. A Division of Wildlife study indicates that those goats fed by humans produce less offspring and have thinner coats. Other above-timberline wildlife includes pikas, marmots, and white-tailed ptarmigan. The ptarmigan changes the color of its plumage to fit the season— brilliant white in winter and mottled brown in summer.

The Mount Evans Highway corridor, from Echo Lake to the summit, is surrounded by the 74,401-acre Mount Evans Wilderness Area. This wilderness, spread across parts of Arapaho and Pike national forests, encompasses both Mount Evans and neighboring 14,060-foot Mount Bierstadt, an almost pristine swath of alpine country, and deep canyons and ridges matted with dense woodlands.

After slowly switchbacking up Mount Evans' southeast flank, the highway and scenic drive reaches its end at a parking lot at 14,150 feet. A short trail climbs north to the peak's rocky 14,264-foot summit. The parking area is small and may be filled on busy weekend days. Restrooms and the burned remains of the old Crest House are found at road's end. Nearby sits the University of Denver's High Altitude Laboratory for research in astronomy, physiology, weather, and biochemistry. There is a twenty-four-inch telescope in the observatory.

The view from atop Mount Evans is breathtaking. Visibility on clear days reaches almost two hundred miles. To the west towers Mount Bierstadt's summit pyramid, and beyond stretches the Continental Divide, the nation's backbone that separates the Pacific and Atlantic ocean watersheds. The famed Mount of the Holy Cross and the rounded summits of the Sawatch Range, including 14,431-foot Mount Elbert, Colorado's high point, run across the horizon. South Park, an immense intermontane basin, spreads between snowy ranges to the southwest. Pikes Peak lifts its bulk in the southern sky, framed by the distant Wet Mountains and the jagged ridge of the Sangre de Cristo Range. The high summits of Rocky Mountain National Park loom to the north, while the limitless, tawny prairie stretches east from Denver's glimmering streets to a flat Kansas horizon.

14 GUANELLA PASS ROAD
Georgetown to Grant

General description: This 22-mile paved and gravel road, a National Forest Scenic Byway, climbs from Georgetown over scenic 11,669-foot Guanella Pass to Grant in the Front Range.

Special attractions: Pike National Forest, Arapaho National Forest, Georgetown National Historic District, Mount Evans Wilderness Area, hiking, backpacking, camping, fishing, scenic views, cross-country skiing, historic sites, aspen colors.

Location: Central Colorado. The drive begins in Georgetown off Interstate 70 west of Denver and ends at Grant on U.S. Highway 285 just east of Kenosha Pass.

Drive route numbers: Clear Creek County 381, Forest Road 118, Park County 62.

Travel season: Year-round. The drive is regularly plowed in winter, although heavy snow may temporarily close it. Carry chains, a shovel, and warm clothes in winter. The drive is not recommended for over-sized RVs or trailers.

Camping: Five national forest campgrounds lie along the drive. 8-site Clear Lake and 17-site Guanella Pass campgrounds sit north of the pass summit, while 26-site Geneva Park, 13-site Burning Bear, and 7-site Whiteside campgrounds lie south of the pass along Geneva Creek.

Services: All services are found in Georgetown.

Nearby attractions: Lost Creek Wilderness Area, Colorado Trail, Kenosha Pass, Fairplay, Como, Boreas Pass, South Park, South Platte River, Silver Plume, Mount Evans scenic drive, Mount Goliath Natural Area, Grays and Torreys peaks, Arapaho Basin Ski Area, Central City and Blackhawk National Historic District, Golden Gate Canyon State Park, Winter Park and Mary Jane ski areas.

For more information: Arapaho National Forest, Clear Creek Ranger District, P.O. Box 3307, Idaho Springs, CO 80452, (303) 567-2901. Pike National Forest, South Platte Ranger District, 11177 West 8th Ave.,

ARAPAHO

To Denver

Republican Mtn.
12,386 ft.

To
Frisco

Silver Plume

Georgetown

★ •Denver

COLORADO

Griffith Mtn.
11,568 ft.

NATIONAL

Clear Lake

Sugarloaf Pk.
12,513 ft.

FOREST

Grays Pk.
14,270 ft.

Clear Lake CG

MT. EVANS

Gray Wolf Mtn.
13,602 ft.

Argentine Pk.
13,738 ft.

Guanella
Pass CG

Mt. Evans
14,264 ft.

WILDERNESS

Guanella Pass
11,669 ft.

Revenue Mtn.
12,839 ft.

Duck Lake

Mt. Bierstadt
14,060 ft.

PIKE

Landslide Pk.
13,238 ft.

Rosalie Pk.
13,575 ft.

GENEVA
PARK

Geneva Mtn.
12,335 ft.

AREA

Geneva Park CG

Burning Bear CG

N

Mt. Logan
12,871 ft.

NATIONAL

Whiteside CG

0 1 2 3 4 5
Miles

Grant

FOREST

Mt. Blaine
12,303 ft.

Kenosha Pass
10,001 ft.

KENOSHA

MOUNTAINS

LOST CREEK
WILDERNESS AREA

116

Lakewood, CO 80215, (303) 236-7386. Georgetown Visitor Information Center, 613 Sixth Street, P.O. Box 426, Georgetown, CO 80444, (970) 569-2888.

The drive: The Guanella Pass scenic drive traverses twenty-two miles of the Front Range, passing abandoned silver mines, sweeping across swatches of alpine tundra littered with wildflowers and willow thickets, dropping down broad glaciated valleys and abrupt canyons, and exploring the range's geologic history. The Front Range, the Rocky Mountains' easternmost range, forms a lofty escarpment that soars over the rolling plains from Canon City into Wyoming. This long, twisting spine, including part of the Continental Divide, is formed by ancient granite, gneiss, and schist rocks that were once the roots of another mountain range over a billion years ago. Repeated faulting, folding, heat, pressure, a final uplifting during the Laramide Orogeny some sixty million years ago, and a final excavation by recent glaciers sculpted the range into its present shape.

Summer and autumn remain the best times to drive over Guanella Pass. Daily summer highs reach the sixties and seventies, while cooler temperatures prevail atop the timberline pass summit. Expect afternoon thunderstorms with heavy rain and lightning. Autumn brings a succession of warm, clear days, chilled nights, and spectacular displays of changing aspen leaves. The first snow usually falls in October and lasts until late May. Winter's white blanket shrouds the undulating flats on the pass summit, making an easily accessible wonderland for cross-country skiers. Spring comes slowly to the high country, but with warmer days the snow fields recede from the woodlands by early June.

The Guanella Pass drive, a National Forest and Colorado scenic byway, begins in Georgetown off I-70 west of Denver. Take Exit 228 off I-70 and follow scenic byway signs through Georgetown to the drive's start on the town's south edge. Georgetown, nestled in Clear Creek's wide upper valley at 8,519 feet, is the centerpiece of the Georgetown-Silver Plume National Historic District which preserves the area's unique architectural and mining attributes. Picturesque Georgetown still remains one of Colorado's richest mining towns, with over $200 million of silver and gold dug from the surrounding mountains.

The town got its start in June of 1859 when George and David Griffith, two Kentucky brothers, heard the siren of gold and plodded westward to claim their fortune. These late arrivers found the best claims already taken at Central City and Idaho Springs, so they trekked further west up Clear Creek Canyon to the confluence of Clear Creek and South Clear Creek in today's downtown Georgetown. Here George's pan revealed specks of gold. The brothers staked their claim and established the Griffith Mining District. George Griffith was named District Recorder and his name affixed to the huddle of cabins along the creek. George's town grew to two thousand residents by the mid-60s, but the best gold was soon exhausted. Silver, however, was plentiful and for the next twenty years Georgetown and Silver Plume, its upstream neighbor, thrived on the silver boom. Only Leadville, the

The Guanella Pass Road climbs past timberline below Mt. Bierstadt and the Sawtooth Ridge.

"Silver King," outshone Georgetown, the "Silver Queen." The town quickly became the commercial hub of the huge mining district, with mills, a brick schoolhouse, numerous churches to minister to the heathen miners, luxurious hotels like the acclaimed Hotel de Paris, four fire companies, saloons and brothels, two newspapers, and, in 1877, the Colorado Central Railroad that linked Georgetown to Denver.

The railroad, operating until 1939 and now rebuilt as a historic attraction, climbed west from Georgetown through rocky Devil's Gate to Silver Plume, two miles west but 638 feet higher. To climb this menacing grade, railroad engineer Robert Blickensderfer designed four miles of track at a four percent grade that spiraled upwards on sharp curves and one huge loop where the track crossed back over itself via a three hundred-foot-long wooden trestle. This grand railroad stretch, called the Georgetown Loop, became a famed tourist attraction due to pioneer photographer William Henry Jackson's promotional photographs. The line was abandoned and demolished in 1939 to make room for the new automobile highway U.S. Highway 6. The railroad was rebuilt and reopened in 1984 to interpret Georgetown's rich mining legacy. The Georgetown Loop Historic Mining and Railroad Park, operated by the Colorado State Historical Society, runs daily train rides along the historic track from Memorial Day to Labor Day.

Georgetown grew until Congress repealed the Sherman Silver Purchase Act in 1893. Overnight the price of silver plummeted and the great mining era ended for the town. By the 1930s a mere two hundred residents lived here amid boarded-up and decaying buildings. In the post World War II period, easy access to the burgeoning Front Range communities brought new life to Georgetown as a quaint mountain community. Today the town's historical character and heritage is well-preserved. A walking tour reveals classic architecture, including the Griffith Mine, the Old Missouri Firehouse, numerous excellent examples of "Gothic Revival"- style residences, the old 1860s stone jail, and the elegant Hotel de Paris, an exquisite hotel that once charmed numerous personages including President Ulysses Grant with fine cuisine and rare wines. Georgetown offers all visitor services and prospers as the gateway to the Summit County ski resorts.

The scenic drive, beginning on the south side of Georgetown, switchbacks steeply up an abrupt mountainside. An excellent view of Georgetown and the broad, U-shaped glaciated valley of Clear Creek is found at a pullout almost a mile up the road. The drive climbs into a hanging valley and after a mile and a half passes the ghost site of Silverdale at the junction of Leavenworth and South Clear Creek. Nothing remains here now, but this area once housed silver miners who worked the Equator, Tilden, Colorado Central, Robinson, and Curtly mines on the slopes above the creek. The town boasted its own post office, but rarely exceeded a population of one hundred. An overlook at 2.6 miles views Leavenworth Creek tumbling through an abandoned mine tunnel. Forest Road 248 begins just to the south. This rough road, best followed in a high-clearance vehicle, ascends seven miles up the abandoned railroad grade of the Argentine Central, the world's highest steam railroad, along Leavenworth Creek to the ghost town of Waldorf at 11,666 feet. Beginning in 1868 Waldorf's mines yielded millions in gold and silver. Early tourists also discovered the thrilling train ride and flocked up its spectacular, curving track. Today, jeeps and mountain bikes can continue up a four-wheel-drive road to almost 13,000 feet on the long ridged summit of Mount McClellan. The view from this lofty vantage point is simply marvelous, encompassing one-sixth of Colorado and 176 peaks from Longs Peak in the north to the distant Sangre de Cristos in the south.

The drive continues south along South Clear Creek, enters Arapaho National Forest, and passes a string of lakes. Green Lake, framed by "No Trespassing" signs, formed when a rock slide dammed the creek. Clear Lake, a deep lake originally excavated by glaciers, makes a good recreation stop. The lake, offering shoreline access only, gives good fishing for rainbow trout and offers a shady picnic area. Lower Cabin Creek Reservoir straddles the valley just beyond Clear Lake. This fenced reservoir, along with Upper Cabin Creek Reservoir to the west, is part of a massive hydroelectric project that pumps water from the lower lake to the upper one and uses the resulting energy to create electricity for Denver.

At five and a half miles the byway passes eight-site Clear Lake Campground. Beyond here the valley broadens, with South Clear Creek meandering through still beaver ponds and dense willow thickets. Anglers can wade out into the silent currents to catch both rainbow and brown trout. This lush valley is a good place to study mountain riparian ecosystems. This valley, like most upper-elevation Colorado valleys, was sculpted by glaciers that left depressions that formed lakes and ponds as they retreated with the warming climate. These shallow lakes slowly filled with sediment, leaving bogs of rich soil behind. Today, streams braid across these wide valleys providing a lush and diverse habitat for many animal species including the beaver—the ubiquitous denizen of high country valleys. Beavers, North America's largest rodent, build dams that flood the bottomlands and create excellent conditions for quaking aspen and willow, the beaver's preferred food and building materials. The dams also fill with silt and slowly turn the moist bogs into mountain meadows. Aspen groves, showy with gold in autumn, line the roadside, while dense forests of blue and Englemann spruce and subalpine fir mat the mountainsides above.

Sixteen-site Guanella Pass Campground sits in the forest below the final ascent to timberline and the pass summit at 10,800 feet. A nearby foot trail climbs one mile west to Silver Dollar, Naylor, and Murray lakes, all glacial lakes tucked into a high cirque below 13,738-foot Argentine Peak. The road begins switchbacking up steep slopes from here. Great views unfold as the road ascends 14,060-foot Mount Bierstadt and its Sawtooth Ridge to the east. The drive passes wind-twisted subalpine fir, called *krummholtz*, at timberline and reaches the broad 11,669-foot-high summit of Guanella Pass. The pass is named for Byron Guanella, a Clear Creek County highway man who supervised the road's construction in 1952.

The pass summit offers not only scenic views, but easy access to a broad swath of beautiful high country that includes the 74,401-acre Mount Evans Wilderness Area. This is a magnificent landscape. Melting snow fields whiten steep slopes and shallow alpine tarns reflect the open sky. Tundra, a delicate carpet of grasses and wildflowers, spreads a mantle of green across the lower peaks, while jumbled granite boulders and cliffs reach to lofty summits. Mount Bierstadt, named for pioneer nineteenth century painter Albert Bierstadt, dominates the view to the east. One of the Front Range's finest wilderness experiences is climbing Bierstadt's broad west face to a high summit that yields superb views. A moderate hike, gaining almost three thousand feet of elevation, begins at the pass parking lot, heads east through willowy bogs, and then up a rough trail through tundra and granite. Other good hikes include the Rosalie Trail and a trail that runs west to Square Top Lakes. The rolling land surrounding the pass summit makes excellent cross-country ski terrain in winter.

The drive descends south from the pass, skirting a rounded ridge and reaching treeline in a half-mile. A mile later the road reaches privately owned Duck Lake, nestled behind a glacial moraine. Grassy slopes of the now defunct Geneva Basin Ski Area slice into the forest west of the drive. Past the lake the road edges down the west flank of 12,335-foot Geneva Mountain through spruce forest and reaches sparkling Duck Creek in a U-shaped glacial valley. The creek, bordering the drive, winds through deep beaver ponds and willows.

At seventeen miles the now-paved road drops into 9,700-foot-high Geneva Park, a broad grassy basin excavated by ancient glaciers. Geneva Creek, originating to the west on the Continental Divide meanders among willow-clad banks and grazing cattle. Forest Road 119 heads northwest up the creek, passing twenty-six-site Geneva Park Campground and Duck Creek Picnic Ground. Bruno Creek, a tributary of Geneva Creek, supports endangered Colorado greenback trout and is closed to fishing. Burning Bear Campground spreads its thirteen sites among open lodgepole pine forest on the southeast corner of Geneva Park. This pleasant campground makes a good overnight stay for wildlife watchers. A walk down to the park's edge in the evening often reveals a wealth of wildlife, including mule deer, elk, and occasional bighorn sheep.

The drive's character changes abruptly past Burning Bear Campground. The road reaches a bouldery terminal moraine left by massive glaciers that formed Geneva Park and switchbacks steeply down Falls Hill into Geneva Creek's steep, V-shaped canyon. The rushing creek tumbles in misty cascades over boulders and bedrock below the road. After a one-mile descent the road again reaches the creek and the pavement ends. The drive's last four miles follow the canyon southward through lush aspen and willow woodlands along the creek. Primitive camping is found along the creek and at five-site Whiteside Campground. Geneva Creek Picnic Ground is a popular lunch spot for byway travelers and anglers. The drive ends on US 285 at Grant, a small hamlet named for former President and Civil War hero Ulysses S. Grant. Denver lies almost sixty miles to the east, and Fairplay, via Kenosha Pass, sits twenty-eight miles to the southwest.

| 15 | **PEAK TO PEAK HIGHWAY**
Central City to Estes Park |

General description: This 63-mile-long drive parallels the forested east flank of the Front Range between Central City and Estes Park.

Special attractions: Clear Creek Canyon, Central City-Black Hawk National Historic District, Golden Gate Canyon State Park, Ward, Roosevelt National Forest, Brainard Lake Recreation Area, Indian Peaks Wilderness Area, Rocky Mountain National Park, Longs Peak, Enos Mills Cabin, Estes Park, hiking, camping, backpacking, rock climbing, historic sites, fishing, scenic views, autumn aspens.

Location: North-central Colorado. The drive begins at the junction of U.S. Highway 6 west of Golden and Colorado Highway 119, and travels north via Colorado Highways 72 and 7 to Estes Park east of Rocky Mountain National Park.

Drive route name and numbers: Peak to Peak Highway, Colorado Highways 119, 72, and 7.

Travel season: Year-round.

Camping: National forest campgrounds along the way, south to north, are Cold Springs, Kelly Dahl, Pawnee, Peaceful Valley, Camp Dick, and Olive Ridge. Longs Peak Campground, tents only, is in Rocky Mountain

National Park. 2 campgrounds lie in Golden Gate Canyon State Park.

Services: All services are in Central City, Black Hawk, Nederland, and Estes Park. Limited services in Lone Pine, Rollinsville, and Ward.

Nearby attractions: Mount Evans Highway, Guanella Pass Scenic Byway, Georgetown, Golden, Arapaho National Forest, Rollins Pass, White Ranch Park, Eldorado State Park, Boulder, Trail Ridge Road, Never Summer Wilderness Area, Arapaho National Recreation Area.

For more information: Arapaho and Roosevelt National Forests, 240 W. Prospect, Fort Collins, CO 80526, (970) 444-6001. Central City PR Office, P.O. Box 249, Central City, CO 80427, (303) 582-5251. Estes Park Area Chamber, P.O. Box 3050, Estes Park, CO 80517, (970) 586-4431, (800) 44-ESTES.

The drive: The Peak to Peak Highway, a designated National Forest Scenic Byway, unfurls for sixty-three miles between Clear Creek Canyon and Estes Park. The drive offers calendar-caliber scenery, with gorgeous views of the skyscraping Continental Divide, high wooded hills, exhilarating canyons and valleys, and the dun-colored prairie to the east. The drive, lying within Roosevelt National Forest, is bordered by both the Indian Peaks Wilderness Area and Rocky Mountain National Park.

The highway, although open year-round, is best driven in summer or autumn when the fall colors peak. Summer temperatures vary according to elevation and range from the forties to the upper eighties. Expect warm days, cool nights, and regular afternoon thunderstorms. September can bring almost perfect weather with warm, clear days and spectacular aspen golds. October begins the cool-down with unpredictable weather. Snow lingers on the cooler slopes in late October and by November the upper elevations are clothed in a mantle of white. Winters are cold and often windy. Days can be warm with highs climbing as warm as the forties, but nighttime temperatures often fall to zero degrees. Spring days are windy and cool. The winter snowpack melts off below timberline in May.

The drive begins at the junction of US 6 and CO 119 twelve miles west of Golden. US 6 twists up Clear Creek Canyon, a precipitous gorge that slices through the lower Front Range escarpment. The same highway junction lies two miles east on US 6 from Interstate 70's Exit 244. The drive, heading northeast up CO 119 alongside North Clear Creek, gently ascends a slicing, dry-walled canyon. Mine tailings, a reminder of the area's golden history, line the creek bank. Occasional placer claims are still being worked by weekend prospectors.

After 6.5 miles the highway enters the Central City-Black Hawk National Historic District and a half mile later enters Black Hawk. The town, along with Central City lying one mile west up Gregory Gulch, sits in what early miners dubbed "The richest square mile on earth." The story began in early 1859 when John Gregory, a Georgia prospector working Cherry Creek's placer gravels in today's Denver, trod up a snowy canyon and found promising color. Gregory had stumbled onto a veritable treasure trove and took out more gold in his first week than all of Cherry Creek had yielded the

The Indian Peaks tower above a lone fisherman and Red Rock Lake along the Peak to Peak Highway.

To Trail Ridge
Estes Park
To Loveland
34

ROCKY
Moraine Park CG
36
To Lyons

CONTINENTAL
Glacier Basin CG

Hallett Pk. 12,713 ft.
MOUNTAIN
Visitor Center
Twin Sisters Pks. 11,428 ft.
ROOSEVELT

NATL.
DIVIDE
Enos Mills Cabin

Mt. Alice 13,310 ft.
Long Pk. 14,255 ft.
7

Olive Ridge CG
Allenspark

PARK
7
To Lyons

Peaceful Valley CG
72
NATIONAL

Sawtooth Mtn. 12,303 ft.
Camp Dick CG

Mt. Audubon 13,223 ft.
To Boulder

Navajo Pk. 13,409 ft.
Pawnee CG
Ward

INDIAN PEAKS WILDERNESS AREA
N. Arapaho Pk.
FOREST

72
To Boulder

119

★ •Denver

COLORADO

Nederland
72

Nebraska Hill 11,534 ft.
Kelly Dahl CG
To Denver

119
Aspen Meadows CG

Cold Springs CG
46

GOLDEN GATE CANYON STATE PARK

Columbine CG
Blackhawk
To Golden

ARAPAHO NATIONAL FOREST
Central City

119

To Frisco
70

To Denver
6

Idaho Springs
70
To Denver

0 2 4 6 8 10
Miles

N

previous summer. Word spread like wildfire and Colorado's first gold rush was on. More than five thousand miners teemed into Gregory's Diggings over the next few months and several camps scattered over the mountain slopes. Two of the camps grew into burgeoning mining towns—Black Hawk, named for the trademark of an early mining company, and Central City, dubbed for the town's central location among the mining camps. By the mid-1860s Central City's population surpassed fifteen thousand and the community boasted a diverse, cultured, and cosmopolitan air. The famed Central City Opera House, active still today, offered its first production, *Camille* in 1861. A darker side existed as well. An 1861 election hosted "217 fistfights, 97 revolver fights, 11 Bowie knife fights, and 1 dog fight." Despite those frightening statistics, no one was killed. The Colorado Territory's first legal hanging occurred here in January, 1864 when a murderer hung.

Central City and Black Hawk thrived on the riches extricated from the surrounding mountains and gulches. Numerous prospectors struck the mother lode and basked in wealth and power. Other millionaires, besides Gregory, included future U.S. Senator Henry Teller and Jeremiah Lee, a twenty-nine-year-old ex-slave of Robert E. Lee. The fabulous Argentine Lode was found in Lee's OK Mine. Teller built the stone Teller House, a town landmark, in 1872. When President Ulysses S. Grant stayed here in 1873, he found the path from his carriage to the Teller House bricked with silver bars. With the rise of the silver towns in the 1880s, the area's fortunes sagged and by 1900 the towns settled into retirement. The Opera House, refurbished and reopened in 1932, brought music lovers and tourists to the quaint towns. Writer Jack Kerouac penned his 1950s Central City experience in his classic novel *On The Road*: "Central City is two miles high; at first you get drunk on the altitude, then you get tired, and there's a fever in your soul. We approached the lights around the opera house down the narrow dark street; then we took a sharp right and hit some old saloons with swinging doors."

Central City and Black Hawk, today preserved in a national historic district, offer many attractions. The Gilpin County Historical Museum displays community history. Tours are given at the Teller House and Opera House. The Central City Opera, the nation's oldest summer opera company, offers excellent productions every summer. Most folks come now for the gambling, which became legal here in 1991. Be prepared in summer and on weekends for traffic congestion and parking problems.

The drive continues up North Clear Creek canyon past Black Hawk, the steep slopes coated in a mixed pine and fir forest and pockmarked with abandoned mine adits and tailings. After a couple miles the highway leaves the drainage and climbs north onto high wooded ridges. The Roosevelt National Forest boundary lies at almost twelve miles. A look back reveals Mount Evans, its snowy 14,264-foot bulk outlined against the southern sky. Atop a ridge crest the drive intersects Colorado Highway 46. This scenic backroad drops east down Ralston Creek to Golden Gate Canyon State Park and meanders on to Golden. As the highway rolls north over undulating ridges and hills, shaggy peaks clothed in conifers and broken by knobby granite crags loom to the east in Golden Gate Canyon State Park.

The park, accessible via a turnoff at sixteen miles, makes a good stopover. The 8,787-acre parkland is ideal for hiking with sixty miles of trails threading the backcountry. Good hikes include 4.6-mile Mule Deer Trail and 2.1-mile Eagle Trail up City Lights Ridge. The evening view from there is marvelous, with bits and pieces of the Denver sprawl glimmering in the twilight. Panorama Point, accessible by car on Tremont Mountain's north flank, overlooks the Indian Peaks stretching north to flat-topped Longs Peak. Thirty-five-site Aspen Meadow and 106-site Reverend's Ridge campgrounds sit on the park's north side just east of the drive.

The road turns north from the state park, dipping through shallow valleys at South Beaver Creek and Lump Gulch before spiraling down Gamble Gulch to Rollinsville. This town, founded in 1873 by John Quincy Adams Rollins, allowed no casinos, dance halls, or saloons. Besides purchasing mines, he built a toll road over 11,671-foot Rollins Pass on the Continental Divide to Middle Park. Later the Denver, Northwestern and Pacific Railroad acquired the right-of-way and built a temporary track with thirty-three tunnels up the route. The line remains the highest altitude reached by an American railroad. The abandoned railbed, converted into a jeep road in 1956, is now one of Colorado's most popular backroad excursions. The jeep road heads west from Rollinsville up South Boulder Creek.

The drive ambles north from Rollinsville and passes forty-six-site Kelly Dahl Campground. The road swings around 8,922-foot Tungsten Mountain and drops down to 8,236-foot-high Nederland and Middle Boulder Creek. Nederland spreads across a broad valley above Barker Reservoir and Boulder Canyon and below the Continental Divide. The town, established in 1877, once boomed with gold, silver, and tungsten mining and now serves as a gateway to the Indian Peaks Wilderness and a getaway for Boulder residents. Author Helen Hunt Jackson described 1870s Nederland as a "dismal little mining town," but now it's a venerable, cozy village with an unpretentious charm. The town works hard at preserving its quiet atmosphere by not becoming a tourist trap or a Boulder bedroom community. It still functions as a regional supply center with a hardware store, auto parts shop, a printer, doctors, and veterinarians. It also offers numerous stores for visitors, including a marvelous rock shop, twelve restaurants, and is home to several activist groups like Amnesty International. Eldora Ski Area, west of town, furnishes 210 acres of skiing and one of Colorado's largest cross country ski areas. CO 119, beginning in Nederland, plunges down Boulder Canyon, a popular rock climbing and hiking area, seventeen miles to Boulder, home of the University of Colorado.

The Peak to Peak Highway, following CO 72, climbs north from Nederland. For nine miles the road twists and curls over forested ridges and through shallow canyons before swinging onto the broad eastern flank of 11,471-foot Niwot Mountain. Vast views unfold from the road. Lower mountains recede east to the great plains and the flat horizon. Ward sits below the drive above upper Lefthand Canyon. Ward, established in 1865, is another mining camp that settled into peaceful retirement after its gold heyday. Calvin Ward discovered the golden Ward Lode here in 1860. The "Switzerland Trail of

America"—the now-defunct Denver, Boulder & Western Railroad—served the town after 1898. A disastrous fire in 1910 destroyed fifty-three buildings in Ward. Ward marks the northern boundary of the Colorado Mineral Belt, a fifty-mile-wide swathe that runs from here to southwestern Colorado and contains most of the state's mineral wealth.

Take Forest Road 112 to Brainard Lake a tenth of a mile past the Ward turnoff. This paved road climbs five miles past picturesque Red Rock Lake to Brainard Lake Recreation Area on the eastern edge of the 73,391-acre Indian Peaks Wilderness Area. The Indian Peaks, including Pawnee, Shoshoni, Navajo, and Arikaree peaks, form a spectacular escarpment along the Continental Divide above the 10,345-foot-high lake. Snow fields and small glaciers cling to the serrated peaks through much of the summer. Glaciers excavated these spiked, weather-beaten mountains and their abrupt alpine cirques. The wilderness area, established in 1978, preserves some of Colorado's best mountain scenery. Its unfortunate proximity to the state's major population centers, however, has caused severe overuse. The USDA Forest Service now imposes restrictions to protect and rehabilitate the area's fragile alpine ecosystems. Permits are needed for overnight camping and limitations placed on fires and pack animals. Bicycles and motorized vehicles are prohibited.

The Brainard Lake Recreation Area, at road's end, makes a good jumping-off point for day hikers and mountain climbers. Mount Audubon, the round-shouldered 13,223-foot peak to the northwest, makes a good climb via a marked four-mile trail. Numerous facilities scatter around the lake, including three picnic areas and fifty-five-site Pawnee Campground. Night temperatures can be frigid at the campground during its May through September season. Snowdrifts often linger in the forest well into July. Both Brainard Lake and Red Rock Lake offer excellent trout fishing.

From Ward the drive continues north over wooded ridges before steeply dipping into Peaceful Valley along Middle St. Vrain Creek. Fifteen-site Peaceful Valley Campground sits just west of the hairpin turn at the canyon bottom. The highway runs down the sharp canyon, its walls studded with towering granite cliffs, before climbing out to its junction with CO 7 from Lyons. CO 72 ends here. The drive turns west on CO 7.

The new highway crosses rolling hills seamed by shallow, grassy valleys. A ponderosa pine woodland veneers the land. Aspen groves tuck into moist ravines and willow thickets border trickling creeks. Ponderosa pine forests dominate Colorado's mid-elevation mountains. These open forests congregate on warm, south-facing slopes where temperatures range as much as twenty degrees warmer than neighboring north slopes. Acidic needles in the springy pine duff on the forest floor inhibits the growth of a shrub and grass understory, allowing the trees to retain all the precious moisture.

A scenic overlook three miles from the junction faces north to Mount Meeker and the Wild Basin in Rocky Mountain National Park. The turn to Allenspark sits a half-mile farther. The town, named for 1859 homesteader Alonzo Allen, caters to visitors with several restaurants, shops, and motels. Olive Ridge Campground, a pleasant fifty-six-site area a couple miles up the road, sits just west of the highway and makes a good base camp for forays into the Wild Basin area.

From Olive Ridge to Estes Park the highway parallels the eastern boundary of Rocky Mountain National Park. This immense parkland spreads across 414 square miles of almost pristine high country, including the Continental Divide. The park, Colorado's largest, boasts 104 peaks above 10,000 feet and seventy-one reaching above12,000 feet. Flat-topped Longs Peak is the park 's high point at 14,256 feet. Glaciers chiseled much of the park's sky-scraping scenery, attacking the ancient 1.7-billion-year-old granite and metamorphic rock core during periodic glacial periods over the last two million years. The ponderous ice sheets draped over the mountain crests and scraped down the valleys, leaving great cirques, horned peaks, sheer cliffs, and huge moraines or piles of boulders as evidence of their passage. The last glacier retreated ten thousand years ago.

The road drops from Olive Ridge and crosses North St. Vrain Creek. Past the creek a turn west leads to Wild Basin, a rugged backcountry cirque in the park's remote southern reaches. Numerous trails lace the basin, threading along sparkling streams to tantalizing above-timberline tarns like Ouzel, Bluebird, Thunder, and Sandbeach lakes. The highway runs north below bulky Mount Meeker, a towering pile of granite rubble, and through Meeker Park, a small hamlet with stables, a lodge, and cabins. Meeker Park Picnic Area lies a mile beyond. As the drive passes Mount Meeker the precipitous east face of Longs Peak monopolizes the view.

Longs Peak, named for 1820 explorer Major Stephen Long, dominates the Front Range like no other mountain save Pikes Peak to the south. Its flat summit, long a pioneer landmark, gleams like an alabaster tower above the sere prairie. The Arapaho Indians called the peak, along with Mount Meeker, "The Two Guides" and early French trappers named them "The Two Ears." An awesome 2,000-foot-high granite wall sliced by glaciers forms the east face of Longs Peak. Mount Meeker and Mount Lady Washington flank the peak. The Diamond, the peak's bold upper face, offers some of North America's best alpine rock climbing on routes like the Yellow Wall and D-1.

After traversing into broad Tahosa Valley between the Longs Peak massif and the Twin Sisters, the highway reaches the Longs Peak trailhead. A short road leads west to twenty-six-site Longs Peak Campground, a tents-only area, and the trailhead. The trail climbs the peak via the Keyhole Route, the peak's only non-technical climb. The trail ascends 7.5 miles and 4,850 feet to the summit. Allow at least twelve hours for the round trip. The park service advises starting the hike by 3 a.m. to avoid the almost daily summer thunderstorms and to carry proper raingear and extra clothes.

A half-mile past the trailhead sits a monument to Enos Mills, Rocky Mountain National Park's founding father. A side-road just up the highway bumps back to his one-room log cabin nestled among pines and wildflowers. Enos Mills came to Longs Peak in 1884, a sickly Kansas lad in search of health among the clean mountains. He first climbed the peak the following year, homesteaded at its base, and began a life-long career as an alpine guide and nature writer. He dubbed Longs Peak "the king of the Rocky Mountains" and made 297 ascents. In 1889 nineteen-year-old Mills met naturalist John Muir in San Francisco and began a friendship with the elder conservationist. In 1902 Mills built rustic Longs Peak Inn in the meadows across today's

The 1885 Enos Mills Homestead Cabin memorializes the life of this famed pioneer naturalist on the Peak to Peak Highway.

highway from his cabin and began writing numerous classic books like *Spell of the Rockies* that detailed his wilderness experiences and the joy of outdoor adventure. Mills wrote, "He who feels the spell of the wild, the rhythmic melody of falling water, the echoes among the crags, the bird songs, the wind in the pines...is in tune with the universe."

Mills, a firm believer in the national park idea and the preservation of America's dwindling wildlands, advocated the creation of a national park surrounding Longs Peak and lectured tirelessly across the country promoting the preserve. In 1915 his dedication bore fruit when Rocky Mountain National Park was created. He died prematurely in 1922. The Enos Mills Homestead Cabin, run by his daughter Enda Mills Kiley, keeps the memory and writings of this legendary Colorado naturalist alive. The cabin displays Mills' photographs, camera, climbing equipment, specimen collections, and original book editions and documents. Enda regales visitors with tales of her famous father.

Twin Sisters Trailhead sits just past the cabin. The trail spirals upward to the top of 11,428-foot Twin Sisters. Excellent views of Longs Peak and the Tahosa Valley stretch to the west. The drive continues north, crosses a broad divide, and begins dropping toward Estes Park. Popular Lily Lake tucks against Lily Mountain along the road. The Lily Lake Visitor Center sits across the road and offers park information. The highway twists down Lily Mountain's steep eastern slope, dropping past rough rock outcrops and scattered ponderosa pines. The road levels out on a wide bench beside Marys Lake before making its final plunge around Prospect Mountain and entering Estes Park and the drive's end at its junction with US 36.

Estes Park forms the eastern gateway to Rocky Mountain National Park. The town, named for the area's first homesteader Joel Estes who settled here in 1859, fills the wooded valley with homes, shops, hotels, restaurants, and tourist traps. The setting is, despite unbridled growth, enchanting with snow-capped peaks and wooded ridges surrounding the town and valley. English traveler Isabella Bird, the first woman to ascend Longs Peak, wrote in 1873: "Never, nowhere, have I seen anything to equal the view into Estes Park." The Beaver Meadows and Fall Creek entrances to the national park lie just west of town. Several park campgrounds sit close to town and Trail Ridge Road, another magnificent scenic drive, begins at Deer Ridge Junction. Lumpy Ridge, called by the Arapaho Indians *Thath-aa-ai-atah* or "The mountain of little lumps," walls in Estes Park on the north. This high ridge, studded with superb granite crags, yields excellent rock climbing. At the drive's end, the junction of CO 7 and US 36, a turn east leads to Lyons while a west turn eases through downtown Estes Park and on to the park.

TRAIL RIDGE ROAD
Rocky Mountain National Park—
Estes Park to Grand Lake

General description: Trail Ridge Road, one of Colorado's most spectacular and popular scenic drives, traverses glaciated valleys and above-timberline Trail Ridge in Rocky Mountain National Park for 45 miles.

Special attractions: Rocky Mountain National Park, Horseshoe Park, Trail Ridge, Tundra Nature Trail, Alpine Visitor Center, Fall River Pass, Milner Pass, Kawuneeche Valley, camping, hiking, scenic views, overlooks, wildlife, fishing, photography, wildflowers.

Location: North-central Colorado. The drive connects Estes Park and Grand Lake.

Drive route name and number: Trail Ridge Road, U.S. Highway 34.

Travel season: May through October. The exact opening and closing dates vary every year due to snow removal in spring and the first big winter snowstorms. Check with the park for current road information, conditions, and closures.

Camping: 5 campgrounds are located in Rocky Mountain National Park, including 2 along the drive. Aspenglen Campground, open on a first-come, first-serve basis, sits near the Fall River entrance 5 miles from Estes Park. Timber Creek Campground, a shaded 100-site campground, lies on the drive's western slope in the Kawuneeche Valley and operates on a first-come basis. Moraine Park and Glacier Basin campgrounds, both on the reservation system in summer, are near the Beaver Meadows Entrance just south of the drive. Longs Peak Campground, a tents-only area, is 11 miles south of Estes Park off Colorado Highway 7.

Services: All services are found in Estes Park, Grand Lake, and Granby.

Nearby attractions: Peak to Peak Scenic Drive, Roosevelt National Forest, Arapaho National Recreation Area, Cache la Poudre-North Park Scenic Byway, Colorado State Forest, Never Summer Wilderness Area, Indian Peaks Wilderness Area, Wild Basin, Longs Peak, Enos Mills Cabin, Bear Lake, Glacier Gorge, Boulder attractions, Arapaho National Forest.

For more information: Rocky Mountain National Park, Estes Park, CO 80517, (970) 586-2371. Estes Park Area Chamber, P.O. Box 3050, Estes Park, CO 80517, (970) 586-4431 or (800) 44-ESTES. Grand Lake Area Chamber, P.O. Box 57, Grand Lake, CO 80447, (970) 627-3402.

The drive: Rocky Mountain National Park, one of Colorado's most spectacular natural areas, protects an immense swathe of pristine high country along the Continental Divide. The divide, the literal roof of the Rockies, twists down North America's mountain backbone splitting the

Atlantic and Pacific watersheds. Jagged peaks march along the divide in the park, lifting glacier-carved ridges and summits into the sky. The forty-five-mile-long Trail Ridge Road scenic drive, the highest continuous auto road in the United States, traverses this superlative parkland—crossing broad valleys with meandering rivers, passing herds of elk, deer, and bighorn sheep, climbing forest-clad slopes, and winding along lofty Trail Ridge.

The 415-square-mile park encompasses 113 named peaks above 10,000 feet, seventy-one over 12,000 feet, and Longs Peak, the park high point, which soars 14,255-feet above sea level. Two small ranges—the Never Summer Mountains and Mummy Range—split from the divide and the Front Range in the park's northwest corner. Besides being a place of mountain splendor, Rocky Mountain National Park is a land of valleys, rivers, and lakes. Over 150 lakes scatter through the park, and almost 500 miles of streams thread its valley and canyons. The park is a mother of rivers with four major rivers arising on the Continental Divide—the Cache la Poudre, Big Thompson, and St. Vrain rivers on the eastern slope and the Colorado River on the western side. Rocky Mountain National Park is also the land above the trees. One-third of the park lies in the alpine zone above timberline, a cold, windswept land where summer visits for a brief two months.

Trail Ridge Road opens in late May, depending on snow removal, and usually closes by late October after the first major snowfall. Unpredictable weather rules during summer and autumn on the drive. Mornings are usually clear, calm, and warm. Temperatures vary from the seventies and eighties in the lower elevations to the forties and fifties above timberline. Expect afternoon thunderstorms along the road with localized heavy rain, hail, snow, and corn snow. High winds usually accompany the storms. Winds exceeding 150 miles per hour have been clocked on Trail Ridge. Snow can fall during any month on the upper elevations. Be prepared by bringing warm clothes, raingear, and sun protection. Lightning is a serious hazard along Trail Ridge. Keep off exposed ridges and trails before and during thunderstorms.

The scenic drive begins five miles northwest of Estes Park where US 34 enters Rocky Mountain National Park at the Fall River Entrance Station. The park's other entrance at Beaver Meadows lies southwest of Estes Park via U.S. Highway 36 and leads to Moraine Park Museum, Glacier Basin and Moraine Park campgrounds, and the Bear Lake area. US 36 also climbs from the Beaver Meadows entrance to a junction with US 34 and Trail Ridge Road at Deer Ridge Junction.

The highway runs west from the entrance station in an open ponderosa and limber pine forest. Aspenglen Campground, with twenty-six sites, sits at 8,230 feet near the Fall River just past the park boundary. The campground operates on a first-come, first-served basis. The road heads up a granite-studded canyon between MacGregor Mountain on the north and Deer Mountain to the south and climbs into Horseshoe Park. A great valley glacier, spilling down today's Fall River drainage from Trail Ridge, excavated this broad U-shaped valley during three ice advances. The last glacial period—the Pinedale—melted away some twelve thousand years ago. Lateral moraines, piles of jumbled boulders, edge the valley, while a giant terminal moraine,

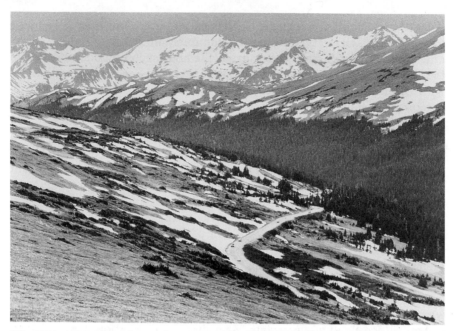

The Never Summer Mountains tower over Trail Ridge Road as it climbs away from Milner Pass and the headwaters of the Cache la Poudre River.

marking the glacier's farthest advance, blocks the valley's eastern end. This terminal moraine also dammed the valley, forming a large, shallow lake. Erosion eventually sedimented the lake, leaving a level, marshy valley floor with the Fall River looping across it.

The flat valley of Horseshoe Park is the bed of a former glacial lake impounded by a terminal moraine. The name might come from the innumerable horseshoe bends Fall River makes as it meanders through the valley; or it might come from the shape of the valley, with the curved top of the horseshoe at the west end near Endovalley Campground, or from a lake shaped like a horseshoe.

The road continues west on the valley's north edge and soon reaches the Sheep Lakes Information Station on the road's south side. The Sheep Lakes, four small glacier-formed kettle lakes, sit in the valley. A couple of pulloffs in Horseshoe Park make good stops to view wildlife. Mule deer, elk, and bighorn sheep regularly graze in the meadows and willow thickets along the Fall River. The mammals are best viewed during early morning or evening when feeding in the park. Elk herds, driven to lower elevations by deep snow pack, congregate in Horseshoe Park in spring, winter, and fall. The autumn rutting period is spectacular when the bull elk bugle their mating calls, vie for herd dominance, and gather harems of females. Two bighorn sheep flocks, totaling around four hundred animals, inhabit Rocky Mountain National Park. While they usually keep to the high country, the Mummy Range flock occasionally descends Bighorn Mountain to natural salt licks in Horseshoe Park. The bighorn sheep road crossing in Horseshoe Park, just past the information station, is closely regulated to protect these elegant animals, the Colorado state animal. Sheep, of course, have the right-of-way, and there is no roadside parking except in designated lots. Visitors are also advised not to approach any wild animals. Mature elk weigh more than one thousand pounds and are unpredictably aggressive during mating season. It's best to view them from the parking areas with field glasses and long telephoto lenses.

The nine-mile-long Old Fall River Road climbs from western Horseshoe Park up Fall River's abrupt glacier gorge to 11,796-foot Fall River Pass on Trail Ridge's northern end. The road, two-lane and paved to Endovalley Picnic Area and then dirt and one-way to its terminus, makes a spectacular side trip. It passes numerous glacial features, thundering twenty-five-foot-high Chasm Falls, and ancient sub-alpine spruce and fir forests. Fall River Road, a property on the National Register of Historic Places, follows an old Arapaho path called the "Dog's Trail." The road, the national park's first high drive, opened in 1920 but saw little use after Trail Ridge Road opened in 1932 because of landslides, avalanches, and sixteen-percent grades.

The highway loops south across Horseshoe Pack, crosses a hilly moraine with aspens, willows, and Colorado blue spruce, and ascends the valley's southern flank. The Horseshoe Park Overlook offers views into the park below. The Mummy Range, a twenty-mile-long Front Range spur, towers to the northwest. A row of jagged peaks, including 13,514-foot Ypsilon Mountain and 13,502-foot Fairchild Mountain, loom above Horseshoe Park.

The viewpoint also offers a look at one of the national park's newest geologic features. Lawn Lake, a small natural lake nestled in the heart of the Mummy Range, was enlarged in 1903 to provide irrigation water for farms near Loveland. In the early morning hours of July 15, 1982, the lake brimmed with snowmelt that slowly seeped around a damaged outlet valve. The water quickly eroded into the earthen dam and at 5:30 a.m. the levee gave way, plunging 674 acre-feet of water down Roaring River's narrow canyon. The thirty-foot-deep deluge scoured the canyon floor, breached Horseshoe Park's north lateral moraine, and deposited a huge alluvial fan near the park's head with up to forty-four feet of debris and boulders weighing over four hundred tons. The relentless water continued toward Estes Park. Horseshoe Park's wetlands, however, slowed the advance and allowed for the evacuation of downtown Estes Park. The flood buried the town's main street under six feet of mud. Three park campers, two in Aspenglen Campground, died in the flood.

The road climbs uphill and reaches Deer Mountain Overlook after 0.6 mile. This point gives great views of the Mummy Range, granite domes on McGregor Mountain's flank, Little Horseshoe Park below, and 10,013-foot Deer Mountain to the east. Deer Ridge Junction, the intersection of US 34, US 36 from Moraine Park, and Trail Ridge Road, sits just ahead. A resort, Deer Ridge Chalet, once sat here, but the Park Service acquired the place in 1960, tore the buildings down, and restored the natural ecosystem. The scenic drive turns west up Trail Ridge Road.

The highway runs northwest and bends into Hidden Valley. The shallow valley, formed by the south lateral moraine of the Fall River glacier on its north side, is a lush, hidden oasis. Dense willow thickets and meadows of grasses and sedges line twisting Hidden Valley Creek. Silted-in beaver ponds form meadows in the east part of the valley. After a couple miles the road reaches active beaver ponds. A wooden boardwalk explores the ponds, traversing out among willows and fresh-cut aspen, a favorite beaver food. Look for these forest engineers swimming in their pools during morning and evening. Hidden Valley Creek also harbors a reintroduced population of threatened greenback cutthroat trout, a Colorado native. This trout, surviving only in isolated lakes and rivers in Colorado's Rockies, almost became extinct due to habitat loss, interbreeding with other trout species, and competition from non-native fish. The downsteam moraine here blocks non-native trout from living in Hidden Valley, allowing the trout to flourish. Fishing for greenback trout is on a strict catch-and-release program. A ten-site picnic area sits by the parking area.

The drive continues up Hidden Valley and after a half-mile loops southeast. The road climbs southeast through a mixed forest of aspen, lodgepole pine, subalpine fir, and Engelmann spruce and reaches Many Parks Curve viewpoint in a mile and a half. The overlook yields dramatic views into several large grassy parks tucked into the Front Range, including Horseshoe Park, Moraine Park, Beaver Meadows, and Estes Park. Forested lateral moraines left by retreating glaciers border the open grasslands. Coarse,

Elk graze in open meadows along Trail Ridge Road in Rocky Mountain National Park's Kawuneeche Valley.

bouldery alluvium, deposited by the Lawn Lake flood, forms a small lake in Horseshoe Park to the north.

The highway bends onto a steep mountainside above upper Hidden Valley, steadily climbing through old-growth spruce and subalpine fir woods. A parking area in the upper valley gives views of the ski area and of open slopes carpeted with a blaze of summer wildflowers. Melting snow irrigates marsh marigolds, paintbrush, lousewort, chiming bells, delphinium, and a forest of spruce and white-barked subalpine fir. The drive continues ascending and after another mile reaches 10,829-foot Rainbow Curve, a lofty viewpoint poised on a ridge over two miles high. Trail Ridge's humped shoulder looms to the south, verdant Horseshoe Park and the twisting highway in Hidden Valley lie far below, and the snowy Mummy Range stretches along the northern horizon. Early mountaineer William Hallett named the range for its fanciful resemblance to a reclining Egyptian mummy.

The road edges west across the north slope of Knife's Edge, a narrow rocky ridgeline. A scattered forest of weathered lodgepole pine and spruce spreads over the hillside. As the road climbs toward timberline, the utmost point where trees will grow, the forest becomes stunted and dwarfed. Severe winds, gusting over Trail Ridge, force the trees to hug the ground or form tree islands. Distinctive "banner trees" form when the branches grow on the tree's eastern or leeward side, out of the wind. Timberline, the elevation that marks the forest boundary, occurs between 10,000 and 11,500 feet in Rocky Mountain National Park. Beyond lies grassy alpine tundra—the land above the trees.

As the highway nears timberline, it passes a small glacier-carved cirque. This amphitheater, the headwaters of Sundance Creek, exhibits a cirque's distinctive features—a moraine of loose rubble, a rocky headwall dissected by the glacier, and a semi-circular shape. Past the cirque, the drive crosses a low timberline gap onto Trail Ridge itself. This 11,440-foot pass, called Ute Crossing, marks the highway's junction with the old Ute Trail that traverses the ridge. The fifteen-mile-long trail, called *Taieonbaa* or "Child's Trail" by Native Americans, begins in Beaver Meadows, threads along the ridgetop, and drops down to Kawuneeche Valley on the west.

Trail Ridge Road is only the latest in an old series of range crossings from the eastern plains to Middle Park's lush grasslands. Trail Ridge, with its gentle contours, forms a natural route over the otherwise cliffed and rugged Continental Divide. Early paleo-Indian hunters used the Ute Trail as long ago as twelve thousand years. A Clovis spear-point found on Trail Ridge confirms their ancient presence. Later Indians built low rock walls to funnel game to hidden hunters. Eagle traps, low pits covered with an animal skin, also dotted the broad ridge. The Ute and Arapaho Indians, settlers, and prospectors regularly crossed the ridge during the nineteenth century. Trail Ridge Road, built in three years, opened in 1932 and bypassed the dangerous Fall River Road.

Trail Ridge Road, the pathway to the high tundra, is America's highest through-highway. It runs above 12,000 feet for four miles and above 11,000 feet for eleven miles. The road, climbing almost 5,000 vertical feet from Estes

Park to the ridge's high point, journeys through three life zones in twenty miles to an alpine climate similar to that in northern Alaska and Canada. Each 1,000 feet ascended is the equivalent of a six hundred-mile trip northward. No other road in the Colorado Rockies offers such a unique opportunity to study, explore, and appreciate the delicate but rigorous world above treeline.

The drive twists along undulating Trail Ridge for the next seven miles to Fall River Pass. Several excellent viewpoints and points of interest scatter along the road. Forest Canyon Overlook, at 11,716 feet, perches high above Forest Canyon. Huge glaciers chiseled this deep U-shaped valley along a major fault line now followed by the Big Thompson River. Ragged peaks, including Mount Ida, Terra Tomah Mountain, and Sprague Mountain, line the Continental Divide's serrated ridge across the abyss. Three small glaciers still tuck under the divide's escarpment. Hanging valleys and cirques hide numerous lakes and tarns below soaring rock buttresses, cliffs, and snow fields. Keep on the paved trail to the overlook to avoid damaging fragile tundra plants.

Almost two miles later the road reaches Rock Cut Overlook, a spectacular 12,110-foot point just past a road cut. The excellent half-mile Tundra Nature Trail climbs east from the parking area to the rounded ridge crest and offers a great introduction to alpine ecology. The tundra inhabitants have superbly adapted to its rigorous climate and short growing season. A scant six to ten week growing season, wind speeds as high as 170 mph, intense ultraviolet radiation, desiccating air, low soil moisture, and intense sunlight all conspire against life. Yet despite the rigors, life not only survives but flourishes atop Trail Ridge. Meadows with thick, wiry grasses spread over the ridge and perennial flowers and herbs huddle against the ground. Over 185 flowering plants grow here, including alpine sunflowers, alpine avens, bistort, moss campion, lousewort, marsh marigold, dwarf clover, and phlox.

Hikers need to keep on the paved walkway and other existing tundra trails. The fragile tundra has almost no carrying capacity, and any human use quickly impacts the plants. Trampled tundra areas take as long as one thousand years to recover. The National Park Service established "tundra protection areas" along Trail Ridge Road to preserve the alpine grassland from being loved to death.

The highway drops north from the Rock Cut to broad 11,827-foot Iceberg Pass and then climbs up the Tundra Curves to a lookout above Lava Cliff cirque. Tall cliffs of 28-million-year-old welded volcanic tuff form the cirque's abrupt wall. The road continues climbing and in 0.8-mile passes Trail Ridge Road's 12,183-foot high point. Edging along immense grassy slopes, the drive gently descends to Gore Range Overlook. This viewpoint, sitting above the head of Forest Canyon, offers expansive views of the Never Summer Range to the west and the Gore Range some seventy-five miles distant. Longs Peak, a pioneer landmark of the northern Front Range, lifts steep slopes broken by granite cliffs to its flat-topped summit. The road swings northeast and steadily drops another mile to 11,796-foot Fall River Pass and the Alpine Visitor Center.

Fall River Pass, the terminus of the Fall River Road, divides the Cache la

Poudre and Fall River drainages. The popular visitor center dispenses park information, sells books and maps, and exhibits tundra ecology and geology. A nearby store sells gifts and lunches. Outside the center are spectacular views into Forest Canyon. The highway begins a serious descent from the pass, dropping steeply down to Medicine Bow Curve, a sharp hairpin turn with an overlook. The road bends west, reaches timberline in another mile, and continues down through spruce forest and lush flower-strewn meadows into the upper Cache la Poudre River valley. Poudre Lake, the headwaters of the seventy-five-mile-long Cache la Poudre River, sits atop the Continental Divide on 10,758-foot Milner Pass. A nearby trail climbs a mile up Specimen Mountain to the Crater where bighorn sheep forage in summer. The trail is closed to hiking until after lambing season in mid-July and the mountain is closed all year to protect a sheep mineral lick.

Lake Irene, a serene lake surrounded by spruce and fir, is nestled just down the highway. A picnic area and restrooms sit near the landslide-dammed lake. The road threads down Beaver Creek's steep canyon, passing Sheep Rock and Jackstraw Mountain to the south, and continues on down to Farview Curve Overlook. This viewpoint, the last lofty overlook on the drive, gazes west into broad Kawuneeche Valley. During the ice ages the park's largest glacier stretched twenty miles down the valley to Grand Lake. The Colorado River, originating at the valley's head, meanders through dense willow thickets and beaver ponds in this flat glacier-carved valley. *Kawuneeche* is Arapaho for "Valley of the Coyote." The Never Summer Range, called *Ni-chebe-chii* or "Never No Summer" by the Arapaho, lifts its craggy crest to the west.

The switchbacking road drops steeply for the next four miles through thick spruce, fir, and pine woods to the valley's eastern edge. The Colorado River Trailhead sits just west of the road. The trail heads north seven miles to Poudre Pass, passing en route the remains of Lulu City, an 1880s mining camp. The highway runs south along the valley edge. Beaver Ponds Picnic Area, one hundred-site Timber Creek Campground, and several trailheads sit along the drive. Never Summer Ranch, just past the campground, makes a good stop. The historic site began as the Holzwarth Homestead in 1883 and later became a dude ranch after the Fall River Road was built. The highway continues south through lodgepole pine forest and open grasslands. Deer, elk, and moose frequently graze in the wide roadside meadows along the road. The Kawuneeche Visitor Center, sitting at 8,720 feet, is the drive's last point of interest. The center offers displays on the park's history, geology, and natural history, gives free park information and permits, and sells books. Trail Ridge Road scenic drive ends almost a mile past the visitor center on the park boundary. Grand Lake sits another mile farther south. US 34 continues past Arapaho National Recreation Area to Granby.

CACHE LA POUDRE - NORTH PARK SCENIC DRIVE
Fort Collins to Walden (North Park)

General description: This 101-mile-long scenic drive follows Colorado Highway 14 between Fort Collins on the eastern edge of the Front Range and Walden in North Park. The road meanders through Poudre Canyon and climbs over Cameron Pass to broad North Park.

Special attractions: Poudre Canyon, Cache la Poudre Wild and Scenic River, Roosevelt National Forest, Cache la Poudre Wilderness Area, Comanche Peak Wilderness Area, Cameron Pass, Rawah Wilderness Area, Colorado State Forest, North Park, Arapaho National Wildlife Refuge, hiking, camping, backpacking, fishing, rock climbing, kayaking, cross-country skiing.

Location: North-central Colorado. The drive begins in Fort Collins just off Interstate 25 and ends in Walden.

Drive route name and number: Colorado Highway 14, Cache la Poudre-North Park Scenic Byway.

Travel season: Year-round. Chains or adequate snow tires might be needed in winter.

Camping: Several national forest campgrounds line the drive including 19-site Ansel Watrous, 7-site Stove Prairie Landing, 15-site Narrows, 45-site Mountain Park, 23-site Kelly Flats, 9-site Big Bend, 15-site Sleeping Elephant, 4-site Big South, 8-site Aspen Glen, and 57-site Chambers Lake. 3 state park campgrounds sit along the Michigan River on the west side of Cameron Pass.

Services: All services are found in Fort Collins and Walden. Limited services are along the drive.

Nearby attractions: Rocky Mountain National Park, Trail Ridge Road, Pawnee National Grassland, Lory State Park, Horsetooth Reservoir, Mount Zirkel Wilderness Area, Rabbit Ears Pass, Arapaho National Forest, Routt National Forest, Never Summer Wilderness Area, Estes Park.

For more information: Roosevelt National Forest, 240 W. Prospect, Fort Collins, CO 80526, (303) 498-1100. Fort Collins Convention & Visitor's Bureau, 420 S. Howes, #101, P.O. Box 1998, Fort Collins, CO 80522, (800) 274-FORT or (303) 482-5821. North Park Chamber, P.O. Box 68, Walden, CO 80480, (970) 723-4600.

The drive: The 101-mile-long Cache la Poudre-North Park scenic drive weaves through the Cache la Poudre River's deep canyon from Fort Collins to the 10,276-foot summit of Cameron Pass before plunging into North Park, a broad intermontane basin ringed by snow-capped mountains. The highway traverses a solid landscape seamed by abrupt canyons, excavated by thick glaciers, and studded with granite cliffs. It climbs over the Medicine Bow Mountains, a windswept gallery of towering peaks, and threads along the Cache la Poudre Wild and Scenic River. Four wilderness areas—the Cache la Poudre, Comanche Peak, Neota, and Rawah wildernesses—in Roosevelt National Forest and the Colorado State Forest abut the drive.

The drive, open year-round, is best in summer and fall. Elevations vary from 5,000 feet to more than 10,000 feet, offering a diverse range of temperatures and climates. Summer high temperatures vary from the eighties at Fort Collins to the fifties atop the pass. Nights in the higher elevations can be cold. Afternoon thunderstorms frequently build over the mountains, bringing localized heavy rain. Autumn yields brisk but mild weather, with colorful aspens lining the highway. Winter days are cold with highs between ten and forty degrees. Heavy snow falls on the pass and the drive's western slope. Be prepared for icy roads, particularly on shaded corners, and carry chains or have adequate snow tires. Spring creeps slowly up the drive from the prairie beginning in April. The roadside snowpack is mostly melted by late May. Expect cool, breezy days and cold nights.

The drive begins at Fort Collins' northern city limit on CO 14/U.S. Highway 287. Fort Collins, sitting two miles west of Interstate 15, sprawls along the Cache la Poudre River at the foot of the abrupt Front Range escarpment. The city, poised on the edge of the Great Plains and the Rocky Mountains, relies on an economic base of agriculture, high-tech industry, and Colorado State University. Started in 1862 as an army fort by two companies of the Kansas Volunteer Cavalry, Camp Collins' mission was to protect travelers, settlers, and the U.S. Mail on the Overland Trail. A flood erased the post in 1864 and a new camp, designated Fort Collins, was erected at today's townsite. After Indian attacks abated, the fort was taken over by the Larimar County Land Improvement Company and streets were platted for a new town in 1873. The town thrived as a farming hub, and in 1879 the Agricultural College of Colorado, now Colorado State University, opened its doors. Points of interest include the Fort Collins Museum, the historic Avery House, and an Anheuser-Busch Brewery. The town, a recreational haven, offers nearby hike and bike trails and fishing areas at Horsetooth Mountain Park and Reservoir and Lory State Park. All visitor services are found in Fort Collins.

The drive heads north and west from Fort Collins on CO 14 across rolling farms and ranches. US 287 makes a quick bypass around Laporte, otherwise CO 14 runs west through the town. Laporte, settled as a fur post by French trappers in 1858, was the area's first settlement. The name, French for "the gate," came from the natural gap in the hogbacks northwest of here where today's highway runs. Antoine Janis, Colorado's first permanent white settler north of the Arkansas River, claimed the river bottom west of Laporte in 1844. Legend says that years earlier Janis, part of an American Fur Company supply train, stashed several hundred pounds of gunpowder and other supplies in a hole along the river one winter to lighten wagon loads, returning the next year to retrieve the goods. Afterwards trappers called the river Cache la Poudre, meaning "cache of the powder."

Just past Laporte is the turn south to Lory State Park. This secluded 2,400-acre parkland is a marvelous, off-the-beaten-track natural area. The park preserves the diverse ecology of the Rockies foothills, with grasslands, upturned sandstone hogbacks, and ponderosa pine forests. Twenty-two miles of marked trails thread through the park, offering adventure to hikers, mountain bikers, and horseback riders. Climbers scale 6,780-foot Arthur's Rock, a granite crag perched above Horsetooth Reservoir. Prairie rattlesnakes are common in summer, especially around talus and on the lower grasslands.

The highway bends northwest, crossing and paralleling long up-ended hogbacks. The hogbacks, high ridges tilted upward when the Rocky Mountains rose, are formed by erosion-resistant sandstone, particularly the seventy-million-year-old Dakota Sandstone. The Dakota Hogback, except for a few faulted areas, can be traced along the foot of Colorado's Front Range from Wyoming to New Mexico. Soft, easily-eroded shales and mudstones form broad vales between the hogbacks. Ten miles from Fort Collins, the drive reaches Ted's Place and the intersection of US 287 and CO 14. Turn west on CO 14. Ted or Edward Irving Herring established his place in 1922 at the scenic entrance to Poudre Canyon.

The highway heads west up a broad valley through low, tawny hills and after a mile and a half enters Poudre Canyon and the Front Range. The highway threads alongside the Cache la Poudre River in the depths of Poudre Canyon for the next fifty miles. The seventy-five-mile-long river, arising from Poudre Lake on Milner Pass and the Continental Divide in Rocky Mountain National Park, dashes through its craggy canyon, empties onto the plains, and ends in the South Platte River near Greeley. Throughout its length the Cache la Poudre remains a wild stream, untamed by dams. The river's marvelous scenery, excellent recreational opportunities, and wild character led to its designation as Colorado's first National Wild and Scenic River. The Poudre Canyon yields excellent fishing for brown and rainbow trout, offers serious whitewater challenges to rafters and kayakers, gives surprisingly good climbing on its cliffs, and boasts numerous national forest campgrounds and picnic areas. The river corridor, close to the urban Front Range cities, is popular, especially on summer weekends.

The drive enters 788,000-acre Roosevelt National Forest just past the canyon entrance. The forest, originally part of the 1897 Medicine Bow Forest Reserve, became Colorado National Forest in 1910 and was renamed for conservationist President Theodore Roosevelt in 1932. Past Picnic Rock

River Access, the highway curves along the river. Steep, dry hillsides, covered with grass and low scrubs, border the blacktop. Grey Rock Trailhead sits seven miles up-canyon. Grey Rock National Recreation Trail, one of the most popular hikes in the canyon, crosses the river on a footbridge and ascends three miles to Grey Rock Mountain's 7,500-foot summit and expansive views.

The road continues west through the town of Poudre Park and passes Poudre Park, Diamond Rock, and Mishawaka picnic areas. Ansel Watrous Campground, with nineteen sites, sits among ponderosa pines in a broad canyon section. A couple miles west the highway swings under granite cliffs, passes through a tunnel, and enters the Little Narrows. The river, making a huge bend, slices through bedrock with the road perched alongside. The canyon again broadens at nine-site Stove Prairie Landing Campground. Stevens Gulch Picnic Area and river access sits another half-mile west. Past the picnic area the highway enters the Big Narrows, an impressive defile filled with soaring buttresses, cliffs, and aretes. The frothy river churns over boulders in a mist of white spray and with a thunderous roar. Moist hanging canyons, filled with Douglas-fir, grass, and ferns, climb above the river's cobbled south bank. Some of the canyon's best rock climbing is found on Ra's Buttress, Pee Wee's Playhouse, and Eve's Cave in the Big Narrows. Narrows Picnic Area and Campground sit just past the confined canyon segment.

The winding canyon, marking an immense horseshoe bend, briefly opens at Big George Flat. The Mount McConnell National Recreation Trail begins near Mountain Park Campground. This five-mile loop trail twists up through fir and pine forest to Mount McConnell's summit on the northern edge of 9,200-acre Cache la Poudre Wilderness Area. This small wilderness, traversed by the river's South Fork, protects a sparsely visited region of rugged mountains and canyons to the south. The Poudre Canyon again constricts down to a rocky, confined gorge. Kelly Flats Campground, with twenty-three campsites spread along the river bank, and several fishing access points line the highway.

As the drive heads west the canyon walls grow and the floor alternately widens and narrows. Mountain mahogany and sagebrush cover the dry south-facing slopes above the highway, while ponderosa pine and Douglas-fir populate the moister north-facing slopes. Open grasslands blanket the wider valley floor at Indian Meadows. Anglers should check signage marking fishing areas restricted to fly and lower catch limits. Rustic and Glen Echo, small resort villages with summer cabins, straddle the broad valley further west. Willows and cottonwoods shade the river banks. Profile Rock, the craggy silhouette of a face, towers south of the river almost three miles past Glen Echo. A small visitor center with national forest information sits a half-mile upriver.

Poudre Canyon assumes a different complexion three miles past Profile Rock. The roadside Home Moraine Geologic Site, an interpretative pullout, marks the easternmost advance of a great valley glacier that excavated the U-shaped canyon to the west. Time and the flow of the river chiseled the confined, V-shaped canyon the drive has followed thus far. The pullout gives

The Cache la Poudre-North Park Byway follows the Cache la Poudre River up rugged Poudre Canyon.

a view of the terminal moraine, a jumble of boulders and cobbles, that marked the glacier's farthest advance eastward.

The highway runs up the broad valley, its flanks stair-stepping up to forested summits. A state fish hatchery, nine-site Big Bend Campground, and Roaring Creek Trailhead sit along the road. At Kinikinik's summer cottages, the Poudre River and canyon make a big bend southwest. The canyon's southern rim forms the northern boundary of 66,000-acre Comanche Peak Wilderness Area, a large swathe of high mountains topped by 12,702-foot Comanche Peak in the Mummy Range. The highway heads southwest up the wide canyon. Sheer crags etched by glaciers perch on steep canyon slopes. Sleeping Elephant Campground, with fifteen aspen-shaded sites, sits along the river while rocky Sleeping Elephant Mountain looms overhead. Tunnel Picnic Area sits along the river by Tunnel Creek. Poudre Falls, a spectacular whitewater cascade, spills over boulders just after the highway crosses from the river's west to east bank. At four-site Big South Campground the highway takes leave of the Cache la Poudre River and Poudre Canyon and begins steeply climbing up Joe Wright Creek's side-canyon.

The road passes Aspen Glen Campground and a Roosevelt National Forest information kiosk. A string of popular fishing lakes and reservoirs scatters through the lodgepole pine forest off the highway. Barnes Meadow Reservoir sits south of the drive and Chambers Lake, named for early trapper Robert Chambers, spreads to the north. The Laramie River, running north to Wyoming and the North Platte River, begins here. The 73,000-acre Rawah Wilderness Area stretches north from the highway, encompassing almost the entire east flank of the Rawah Range, a southern extension of Wyoming's

Medicine Bow Mountains. The Arapaho Indians used their word for "wilderness," *rawah*, to describe this pristine sierra of high peaks and crystal lakes. The drive continues climbing above the shallow creek valley, edges past Joe Wright Reservoir, and reaches the broad summit of 10,276-foot Cameron Pass. The col, named for pioneer railroad builder General Robert Cameron after he discovered it in 1870, is flanked by white fir forest that climbs to timberline on snow-capped 12,951-foot Clark Peak. Small 9,900-acre Neota Wilderness Area protects an above-timberline region of flattened ridges fringed by fir and spruce.

The drive plunges abruptly down the pass's west slope and after a mile bends west above Michigan River's wide glaciated valley. The highway edges past a scenic overlook that offers a superlative view south of ragged 12,485-foot Nokhu Crags and 12,940-foot Mount Richtofen on Rocky Mountain National Park's northwest corner. The road continues to descend and passes a turnoff that leads south to the Lake Agnes trailhead. The half-mile trail climbs over glacial moraines to Lake Agnes, a timberline lake cupped in a deep basin below the Nokhu Crags. Nokhu is an abbreviated name derived from *Nea ha-no-Xhu* or Eagle's Nest in Arapaho. Crags Campground, administered by the Colorado State Forest, scatters through spruce forest along the side-road.

The byway drops into the Michigan River's broad, willow- covered valley. This area, along with the western flank of the Rawah Range, is part of the Colorado State Forest State Park. This 72,000-acre parkland, Colorado's largest state park, is administered by the Colorado Division of Parks as a trust land of funding the state's public school system. Besides recreational uses, grazing, logging, and hunting are permitted. The park offers three campgrounds with seventy-five sites, almost twenty miles of trails, and fishable lakes and streams. Kelly Lake, just below the range crest, is one of the few places in Colorado that houses the rare golden trout, an introduced California species. The park's diverse habitat also shelters more than 125 bird species, as well as mammals including marmot, marten, beaver, red fox, coyote, mink, bighorn sheep, and moose. The park's small moose population usually shelters among the willows along the upper Michigan River on the drive.

Past the campground at Ranger Lakes, the highway and river swing northwest around 10,390-foot Gould Mountain. A dense lodgepole pine forest, broken by scattered aspen groves, borders the asphalt. The small town of Gould offers gas and groceries. The state park headquarters and the turnoff to North Michigan Reservoir and Campground sits a couple miles farther.

The drive bends west and crosses the broad Michigan River valley. The ragged crest of the Rawah Range forms an immense wall to the east, while low-browed hills stretch along the valley's western rim. Wide grasslands, sprinkled with grazing cattle, spread along the meandering river. The highway, running northwest along rolling hills, passes open lodgepole pine and aspen woodlands before leaving the river valley and the mountains behind.

North Park, a huge glacial basin hemmed in by mountains, lies ahead. The basin, thirty-five miles wide and forty-five miles long, is characterized by sagebrush rangelands and slow meandering rivers. The Ute Indians, who frequently hunted the park's bison in summer, called it "Cow Lodge" and "Bull Pen." Lieutenant John C. Fremont, one of its first explorers, noted in his 1844 journal "...a beautiful circular valley of thirty miles in diameter, walled in all around with snowy mountains, rich with water and grass, fringed with pine on the mountain sides below the snow, and a paradise to all grazing animals." The road crosses low, sagebrush-covered bluffs and dips across Owl Creek's shallow valley. Seven miles after leaving the Michigan River the highway reaches Brocker Overlook above Arapaho National Wildlife Refuge.

The twenty thousand-acre refuge, established in 1967, provides important nesting habitat for migratory waterfowl along the twisting Illinois River. Water, diverted from the river, irrigates meadows and fills shallow ponds. After the ice melts in the refuge in late May, thousands of ducks, including pintail, mallard, gadwall, and American wigeon, as well as Canada geese begin arriving to nest and raise their broods. Other shore and water birds seen are Virginia rails, Wilson's phalaropes, avocets, sandpipers, great blue heron, bitterns, and grebes. Numerous raptors—eagles, hawks, and prairie falcons—wheel across the sky in search of prey. Moose, elk, and mule deer range across the refuge, particularly during winter. A six-mile self-guided auto tour, beginning three miles south of Walden on Colorado Highway 125, explores the wildlife area.

The byway continues northwest along a bluff above the river and three miles later enters Walden and the scenic drive's end. Walden, North Park's largest town and a ranching center, is named for Mark Walden, the former postmaster of the nearby ghost town of Sage Hen Springs. The town, founded in 1889, was originally called Sagebrush for the ubiquitous stands of grey *Artemisia tridentata* that blanket North Park. Walden offers all visitor services, including gas, restaurants, and lodging.

18 INDEPENDENCE PASS DRIVE
Buena Vista to Aspen

General description: This 44-mile-long drive climbs over 12,095-foot Independence Pass, Colorado's highest paved pass, and the Continental Divide between the upper Arkansas River Valley and Aspen.

Special attractions: Twin Lakes, Mount Elbert, Colorado Trail, La Plata Peak, Independence Pass, Independence ghost town, Hunter-Fryingpan Wilderness Area, Collegiate Peaks Wilderness Area, Continental Divide, Braille Nature Trail, San Isabel National Forest, White River National Forest, camping, mountaineering, rock climbing, fishing, hiking, backpacking, scenic views.

Location: Central Colorado. The drive runs between U.S. Highway 24 twenty miles north of Buena Vista to Aspen.

Drive route name and number: Independence Pass Road, Colorado Highway 82.

Travel season: Spring through fall. The highway usually opens sometime in May and closes after the first major autumn snows in late October or early November.

Camping: Several national forest campgrounds are scattered along the drive. 71-site Lakeview, 26-site Parry Peak, and 35-site Twin Peaks campgrounds sit on the east side of the pass. 9-site Lost Man, 6-site Lincoln Gulch, 11-site Weller, and 47-site Difficult campgrounds lie on the west side.

Services: All services are found in Aspen, Buena Vista, and Leadville. Limited services are at Granite and Twin Lakes.

Nearby attractions: Leadville National Historic District, National Mining Hall of Fame, Leadville National Fish Hatchery, Arkansas River, Mosquito Pass, Turquoise Lake, Holy Cross Wilderness Area, Clear Creek Canyon, Cottonwood Pass, Buena Vista, Mount Massive Wilderness Area, Ashcroft, Pearl Pass, Maroon Bells-Snowmass Wilderness Area, Maroon Lake, Buttermilk Mountain and Snowmass ski areas, Roaring Fork River.

For more information: San Isabel National Forest, 1920 Valley Drive, Pueblo, CO 81008, (719) 545-8737. White River National Forest, P.O. Box 948, Glenwood Springs, CO 81602, (970) 945-2521. Aspen Chamber Resort Assn., 425 Rio Grande Pl., Aspen, CO 81611, (970) 925-1940.

The drive: This forty-four-mile scenic drive crosses 12,095-foot Independence Pass, Colorado's highest paved pass, perched atop the Sawatch Range in central Colorado. The Sawatch Range, crested by the twisting Continental Divide, is one of the state's main mountain ranges. It stretches over one hundred miles from the Eagle River and Interstate 70 south to Marshall Pass and the Cochetopa Hills above the San Luis Valley. Sawatch, a Ute word meaning "water of the blue earth," describes an ancient lake that once filled the San Luis Valley. Later explorers, including Captain John Gunnison in 1853, applied the name to the mountain chain. The spelling of Sawatch was also changed from Saguache, which one wag said could only be pronounced by sneezing.

The Sawatch Range, lying within the San Isabel and White River national forests, contains fifteen of Colorado's fifty-four 14,000-foot peaks, including four of the five highest. Mount Elbert, the state's rooftop at 14,433 feet, tops the list, followed by 14,421-foot Mount Massive, 14,420-foot Mount Harvard, and 14,336-foot La Plata Peak. Large tracts of wild lands—the Holy Cross, Mount Massive, and Collegiate Peaks wilderness areas—straddle the range and preserve large areas of pristine, roadless mountains. The range's snowy crest also gives birth to numerous rivers, including the Arkansas, Taylor, Roaring Fork, Frying Pan, and Eagle rivers. On the east the Independence Pass scenic drive follows Lake Creek's deep, glaciated valley between Mount Elbert and La Plata Peak, while on the west the drive plunges down the Roaring Fork River corridor surrounded by the Hunter-Fryingpan and Collegiate Peaks wilderness areas.

Heavy snow shuts down the highway in winter. The road opens, usually in May, when deep drifts on the upper section melt back enough for snowplows to scour the roadway clean. It closes again when snow flies, usually in late October. Expect cool temperatures atop the pass from May through October, with possible afternoon thunderstorms and even summer snow. Summer temperatures can reach into the seventies, but breezes usually cool the air. If hiking on ridges atop the pass, watch for lightning on summer afternoons. Also use caution when crossing snowfields, they are deceptively dangerous. Carry and know how to use an ice axe and wear proper footwear. As a rule of thumb, air temperatures decrease three degrees for every one thousand feet of elevation ascended. Consequently the lower elevations, including Aspen and Twin Lakes, are warmer than the pass summit with temperatures reaching eighty degrees.

The drive begins at the intersection of US 24 and CO 82 twenty miles north of Buena Vista and fifteen miles south of Leadville in the Arkansas River valley. Granite, almost three miles south of the intersection, was the site of the area's first gold discovery in 1859. The camp was short lived as richer deposits were found upstream at California Gulch near today's Leadville. Turn west on CO 82, the Independence Pass Road. **Vehicles over thirty-five feet long are prohibited on the pass.** The highway runs east alongside turbulent Lake Creek as it rushes across a huge boulder-strewn moraine left by the ancient Lake Creek Glacier, an immense glacier that scoured out the deep valley to the west. The moraine forms Twin Lakes, two large lakes that have been enlarged for water storage as part of the Fryingpan-Arkansas Project. This huge water project, supplying water primarily to Colorado Springs and Aurora on the Front Range, pumps water from the western slope of the Continental Divide to Turquoise Lake west of Leadville. The water is piped south to Twin Lakes, where it generates electrical power before being divided and sent to thirsty Front Range cities.

The highway reaches the north side of Twin Lakes and Mountain View Overlook after a mile and a half. The drive continues west across sagebrush-covered slopes above the lake. At 2.4 miles the road passes Dexter Point Campground and a boat ramp, both part of Twin Lakes Recreation Area. Farther west a side road leads north to twenty-four-site Lakeview Campground and Mount Elbert Picnic Ground. The Frying Pan-Arkansas Project Visitor Center is reached at 4.5 miles. The center explains the history and hydraulics of the project. The lakes offer excellent fishing, with lake trout exceeding thirty pounds as well as rainbow and cutthroat trout. Beyond the center the highway bends southwest through piney hills, passes White Star Campground on the lakeshore, and enters the town of Twin Lakes.

This picturesque community, set at 9,015 feet at the foot of Mount Elbert, was settled around 1880 after the initial silver rush to nearby Leadville. The valley yielded a few prosperous lodes like the Little Joe, Bartlett, and Fidelity mines, but it was the natural beauty that attracted newcomers then and now. The town, offering few services, lies near a major avalanche chute that erased the western part of town. Look for some overgrown cabin foundations in the meadows below 12,682-foot Parry Peak, a spur of Mount Elbert. The town hosts an infamous tomato war every September. While driving through keep an eye out for the uniformed police officer mannequin in his roadside patrol car.

Past Twin Lakes the highway bends southeast for a mile, skirting marsh and willow thickets on the west edge of the lake before swinging into Lake Creek's narrowing valley. The creek rushes over worn cobbles and boulders in a shallow canyon below the road. Dense forests of lodgepole pine and aspen line the way and blanket steep mountainsides. Parry Peak Campground, with twenty-six sites, lies near the valley entrance. Thirty-five-site Twin Peaks Campground spreads alongside the highway a mile further west. Monitor Rock, a bold white cliff, looms over the drive on the southern flank of Mount Elbert. Glacial striations, scratched by boulders imbedded in a deep valley glacier as it crept down the valley, scar the massive rock. A short walk to the cliff's rounded southern buttress reveals deep, parallel grooves in the smoothed rock surface. Over the last few million years glaciers periodically excavated this valley and the rest of the Sawatch Range. The scenic drive travels through characteristic U-shaped valleys on both sides of the pass. The glaciers that once rested here were several thousand feet thick, with only the high peaks poking above the whiteness. The glaciers sculpted today's mountain scenery, leaving cirques, aretes, hanging valleys, and moraines as evidence of their passage.

The valley broadens past Monitor Rock and the creek swings between willow-lined banks. Thick stands of aspen border the drive and offer spectacular color in late September. La Plata Peak dominates the valley. It's long ridges, corniced with winter snow and studded with rock pinnacles and crags, sweep south to the peak's sharp 14,336-foot apex. La Plata Peak, one of the range's most satisfying climbs, was named by pioneer surveyor Ferdinand Hayden in 1874 with the Spanish word for silver. The summit is best reached via the La Plata Trail. Park alongside the highway at the turnoff for Forest Road 391, the South Fork of Lake Creek road, almost fifteen miles from the drive's start. The trail drops down and crosses Lake Creek, wanders through thick spruce forest into La Plata Gulch, and then ascends east up a grassy, above-timberline spur to the summit ridge.

At fifteen miles the highway heads northwest up Lake Creek's North Fork into a wide, flat-bottomed valley. Dense willows carpet the damp valley floor and hem in the meandering creek. Beaver ponds still the tumbling stream and make good fishing holes. A few miles later the highway makes a sharp switchback and begins climbing steeply up a shelf road chiseled into the mountain slope. Watch for fallen boulders on this road section. Just over a mile later the highway exits the shelf into Mountain Boy Gulch, a hanging valley with verdant meadows and dense forest. A waterfall sweeps over a cliff band at timberline west of the drive and thick snow cornices line the Continental Divide's ridgeline above. The road switchbacks up the valley's north slope, twisting through stunted, windswept trees at timberline. Just past treeline the drive bends sharply west and begins the final ascent to the pass summit.

Americans have long been a pass-loving people. A sense of freedom is

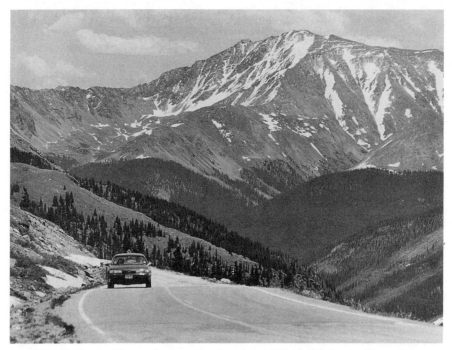

La Plata Peak rises beyond a car nearing the summit of Independence Pass.

found in crossing a wild sierra. Out there, beyond the summits, stretches a whole new world, waiting patiently to be discovered and explored. On surmounting a pass, the first instinct is to continue, to plunge down into the unknown valleys below. But here, atop 12,095-foot Independence Pass, stop and linger. Breathe in this moment and this majestic panorama.

A parking area and sign mark the lofty summit. A short trail wends south to a lookout point poised above Mountain Boy Gulch. Mountains surround this overlook—La Plata Peak to the south; Mount Elbert and its high satellites dominate the eastern skyline; and rows of peaks and ridges march westward to the Maroon Bells, Snowmass Mountain, and Capitol Peak. The pass summit introduces the world above the trees, a world more similar in climate and flora to the lands beyond the Arctic Circle thousands of miles to the north than that of nearby lowland valleys. Mats of wiry grass sprinkled with delicate wildflowers brighten the broad crest. Deep snowdrifts, persisting well into August, cling to leeward edges and deep ravines. Frigid tarns of snowmelt fill shallow depressions with sky and cloud reflections. Beyond the pass, rounded ridges clad in tundra plants sweep up to boulder fields, rocky buttresses, and windy summits.

The highway falls abruptly west, edging north down a steep shelf road for over a mile. Watch for fallen boulders. No guardrail or shoulder comforts the nervous driver here. On reaching the valley floor and timberline, the drive bends south above the infant Roaring Fork River and heads downhill through subalpine fir forest and open meadows. The ghost town site of Independence sits two miles down. Gold was discovered on Independence Day, 1879 in this alpine valley, bringing a stampede of prospectors to the new town dubbed Independence. By 1880 the path over what was then called Hunter's Pass and later Independence Pass became a horse trail operated by the Twin Lakes and Roaring Fork Toll Company. On November 6 the following year, they opened a frightful wagon road that climbed the lofty pass between Leadville and the burgeoning silver town of Aspen. The road was an instant success with freight traffic swarming over the divide. Hefty tolls ensured temporary prosperity. For five winters, an army of snow shovelers labored to keep the road open—a feat today's highway department will not undertake with the area's high avalanche danger. The stagecoach trek over the pass took twenty-four hours, five changes of horses, and three toll gates. In 1888 the railroad reached Aspen and the trail closed down until resurrected as an automobile road in the 1920s. The town of Independence, at its peak in the early 1880s, boasted a population of two thousand, and ten saloons. By the turn of the century, the last prospector had pulled up stakes, leaving the town for the owls and mice. Weather-beaten cabins and a few crumbling buildings are all that remain of Independence today. The ghost town, preserved through the efforts of the Aspen Historical Society, makes a good stop. Walk through the grassy streets today and imagine the daily rigors and trials faced by the nineteenth-century miner.

The highway passes Lost Man Trailhead, the jumping-off point for a popular hike into the Hunter-Fryingpan Wilderness Area, and nine-site Lost Man Campground two miles past Independence. A dense forest of lodgepole pine, spruce, and fir shades this pleasant 10,700-foot-high campground. The Braille Nature Trail, a barrier-free pathway, explores the forest farther down the road. Past the trail the highway narrows and winds down a steep canyon above the Roaring Fork River. Numerous granite crags nestle in the woods between here and Aspen, offering a diverse selection of routes for rock climbers. Some of the best cliffs include the Grotto Walls, Whirlpool Rock, and Weller Slab. More information can be found at the climbing shop in Aspen.

The Lincoln Creek Road, Forest Road 106, starts ten miles west of Lost Man. This road, rapidly turning to rough four-wheel drive, leads southeast up Lincoln Creek to Grizzly Reservoir and Portal Campground. Past the turn the road narrows and twists underneath the looming Grotto Walls. Look for another pullout just past the bends. A trail begins at the road's end, crosses the river on a footbridge, and heads east across glacier-polished granite a hundred yards to the Grottos. The Grottos are a series of caverns chiseled by the Roaring Fork River before it cut its present channel. The cavern, roofed by a slit of light, are best accessed via their west end. It is generally dry, although snow and ice linger inside the Grottos through the early summer.

The drive continues west to eleven-site Weller Campground, its sites surrounded by a lush aspen grove. Aspens sprinkle among fir and spruce forests along the road or form moist glades with a thick understory of grass, columbines, and ferns. In late September, the aspens drape sheer mountainsides with their rippling gold color. Past the campground, the highway abruptly narrows to one-and-a-half lanes and creeps shelf-like above a granite slab. After a quarter-mile the highway widens and drops onto a broad glaciated valley. The road stairsteps down to a lower valley. Difficult Campground, with forty-seven sites, sits along the river among dense willow thickets and beaver ponds. Heading west the highway crosses wide meadows below steep aspen-covered hillsides. North Star Wildlife Preserve, threaded by a footpath, protects critical elk habitat along the valley floor. The highway reaches 7,908-foot-high Aspen and the drive's end a mile farther downstream.

Aspen, Colorado's famed ski resort, began as a silver mining camp in 1879. Prosperity poured from its wealthy lodes, including the Smuggler, Montezuma, Midnight, and Molly Gibson mines, until the great silver crash of 1893. At that time, Aspen, with a population of twelve thousand, was the state's third largest city. The town, one of the first to run on electricity, boasted six newspapers, two banks, the Wheeler Opera House, and the fabulous Hotel Jerome. Victorian homes and buildings from that era still line the streets. Skiers began sampling Aspen's deep snow in 1936, and by the late 1940s the town stood poised to become one of America's great ski resorts. Aspen, besides its four ski areas, offers all visitor services as well as numerous festivals and events.

19 COTTONWOOD PASS SCENIC DRIVE
Buena Vista to Almont

General description: A 60-mile-long paved and gravel road that crosses 12,126-foot Cottonwood Pass on the Continental Divide and follows the Taylor River to Almont.

Special attractions: Collegiate Peaks Wilderness Area, Mount Yale, Cottonwood Pass, Taylor Reservoir, Taylor Canyon, Continental Divide, Colorado Trail, camping, hiking, backpacking, rock climbing, fishing, fly-fishing.

Location: Central Colorado. The drive runs from Buena Vista in the Arkansas Valley to Almont, eleven miles north of Gunnison.

Drive route name and numbers: Cottonwood Pass Road, Forest Roads 306, 209, and 742.

Travel season: Late spring through autumn. The drive closes in winter after the first big snowfall and opens in late spring after snowmelt. Check with the national forest offices for opening and closure dates.

Camping: 9 national forest campgrounds lie along the drive.

Services: All services are in Buena Vista. Limited services are in Almont, with complete services nearby in Gunnison and Crested Butte.

Nearby attractions: Elk Mountains, Crested Butte, West Elk Scenic Byway, Gunnison, Curecanti National Recreation Area, West Elk Wilderness Area, Tincup, Cumberland Pass, Alpine Tunnel, St. Elmo, Mount Princeton Hot Springs, Arkansas River State Recreation Area, Buffalo Peaks Wilderness Area.

For more information: San Isabel National Forest, 1920 Valley Dr., Pueblo, CO 81008, (719) 545-8737. Gunnison National Forest, 2250 Hwy. 50, Delta, CO 81416, (970) 874-7691. Buena Vista Chamber, P.O. Box 2021, Buena Vista, CO 81211, (719) 395-6612.

The drive: The Sawatch Range lines the west side of the Arkansas River Valley, its high peaks soaring to meet the clouds and sky. This long range, stretching almost one hundred miles from the Eagle River to Marshall Pass, is studded by fifteen 14,000-foot peaks including 14,433-foot Mount Elbert, Colorado's highest point. Only two highways—Independence and Monarch passes—and a handful of gravel roads cross the range. The Cottonwood Pass Road, surmounting the Continental Divide at a lofty 12,126 feet, is the only one of these latter roads passable in a standard two-wheel-drive passenger car. The road makes a spectacular backcountry tour that is easily accessible from the Front Range cities. It threads up Cottonwood Creek past beaver ponds and the Collegiate Peaks Wilderness Area, loops above timberline to the pass summit, and drops down through broad Taylor Park and the Taylor River Canyon to Almont and the Gunnison River.

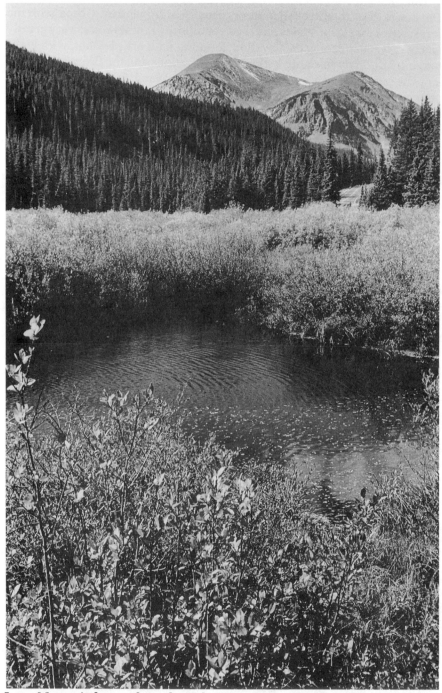

Jones Mountain looms above the Holy Water Beaver Ponds and the Cottonwood Pass Drive.

Cottonwood Pass opens in May or June depending on snowfall amounts and closes after the first major snow, usually in November. Check with the forest office for closure dates and road conditions. Temperatures vary greatly on the drive, depending on elevation. Summer days are pleasant, with highs ranging from sixty to eighty in the lower elevations and the fifties and sixties atop the pass. Expect afternoon thunderstorms. Watch for lightning if hiking on ridges. Temperatures begin declining in early September, with the difference between day and night temperatures differing as much as forty degrees. Highs are in the sixties and low seventies with nighttime lows dipping below freezing. September and October are generally dry, although cold fronts often bring rain and snow to the high country. The first heavy snow occurs in mid-October.

The Cottonwood Pass scenic drive begins at the traffic light marking the intersection of U.S. Highway 24 and Chaffee County Road 306 in Buena Vista. The town, at an elevation of 7,954 feet, was settled by silver miners in 1879. The Denver and Rio Grande Railroad arrived in 1880 en route to the upstream Leadville mines. The town grew as a supply and transportation center for towns and mines in outlying canyons including Clear Creek and Chalk Creek canyons. A mill and smelter built in 1881 brought additional prosperity. Buena Vista quickly outgrew Granite, the county seat, twenty miles upriver and the town was voted the new county seat. When Granite refused to yield the county records, Buena Vista locals broke into the courthouse at night and claimed the papers and county business. Buena Vista was a rowdy town, and thirty-six bars did their best to fuel the brashness.

Today Buena Vista thrives on tourism and bills itself as the "Whitewater Capital of Colorado." The nickname is no lie—the nearby Arkansas River offers some of the nation's best kayaking and rafting adventures. The Numbers rapid, just upstream from town, gives a technical and treacherous run for kayakers. Brown's Canyon, the most popular river run in Colorado, lies a few miles downstream. The river plunges through a series of demanding rapids with names like Widowmaker, Big Drop, and Zoom Flume. Numerous outfitters offer guided river trips. The Arkansas River here is part of the 148-mile-long Arkansas Headwaters Recreation Area.

Buena Vista, meaning "good view" in Spanish, sits in a superlative location at the confluence of Cottonwood Creek and the Arkansas River. Towering mountains, flanking the broad river valley, form a staggering presence. Low peaks, covered with brushy pines, climb eastward to the Buffalo Peaks at the southern end of the Mosquito Range. Westward looms the Collegiate Peaks section of the Sawatch Range rising 6,000 feet from the valley floor. Bulky 14,197-foot Mount Princeton, with long, sweeping ridges, dominates the view. Another fourteener, Mount Yale, lies half-hidden by lower mountains to the north. The drive heads west from Buena Vista toward the deep cleft chiseled by Cottonwood Peak between the two massive peaks.

The road leaves Buena Vista behind after a mile, running over a gravel bench past scattered homes. Cottonwood Creek hides beneath tall cottonwoods north of the road, while Mount Princeton looms to the southwest. After four and a half miles the road enters San Isabel National Forest, an immense 2.5-million-acre forest that stretches across central and southern Colorado. The road enters the mountain rampart and Cottonwood Creek's canyon a quarter-mile farther up. The drive twists along the tumbling stream, its banks a tangle of cottonwoods and willows. Abrupt slopes climb north of the road, broken by white cliffs, scree, and ponderosa and pinyon pines. A couple miles past private Cottonwood Hot Springs, the road, now FR 306 bends up the creek's main fork. A left turn on FR 344 runs southwest to Cottonwood Lake. This small lake nestled in woods offers good rainbow trout fishing from its banks. Twenty-eight-site Cottonwood Lake Campground sits on the south shore.

The paved drive ascends the broad, glaciated valley for eight miles, before steeply switchbacking for five miles through spruce forest and open meadows to reach timberline and the cloud-scraping pass summit. The rugged country abutting the drive on the north lies within 131,000-acre Collegiate Peaks Wilderness Area, an untrampled swathe of peaks and valleys spreading north to the Independence Pass highway. Several roadside trailheads offer access to the area. The Avalanche Trailhead at nine miles climbs Avalanche Gulch via the Colorado Trail. Denny Creek Trailhead, at twelve miles, scales scenic Denny Creek to Brown's Pass. The twenty-nine-site Collegiate Peaks Campground, a mile east of Denny Creek, is the jumping-off point for walkers to climb 14,196-foot Mount Yale. The hike begins just west of the campground on an old, unmarked jeep road that zigzags up Denny Gulch before turning into a well-traveled trail that scrambles up ridges above timberline to the summit. Ptarmigan Trail, in the upper valley, wends south to Ptarmigan Lake nestled below Jones Mountain.

Jones Mountain, a round-shouldered 12,995-foot peak, dominates the upper valley. Good views of the mountain are found at Holy Water Beaver Ponds at mile thirteen. A paved parking lot allows travelers to stop and perhaps catch a glimpse of an elusive beaver swimming across a still pond densely lined with willows, a favorite beaver food. The beaver, North America's largest rodent, builds numerous dams that stairstep up most of Colorado's high mountain valleys. The chains of lakes constructed by this small conservationists combat erosion, provide flood control, and create habitat for birds and fish. Their ponds silt up over time, creating rich soil for mountain meadows. Forests of spruce, set off with glades of quaking aspen, cover the mountain slopes above the beaver ponds. The Cottonwood Pass drive is one of Colorado's best foliage tours in late September.

Just before the pass summit the road curves across an above-timberline cirque etched by ancient glaciers. Low willows clot the roadside. The climbing road makes a last hairpin turn, and edges along a shelf road for a half-mile to the 12,126-foot summit of Cottonwood Pass. This saddle lies on the Continental Divide, the twisting mountain backbone that separates the Atlantic from the Pacific watershed. Cottonwood Pass has long been an important mountain crossing. An early wagon track, roughly following today's pass road, served as the main route into Aspen until the Independence Pass trail opened in 1881. The road, although serving Tincup and Taylor Park, fell into relative disuse until the Forest Service reconstructed the

Mt. Yale in the Collegiate Peaks Wilderness Area towers above the Cottonwood Pass Drive.

road in 1960. The summit allows a great panoramic view that encompasses Taylor Park and Castle Peak to the west and the Sawatch Range to the north. A short hike climbs south up the divide ridge to a higher viewpoint. The pavement ends atop the pass. The west side is gravel for the fourteen downhill miles to Taylor Park Reservoir.

The drive drops northwest above a high cirque and reaches Timberline Overlook, a roadside pullout, after a mile. Here the road begins lacing down toward the cirque floor and timberline. Spiraling down, the road parallels Pass Creek, running through spruce forest and below open slopes. Numerous beaver ponds step down the valley floor. As the road descends, the forest is mixed lodgepole pine and aspen. After eight miles the road reaches the edge of rolling Taylor Park, a high intermontane basin covered with forest and sagebrush meadows. The park is named for James Taylor, leader of a group of 1860 prospectors. The drive gently descends over undulating ridges and through shallow valleys. Taylor Park Ranger Station sits twelve miles from the pass summit at 9,524 feet. A mile and a half later the drive intersects paved FR 742 and turns southward. An overlook with picnic tables sits at the junction.

Taylor Park Reservoir, with 2,033 surface acres, spreads across the valley floor west of the road. The drive twists south on gravel benches above the lake. Forest Road 765 heads east a couple miles down the drive. This road leads to the picturesque mining town of Tincup, named for prospector James Taylor who washed gold ore from Willow Creek gravel in his tin cup. The road climbs over Cumberland Pass from Tincup and provides access to several excellent jeep trails. Past the junction the drive crosses Willow Creek and turns west above the lake. A viewpoint offers excellent views of the wind-tossed lake and a long row of peaks perched on the Continental Divide. Lakeview Campground, with thirty-five sites, sits south of the drive, while another road offers lake access at the Taylor Lake Boathouse. The regularly stocked lake yields excellent fishing for large lake trout, pike, Kokanee salmon, and rainbow, brown, and Snake River cutthroat trout.

The road continues along the lake's southern shore, winding through lodgepole pines and blue spruces. After two miles the drive reaches the large earthen dam that forms the reservoir and drops into Taylor Canyon. Taylor Dam Vista Point overlooks the dam. The 206-foot-high dam, finished in 1937, backs up 106,200-acre feet of snowmelt used for summer irrigation water.

The drive, paved FR 742, follows the Taylor River for twenty-one miles through Taylor Canyon to Almont and the river's confluence with the East River. Steep walls, blanketed with spruce, pine, and aspen, and broken by ragged cliffs, climb above the river to 12,100-foot Park Cone and 11,655-foot Baldy Mountain in the upper gorge. The large river rushes through cobbled rapids and pools in deep ponds by dark boulders. The Taylor River offers great fly-fishing for rainbow and brown trout. Be aware that private property borders much of the river. Look for public access areas. A trio of forest campgrounds—twenty-three-site Lottis Creek, six-site Cold Spring, and sixteen-site Lodgepole—scatter above the river in the central canyon. Further west are twenty-site Rosy Lane, twenty-seven-site Onemile, and seventeen-site North Bank campgrounds. Decent rock climbing is found on the towering granite cliffs near North Bank. More broken cliffs scatter along the canyon flank.

The canyon widens past the campgrounds and leaves Gunnison National Forest. Dry, rolling hills colored gray with sagebrush surround the canyon, with groves of spruce and fir tucked into moist side-ravines. Hay fields and cattle spread across the wide canyon floor, before the river again plunges into a cliff-lined gorge. Gunnison Mountain Park, with picnic facilities and a nature trail, lies below cliff bands in this lower canyon. Cottonwoods and willows border the Taylor River. At Almont, a small resort town, the road and drive deadends on Colorado Highway 135. The East and Taylor rivers join here in this shallow valley to form the Gunnison River. Almont, established in 1881 as a railroad stop, was named for Almont, a famed Kentucky racehorse. A turn north on CO 135 leads seventeen miles to Crested Butte, while a south turn heads eleven miles to Gunnison and U.S. Highway 50.

General description: A 164-mile-long loop drive that encircles the West Elk Mountains, passing numerous geologic features, dense aspen woodlands, and spacious valleys.

Special attractions: Curecanti National Recreation Area, Dillon Pinnacles, Blue Mesa Reservoir, Morrow Point Reservoir, Gunnison National Forest, West Elk Wilderness Area, Crawford State Recreation Area, Paonia State Recreation Area, Raggeds Wilderness Area, Lost Lake, Kebler Pass, Crested Butte National Historic District, Crested Butte Mountain Resort, hiking, camping, backpacking, sail boarding, skiing, scenic views, fall colors, fishing.

Location: West-central Colorado. The drive makes a huge loop around the West Elk Mountains to the north and west of Gunnison.

Drive route numbers: U.S. Highway 50, Colorado Highways 92, 133, 135, Gunnison County 12.

Travel season: The paved highway portions are open year-round, although snow may temporarily close the highways. Adequate snow tires or chains are advised. The gravel road over Kebler Pass closes in winter and opens in late spring when the snow melts away.

Camping: Numerous campgrounds lie along, or just off, the drive. Curecanti National Recreation Area offers 188-site Elk Creek, 9-site Dry Gulch, 7-site Red Creek, and 8-seven-site Lake Fork campgrounds along the drive. Gunnison National Forest has 5-site Mesa Creek, 18-site Erickson Springs, 11-site Lost Lake, 32-site Lake Irwin, and 10-site Almont campgrounds. Paonia State Recreation Area with 15 sites and Crawford State Recreation Area with 57 sites are found on the drive. The North Rim of the Black Canyon of the Gunnison National Monument's campground lies south of Crawford.

Services: All services in Gunnison, Crawford, Hotchkiss, Paonia, and Crest Butte.

Nearby attractions: Black Canyon of the Gunnison National Monument, Grand Mesa, Lake City, McClure Pass, Maroon Bells-Snowmass Wilderness Area, Glenwood Springs, Marble, Cottonwood Pass, Taylor River Canyon, Tincup, Uncompahgre National Forest.

For more information: Gunnison National Forest, 2250 Hwy. 50, Delta, CO 81416, (970) 874-7691. Crested Butte Chamber, P.O. Box 1288, Crested Butte, CO 81224,(970) 349-6438 or (800) 545-4505. Gunnison Country Chamber, P.O. Box 36, Gunnison, CO 81230, (970) 641-1501 or (800) 274-7580.

The drive: The 164-mile-long West Elk scenic drive loops around the rugged West Elk Mountains in western Colorado. The drive explores a diverse landscape. Precipitous peaks lift snow-capped summits into the

CO 92 traverses steep slopes above Morrow Point Reservoir and the upper Black Canyon on the West Elk Scenic Drive.

turquoise sky. Aspens spread golden tapestries across rolling hillsides. Granite cliffs stud sharp canyons, their abrupt walls chiseled by time and the river flowing. It's a land of majestic grandeur, but it's also a land of details waiting to be discovered. It's in those close-up vignettes that the world comes more alive—the clarity of a jewel-like dewdrop on a shaft of grama grass; the rustle of scrub oak leaves from a rufous-sided towhee; the cold smoothness of a river-worn cobble; ridgeline trees silhouetted against an evening thunderstorm.

Traffic along the drive's 132 paved miles and 32 gravel miles is generally light, although the US 50 section west of Gunnison can be heavy in summer. The mountain roads are winding and narrow, with occasional pulloffs. Watch for blind corners. The gravel segment is easily driven in summer and fall by passenger cars. Muddy and slick patches linger after heavy rain. Winter snow closes Kebler Pass, although the rest of the route remains open.

Summer and autumn are the best times to drive the roads, with pleasant daily high temperatures between sixty and eighty degrees depending on the elevation. A wide range of elevations, from 5,351 feet at Hotchkiss to the 9,980-foot summit of Kebler Pass, and the diverse topography lend a variety of climates and ecosystems to the drive. Expect regular afternoon thunderstorms in summer, with localized heavy rain on the mountains. Occasional cool, rainy periods occur in September and by late October snow begins falling on the high country. Winters are frigid. Every winter Gunnison, lying in a valley, records a number of national lows with below zero temperatures. Daily highs climb into the twenties. Crested Butte tends to be a little warmer, but an annual average of 230 inches of snow falls on its ski slopes. Warmer winter weather and less snow is found in the North Fork Valley at Paonia and Hotchkiss. Spring begins in April at the lower elevations and slowly creeps up the slopes until early June when most of the snow is melted. Spring brings unpredictable weather with warm, breezy days and unsettled periods with rain and sleet.

The drive begins in Gunnison on US 50. Gunnison, at 7,703 feet, sits in the broad Gunnison Valley at the confluence of the Gunnison River and Tomichi Creek. Low sagebrush-blanketed hills lift their rounded shoulders above the town. Gunnison has strong farming and ranching roots, although it was established in 1880 as a railroad stop and supply center for nearby mining areas. Originally called Richardson's Colony for local town organizer Dr. Sylvester Richardson, the community was renamed for ill-fated railroad surveyor Captain John Gunnison. Gunnison and his party, surveying a possible transcontinental railroad route, camped here on September 6, 1853. The group explored westward along today's US 50, before being massacred by Indians in Utah's Sevier Valley in late October. Gunnison, home of Western State College, thrives as a ranching and tourism hub.

The drive's twenty-eight-mile first segment goes west on US 50. The highway quickly leaves Gunnison and runs through a broad valley lush with cattle paddocks and hayfields. Narrowleaf cottonwoods densely line the Gunnison River's banks. After a few miles the highway and river enter Curecanti National Recreation Area, a 42,000-acre site managed by the National Park Service. Blue Mesa, Morrow Point, and Crystal lakes, part of the Bureau of Reclamation's Colorado River Storage Project, offer fishing, camping, and boating recreation as well as provide water for irrigation and hydroelectric power. The two lower reservoirs fill the narrow floor of the Gunnison River's upper Black Canyon, forming long, fjord-like lakes, while Blue Mesa Lake, the upper reservoir, drowns a wide valley.

The highway enters a shallow canyon and passes Neversink, Crystal Ranch, and Beaver Creek picnic areas. All three offer Gunnison River fishing access. Past Beaver Creek the highway winds alongside upper Blue Mesa Lake, a narrow lake amid granite bluffs and sagebrushed hillsides. At the Lake City Bridge and the junction with Colorado Highway 149, the lake opens into broad Iola Basin. The highway borders Blue Mesa Lake for the next nineteen miles to its dam. Blue Mesa Lake, Colorado's largest lake, stretches twenty miles from dam to inlet, covers nine thousand surface acres when full, boasts ninety-six miles of shoreline, and reaches 330 feet in depth near its dam. Blue Mesa is Curecanti's most accessible and most popular recreation site. The lake yields excellent fishing, particularly for big mackinaw lake trout. The largest "macs," preferring deep, cold water, reach weights exceeding thirty pounds. Kokanee salmon, brown, and rainbow trout also flourish in Blue Mesa Lake. The lake also offers great winter ice fishing.

High, flat-topped mesas, capped with a layer of volcanic West Elk Breccia, surround Blue Mesa Lake. The breccia, a mixture of ejected rock fragments and ash, exploded from immense volcanoes in today's West Elk and San Juan mountains. Below the mesa rims, erosion chisels strange shapes from the volcanic palisades. The Dillon Pinnacles, a bizarre collection of spires, buttresses, gargoyles, fins, and hoodoos, sits prominently above the drive near the lake's west end. A two-mile trail climbs to a bench below the pinnacles. Sagebrush colors the rounded mesa slopes above the lake a dull gray, while green cottonwoods and scrub oak tint side-canyons and ravines.

Several picnic areas and campgrounds are scattered along the lake and highway. Stevens Creek Campground, twelve miles west of Gunnison, offers fifty-four lakeside sites. Elk Creek Campground spreads 188 sites across a dry vale. Nearby is the park visitor center with informative displays on area natural history, history, geology, and recreational opportunities. The Bay of Chickens, a mile past Elk Creek, is the lake's best board sailing area. Nine-site Dry Gulch and seven-site Red Creek campgrounds are located just off the drive in their respective side-canyons. The Dillon Pinnacles Trail and Picnic Area begins on the north side of the Middle Bridge between the lake's Sapinero and Cebolla basins. The drive crosses the bridge, passes a scenic overlook above the south shore, and loops around Sapinero Mesa's broad north flank to the Lake Fork Bridge over the Lake Fork Arm. The highway climbs a hill and intersects CO 92, the second leg of the byway journey.

Turn north on CO 92. The drive's second segment travels fifty-two miles to Hotchkiss in North Fork Valley. The two-lane highway drops past eighty-seven-site Lake Fork Campground, a pull-through RV camping area, and crosses Blue Mesa Lake's 342-foot-high earth and concrete dam. The dam, completed in 1965, plugs the narrow river channel with over three million cubic yards of fill. The highway creeps over the eight hundred-foot-long dam and twists onto a bench above Morrow Point Lake and the precipitous upper Black Canyon of the Gunnison River. The Black Canyon, one of Colorado's most startling earth features, stretches fifty miles through the Gunnison Uplift. The Gunnison River, the state's fourth-largest river, sliced into ancient two-billion-year-old bedrock over the last three million years to create this marvelous chasm. The river, using a steep gradient and its watery knife, cuts downward about one inch per century. The lower canyon is protected in Black Canyon of the Gunnison National Monument, while the upper canyon hides two fingering reservoirs beneath somber canyon walls.

The highway winds along a granite bench above the canyon. Geologists say the bench is the erosional remnant of a gentle highland that rose here over two billion years ago. Above the bench lie multi-colored layers of the Morrison Formation and Dakota sandstone, and rimming the mesas above is West Elk Breccia. The road passes several scenic viewpoints before reaching Pioneer Point. This spectacular overlook views the inner gorge. Curecanti Needle, one of the canyon's prominent landmarks, juts into Morrow Point Lake far below. The seven hundred-foot-high pyramid-shaped Needle once was the emblem of the Denver & Rio Grande Railroad which traversed the canyon in the 1880s. Trains often stopped for travelers to admire Curecanti Needle. The excellent Curecanti Creek Trail drops two miles down from the overlook to the lake via a steep rock canyon.

The drive bends away from the gorge at Pioneer Point and runs north up Curecanti Creek's broad valley before crossing the creek and climbing southward through thick aspen forest. The road clings to steep slopes above Morrow Point Lake. The southern edge of Black Mesa forms a cliffed palisade above the road. Aspens and scrub oaks blanket the roadside. Hermits Rest, the next stop, is a lofty viewpoint poised almost 2,000 feet above the lake. Steep slopes loom above the green water, breaking to crags and forested ridges. Beyond towers the San Juan Mountains, including bulky 14,309-foot Uncompahgre Peak and pointed 14,017-foot Wetterhorn Peak. Restrooms, picnic tables, and interpretative signs sit at the point. Three-mile-long Hermits Rest Trail descends sharply to the lake and a primitive campground.

The highway bends away from the canyon brink, doglegs through a couple moist ravines filled with trickling creeks and aspen groves, and emerges on the rounded rim above Crystal Lake. Crystal Creek Trail leads 2.5-miles west to a sweeping 8,900-foot overlook above the lake. A picnic area sits by the pullout. The road descends north through Gambel oak thickets into Crystal Creek's shallow valley. Past Big Hill, the highway skirts Crystal Valley and drops into Onion Valley. Low hills covered with pinyon pine and juniper flank this valley. The road passes Gould Reservoir and numerous ranches before reaching Crawford State Recreation Area and its four hundred-acre reservoir. This remote state parkland offers excellent perch fishing, boating, swimming, and a fifty-seven-site campground. A turn here leads eleven miles south to the North Rim of the Black Canyon of the Gunnison National Monument. The monument holds great views into the abyss, a scenic drive, and a primitive campground.

The highway crosses the Smith Fork River and enters Crawford. This pleasant ranching town, named for Indian scout and former Kansas governor Captain George Crawford, began as a layover on the arduous Hartman Cattle Trail between Gunnison and the North Fork Valley. By 1881 ranchers had settled the area, bringing cattle herds to graze the upland meadows and the town was established in 1883. Crawford sits in a spectacular setting. Grand Mesa rims the northern skyline and the spiked peaks of the West Elk Range fill the eastern horizon. Most of the West Elks are protected in the 176,000-acre West Elk Wilderness Area, one of Colorado's largest wildernesses. The range boasts numerous high peaks, including the high point 13,035-foot West Elk Peak. Needle Rock, sitting just east of Crawford, is a volcanic plug. The rock, once the inner conduit of an extinct volcano, is solidified lava that remained after the volcano's softer outer layers eroded away.

The drive turns northwest from Crawford onto fertile Crawford Mesa and drops eleven miles through barren Mancos shale hills to, 5,351-foot-high Hotchkiss in the North Fork Valley. Hotchkiss, nicknamed "The Friendliest Town Around," was the first hamlet established in the fertile North Fork Valley along the North Fork of the Gunnison River. Enos T. Hotchkiss wandered into the valley, a popular Ute Indian wintering site, in 1879 and returned with others in 1881 after the Utes were removed to reservations. Hotchkiss homesteaded the area and planted an orchard. A small community composed of homesteaders, ranchers, and farmers sprang up and the town incorporated in 1901. The town's first commercial building, listed on the National Register of Historical Places, is an old hotel that now houses several shops. The railroad, en route to the up-valley coal mines, came through in 1902. Hotchkiss continues its rural tradition with an economy based, as it was a hundred years ago, on cattle, sheep, fruit, logging, and the annual Delta County Fair each August.

The drive intersects CO 133 in Hotchkiss. Turn east on CO 133 for the drive's twenty-four-mile third leg. The highway crosses corn fields and climbs onto a shale bluff north of the river. A couple of pullouts overlook the broad valley. The river riffles below over gravel bars. Thick cottonwoods broken by pastures cover its floodplain. The West Elk Range, including 11,396-foot Lamborn Mountain and 10,906-foot Landsend Peak, dominate the valley view. The highway descends onto the valley's north edge and runs through a pastoral countryside with hay fields and grazing cattle and horses. Paonia is reached after nine miles.

While the drive and highway bypass Paonia on its north side, it's worth a turn on Colorado Highway 187 to visit the town. Paonia, situated on the south bank of the North Fork of the Gunnison, lies at the upper end of North Fork Valley with mountains and mesas looming above. The town, established in 1881 by rancher Samuel Wade, was named Paonia, a misspelling of the Latin name for peonia, a common area flower. In 1882 Wade brought a trunk of young fruit saplings from Gunnison on a difficult, cold two-week trek, giving the town its main business for the next century. The orchards flourished in the valley's mild climate, with over three hundred sunny days a year and its cool nights. Paonia, with more than three thousand residents, flourishes with its orchards, nearby coal mining, sheep and cattle, and its

Mt. Lamborn and Landsend Peak rise beyond the North Fork Valley's agricultural fields and pastures along the West Elk Scenic Drive.

many artists and artisans. The town once made "Ripley's Believe It or Not" with its record twenty churches per capita. A chamber of commerce visitor center sits along the drive just north of Paonia.

Past Paonia the valley begins to narrow, with steep shale hillsides covered with pinyon pine, juniper, and scrub oak climbing away from the river. Orchards, including apple, pear, peach, and cherry, line the highway and perch on river terraces. Delta County, with over 450,000 apple trees, produces two-thirds of Colorado's apples. The narrow, fifteen-mile canyon between Paonia and Paonia Reservoir boasts a long history of coal mining. The highway runs past several working mines and mining towns including Somerset. Coal, first discovered in 1883, boomed during World War I and again in the 1970s. Four working mines—Somerset, Bear, West Elk, and Cyprus—now produce over three million tons of coal annually. The coal silos along the highway allow for rapid loading of railroad cars. The canyon narrows past Somerset and the road winds shelf-like above the river. Below Paonia Dam the drive intersects Gunnison County 12, the thirty-two-mile fourth segment of the drive. CO 133 continues north past Paonia State Recreation Area, and over McClure Pass to Carbondale.

Turn east on County 12 and head up Anthracite Creek's canyon. This gravel road section to Crested Butte offers some of Colorado's best backroad scenery and spectacular aspen foliage in late September. The road runs up the canyon for six miles, its south-facing flank coated with scrub oak and mountain mahogany and its cross-river north-facing flank dense with aspen, spruce, and fir forest. Erickson Springs Recreation Area, with eighteen campsites, restrooms, tent pads, and a well, nestles below the Raggeds Wilderness Area. The road crosses the creek here and begins steeply switchbacking up the valley's south slope. After a couple miles of climbing the angle eases and the road bends across Watson Flats through oak thickets and open meadows. The drive bends east and heads toward towering 11,348-foot Marcellina Mountain, an immense rocky peak seamed with snow gullies and serrated ridges. The West Elk Range looms to the south across a broad aspen-filled valley, including 12,185-foot West Beckwith Peak and 12,432-foot East Beckwith Peak.

The road, following an old Ute trail, runs across a rolling bench below Marcellina Peak through lovely aspen groves. Two wilderness areas flank the drive. The 64,000-acre Raggeds Wilderness Area protects a magnificent swathe of high peaks, including Marcellina Peak, north of the byway. The West Elk Wilderness encompasses the volcanic West Elk Range to the south. Both Beckwith peaks as well as the Anthracite Range south of Kebler Pass lie in the area. The road scales a rounded ridge below Marcellina Peak, passes the Ruby/Anthracite Trail, and a mile and a half later reaches the turn to Lost Lake Slough. This rough national forest road climbs two miles south to the lake, a tranquil pond cradled in a glacier-carved basin beneath East Beckwith Peak. The peak soars above aspen and spruce forest and cliffed ridges. This idyllic spot, with an eleven-site campground and good fishing, makes a wonderful overnight stay.

The drive continues over aspen-covered hills and twists down to Anthracite Creek and Horse Ranch Park, a spacious valley filled with low willows. The road bends east along the creek and skirts The Dyke, a sawtoothed Chinese Wall of pinnacles that climbs the southern end of the Ruby Range. The Ruby Range is a small sierra that connects the Elk Range on the north to the West Elk Range. It's a long ridge decorated with numerous sharp peaks. Ruby Peak and Mount Owen, the 13,058-foot range high point, tower north of The Dyke. The road gently climbs out of the valley through a thick spruce woodland and tops out on the wide 9,980-foot summit of Kebler Pass. A few lonely gravestones sit in the old Irwin Cemetery atop the pass. The silver mining town of Irwin once roared near here, with over five thousand residents in 1879 despite the town's location on Ute Indian territory. The town once boasted a bank, the *Pilot* newspaper, hotels, three churches, six sawmills, twenty-three saloons, and the exclusive Irwin Club which hosted ex-president Ulysses Grant in 1880. Irwin quietly faded away after the great silver crash of 1893.

Forest Road 730 begins immediately below the Kebler Pass summit and heads south to 10,033-foot Ohio Pass and down Ohio Creek to Gunnison. The drive swings north from the pass and descends into Coal Creek's glaciated valley. The road bends east almost a mile from the pass. A left turn here bumps north to Lake Irwin, a picturesque lake tucked into the east flank of the Ruby Range. A thirty-two-site campground sits alongside the popular lake. The drive drops down Coal Creek's narrow canyon seven miles to Crested Butte along a wide road that follows the abandoned Crested Butte Branch of the Denver & Rio Grande Railroad.

Crested Butte, a charming, unpretentious Victorian town, offers superb powder skiing in winter and is reputed to be Colorado's mountain bike capital in summer. The town, hiding in the morning shadow of 12,162-foot Crested Butte, sits at 8,885 feet in a wide basin surrounded on three sides by lofty peaks.

Crested Butte began as a gold camp and supply center in the early 1880s. As the gold and silver boom abated, discoveries of nearby high-grade coal deposits turned Crested Butte into a Colorado Fuel & Iron company town until the mine closed in 1952. The opening of the ski area and the spectacular mountain scenery ringing the town now fuel the economy. Much of old Crested Butte, a national historic district, retains its nineteenth century ambiance. A forty-site walking tour explores historical Crested Butte. The ski resort boasts over twenty feet of winter snow, eighty-five trails spread over 1,150 ski-acres, and 550 acres of double black-diamond terrain. Excellent cross-country ski trails thread through surrounding Gunnison National Forest. The area also offers some of the Rockies' best mountain biking, with numerous trails and jeep roads lacing the backcountry. Crested Butte has all visitor services, with fine hotels and excellent restaurants.

After entering Crested Butte, follow Whiterock Avenue for a half-mile to Sixth Street and CO 135. Turn south on CO 135. This last part of the journey travels twenty-eight miles south to Gunnison and the drive's endpoint. The highway runs along the Slate River in a broad grassy valley. Whetstone and Red mountains, their lower slopes cloaked in aspens and evergreens, loom to the west. After a few miles the Slate joins the East River. The road continues along East River and passes through a narrow canyon below humpbacked 10,878-foot Round Mountain. Low sagebrush-covered hills border the valley and highway. At Almont the East and Taylor rivers combine to form the Gunnison River. The highway runs through low bluffs along the Gunnison, passes ten-site Almont Campground, and emerges into a broad valley. The last eleven miles traverse the Gunnison River's cottonwood-lined banks. Small ranches and fields full of grazing cattle and horses abut the asphalt. The highway passes the Ohio Pass turnoff and bends south to Gunnison and US 50.

21 SILVER THREAD SCENIC BYWAY
South Fork to Lake City

General description: A 75-mile route that follows the Rio Grande, climbs over Spring Creek Pass and the Continental Divide, and ends in Lake City in the heart of the San Juan Mountains.

Special attractions: Wagon Wheel Gap, Creede National Historic District, Rio Grande, Clear Creek Falls, Spring Creek Pass, Slumgullion Earthflow, Rio Grande National Forest, Colorado Trail, La Garita Wilderness Area, Weminuche Wilderness Area, Gunnison National Forest, Lake San Cristobal, Lake City National Historic District, hiking, camping, fishing, backpacking, scenic views.

Location: South-central Colorado. The highway runs between South Fork on the west edge of the San Luis Valley to Lake City 55 miles southwest of Gunnison.

Drive route name and number: Silver Thread Scenic Byway, Colorado Highway 149.

Camping: 7 national forest campgrounds—Palisade, Marshall Park, Rio Grande, Bristol View, Silver Thread, North Clear Creek, and Slumgullion Pass—lie along the drive.

Services: All services are found in South Fork, Creede, and Lake City.

Nearby attractions: San Luis Valley, Los Caminos Antiguos Scenic Byway, Wheeler Geologic Area, San Luis Peak, San Juan National Forest, Alpine Loop Back Country Byway, Handies Peak, Big Blue Wilderness Area, Uncompahgre Peak, Curecanti National Recreation Area.

For more information: Rio Grande National Forest, 1803 W. Hwy. 160, Monte Vista, CO 81144, (970) 852-5941. Creede-Mineral County Chamber, P.O. Box 580, Creede, CO 81130, (719) 658-2374. Lake City Chamber, P.O. Box 430, Lake City, CO 81235, (970) 944-2527.

The drive: The seventy-five-mile Silver Thread Scenic Byway, following CO 149 between South Fork and Lake City, traverses a spectacular, off-the-beaten-track part of Colorado. The drive parallels the Rio Grande below cliffed palisades, passes through historic Creede, climbs over lofty Spring Creek and Slumgullion passes, crosses an active earthflow, and ends in Lake City in the heart of the rugged San Juan Mountains. The San Juans, Colorado's largest mountain range, is a tumble of peak and canyon that spreads across ten thousand square miles, an area the size of Vermont. The range encompasses almost all of southwestern Colorado south of the Gunnison River and west of the San Luis Valley, and includes nine sub-ranges—Sneffels Range, San Miguel Range, La Plata Mountains, La Garita Mountains, Needles Range, West Needles Range, Rico Mountains, Grenadier Range, and Piedra Mountains. The San Juans also boast ten 14,000-foot peaks, a million acres preserved in wilderness areas, and is the headwaters of numerous rivers including the Rio Grande, and Dolores, Animas, and Uncompahgre rivers.

Climate and weather differs dramatically along the byway because of a wide range of elevations from 8,180 feet at South Fork to 11,361 feet atop Slumgullion Pass, the drive high point. Summer days along the Rio Grande range into the eighties, but are usually cooler at the upper elevations. Expect afternoon thunderstorms, particularly in July and August, with locally heavy rain. Nights at the campgrounds are cool. Autumn offers warm weather, with generally clear skies and golden aspens. Cold fronts sweeping out of the north often color the high country white with fresh snow in October. Winter arrives by late October and locks the land in a blanket of white until March or April. The road will occasionally be closed by heavy snow. Carry chains, a shovel, and extra clothes in winter. Snow lingers on the higher elevations well into early summer. The San Juan Mountains, the wettest part of Colorado, receives as much as fifty inches of annual precipitation and 350 inches of snow. Spring weather is unpredictable with rain, snow, sleet, sun, and wind possible—all on the same day.

The Silver Thread Scenic Byway, a designated national forest byway, begins at the junction of U.S. Highway 160 and CO 149 in South Fork, forty-eight miles west of Alamosa on the western edge of the broad San Luis Valley. South Fork, a small resort and lumber town, sits at the confluence of the Rio Grande and the South Fork of the Rio Grande. Head northwest on CO 149.

The road leaves South Fork and crosses the Rio Grande after a half-mile and enters 1.8-million-acre Rio Grande National Forest almost five miles up. Collier State Wildlife Area, providing crucial winter habitat for deer and elk, spreads along the river bottomlands here. The highway parallels the river in the bottom of a deep, broad canyon. Long cliff bands, composed of welded volcanic tuff, stairstep upwards forming the Rio Grande Palisades. Open ponderosa pine forest scatters across the warm south-facing slopes, while glades of aspen mix with spruce and fir woodlands on the cooler north-facing mountainsides. Tall cottonwoods and dense willow thickets line the rushing Rio Grande. At six miles the wildlife area offers picnic tables and restrooms for picnickers and anglers. Farther up, the canyon narrows and its cliffs steepen. Palisade Campground, with thirteen pine-shaded sites, sits along-

Creede, along the Silver Thread Scenic Byway, attracts visitors with its historic mining past.

side the river at ten miles. The campground, lying in the shadow of the looming Palisades, is a popular put-in point for river rafters. The river section from here to South Fork yields an easy and scenic half-day run. The Rio Grande from South Fork to Wagon Wheel Gap is also designated Gold Medal fishing waters, with anglers catching rainbow and brown trout.

After eleven miles the highway swings under an abrupt escarpment of tall cliffs broken into flying buttresses, aretes, gargoyles, and castles. Immense talus slopes cascade down to the highway. These volcanic cliffs form Wagon Wheel Gap, a narrow gorge named for an abandoned wagon wheel found here in 1873. The wheel was supposedly left by the 1861 Baker prospecting party after being ordered by Utes to vacate their upstream camp. The party left so quickly that equipment and supplies were scattered along their retreating trail.

Forest Road 600 begins just past the gap and winds twelve miles north to Hansons Mill, the former site of a lumber mill. Road's end, in a high grassy park below Pool Table Mountain, is the jumping-off point for visitors who either walk or jeep seven miles to Wheeler Geologic Area. The area, tucked into a shallow canyon below Halfmoon Pass and the crest of the La Garita Mountains, is a rough landscape of fantastic rock formations. Erosion sculpted the soft volcanic rock into a fairyland of spires, minarets, goblins, fluted cliffs, and jumbled badlands. The area, now part of La Garita Wilderness Area, was designated the nation's first national monument in 1906. Its isolation and low visitation, however, prompted the tract's removal from the national park system in 1950.

The scenery changes dramatically past Wagon Wheel Gap. The canyon opens into a broad grassy valley, flanked by sagebrush slopes on the north and spruce and fir forest on the rounded ridges to the south. The drive runs up the south side of the widening valley for five miles, crosses the Rio Grande at the abandoned site of Wason, now the Wason Ranch, and bends northwest up Willow Creek to Creede. This historic mining town, nestled at the foot of a cliffed canyon, got its start in 1889 after prospector Nicholas Creede stumbled onto a rich silver lode at a lunch stop. He supposedly exclaimed, "Holy Moses, I've struck it rich." His wealthy Holy Moses Mine attracted thousands of fortune seekers.

Almost overnight the camp erupted into a tent city. The boom town grew by three hundred people a day in the frenzied summer of 1890. By 1892 more than ten thousand lived in Creede. The town just as quickly developed a boisterous, hell-raising reputation. Writer Cy Warman, who founded the town's first newspaper, immortalized Creede in a popular poem that read, "It's day all day in the daytime, And there is no night in Creede." Another writer noted, "At night there are no policemen to interfere with the vested right of each citizen to raise as much Cain as he sees fit and...three-fourths of the population are of the kind that does see fit." The infamous town attracted numerous outlaws, gamblers, gunslingers, madams, murderers, and preachers. It's cast of characters included con man Soapy Smith, quick-draw artist Calamity Jane Canary, cigar-smoking cardshark Poker Alice, lawman Bat Masterson, and Bob Ford, killer of Jesse James. Saloon keeper Ford got his due when Ed O'Kelly, a Missouri friend of James, murdered him with a double-barreled shotgun in 1892. In 1892 Creede, nicknamed "Colorado's Silver Ribbed Treasure Trove," yielded a million dollars of silver ore a month. The following year Congress enacted the Silver Act and the price of silver plummeted from $1.29 an ounce to fifty cents and Creede almost shut down. Catastrophic fires and floods destroyed the town several times, but townspeople, overcoming adversity, rebuilt. The mines, far from exhausted, continued to work well into the twentieth century. In 1939 some 500,000 ounces were shipped every week and in 1966 Mineral County produced almost 150,000 ounces of silver.

Creede, now a national historic district, makes a delightful stop on the scenic drive. The picturesque town boasts numerous visitor attractions including an underground fire station and the renowned Creede Repertory Theater, which rotates plays and dramas nightly through summer in the old Creede Opera House. The town makes a good base camp for exploring the surrounding high country and enjoying the myriad fishing, hiking, and mountain biking possibilities. A seventeen-mile-long auto trip, the Bachelor Historic Tour, begins on Creede's south side and climbs to the Equity Mine before returning on Bachelor Road. The tour offers sixteen interpretative stops, including ghost towns, old mines, and the Sunnyside Cemetery, and several scenic overlooks.

The highway runs south from Creede and after a mile bends into the Rio Grande valley. The road heads southwest across terraced benches deposited on old river floodplains. Marshall Park Campground, with sixteen sites,

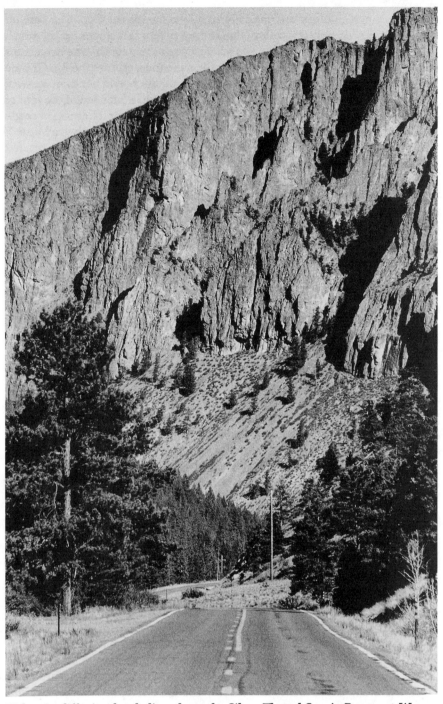

Volcanic cliffs rim the skyline above the Silver Thread Scenic Byway at Wagon Wheel Gap.

spreads along the river west of Seven-Mile Bridge. Forest roads 523 and 528 head south from here to Spar City, a ghost town that was contemporary with Creede. Four-site Rio Grande Campground sits a few miles farther upstream along the river and provides good fishing access. At mile thirty-five the highway and Rio Grande swing northwest up a broad valley flanked by rounded mountains. The river, its headwaters on Stony Pass atop the Continental Divide west of here, uncoils in long, lazy loops across the flat valley meadows. The valley here was not actually carved by the river, but is a down-dropped block with faults on either side. A roadside overlook near the valley head offers views west toward the Rio Grande headwaters and the remote backcountry of Weminuche Wilderness Area, while rocky 12,706-foot Bristol Head's high volcanic cliffs hem in the eastern skyline and form, along with its long northern ridge, the uplifted border of the valley. Jim Stewart's hidden treasure still resides somewhere on Bristol Head's western flank. In 1852 Stewart, an Army mail courier, detoured through these mountains to avoid Indian trouble. While crossing a creek, he accidently dropped his mail bag into the water. While drying out the mail he panned the stream and found gold nuggets. Noting the location, Stewart later returned but was never able to find his placer gold stash.

Forest Road 520 leaves the drive at the valley's northern end and heads west nine miles up a narrow canyon to Rio Grande Reservoir, a long fjord-like lake that offers excellent fishing and camping opportunities. Road Canyon Reservoir, off FR 520, yields rainbow trout up to six pounds, while numerous backcountry lakes and streams in the Weminuche Wilderness south of Rio Grande Reservoir give excellent fishing. The road, continuing west from the reservoir as a four-wheel-drive track, climbs another twenty miles to the lofty 12,594-foot summit of Stony Pass along a historic wagon route before dropping steeply to Silverton.

The scenic drive, leaving the Rio Grande's valley, heads north up Spring Creek's shallow valley and passes Spring Creek Reservoir Rest Site. This national forest area offers fishing in a small lake and picnicking. The road twists up rolling ridges coated with stands of spruce, fir, and quaking aspen and grassy meadows. Several campgrounds—Bristol View, Silver Thread, and North Clear Creek—lie on the drive or just off, on Forest Road 510, North Clear Creek Road. Silver Thread Campground, with eleven sites, lies on a highway hairpin-turn. A short trail leads east to South Clear Creek Falls from the campground. A couple miles higher sits a scenic overlook on the edge of an aspen-fringed meadow. The marvelous view west looks up the glaciated valley of South Clear Creek. Brown and Hermit lakes glimmer on the valley floor, while 13,821-foot Rio Grande Pyramid dominates the Continental Divide above. The 1874 Wheeler Survey called the pyramid "one of the handsomest and most symmetrical cones in Colorado."

The drive crosses a low divide and drops northeast into North Clear Creek's broad drainage. FR 510 heads east for a half-mile from the drive to Clear Creek Falls, one of Colorado's most spectacular waterfalls. North Clear Creek meanders across its broad valley, through willow-lined banks before plunging almost one hundred feet over a cliff of hard basalt in a craggy chasm.

The frothy creek continues down the steep, rocky canyon to the Rio Grande. The falls observation area offers a fenced overlook, picnic tables, and restrooms.

From the falls the highway runs north up Spring Creek's brushy valley, past aspen groves and grasslands. After seven miles the drive reaches the crest of 10,898-foot Spring Creek Pass atop the Continental Divide, the nation's great spine that separates the Atlantic and Pacific watersheds. East of here towers Baldy Cinco, a 13,383-foot peak in the 104,000-acre La Garita Wilderness Area. The Colorado Trail, a 469-mile-long footpath from Denver to Durango, crosses the highway here while following the divide westward. A kiosk on the pass gives information on local geology, recreation, and hiking.

The byway drops down across the headwaters of Cebolla Creek and winds west through moist spruce forest for six miles to 11,361-foot Slumgullion Pass. This high point, not a true pass, divides Cebolla Creek from the Lake Fork of the Gunnison River. Twenty-one-site Slumgullion Campground sits just north of the highway on the west side of the pass. The drive begins steeply descending on seven-percent grades through dense spruce and aspen woodlands. Windy Point Overlook yields great views west into the San Juans. To the southwest towers the Continental Divide ridgeline and 14,001-foot Sunshine Peak, 14,034-foot Redcloud Peak, and 14,048-foot Handies Peak; to the northeast looms pointed 14,017-foot Wetterhorn Peak and bulky 14,309-foot Uncompahgre Peak, the San Juans' highest mountain. Steep hillsides fall away below to the river's deep canyon. A sign identifies the peaks and other notable features.

Below the overlook the highway passes the Slumgullion Earthflow, one of Colorado's most unique natural wonders. The earthflow or mudslide occurred some seven hundred years ago on the southern flank of Mesa Seco to the north when weak volcanic tuff and breccia, lubricated by heavy rains, slumped five miles down the steep mountainside to the valley floor. The 2,700-foot-high flow blocked the river and formed narrow Lake San Cristobal, Colorado's second largest natural lake. A second flow some 350 years ago overlies the upper part of the flow. This active new slide sporadically lurches as much as twenty feet downhill every year. The trees studding the active flow are readily apparent by their drunken angles. The pass and earthflow were named for slumgullion, a yellowish stew concocted by hungry miners who tossed whatever ingredients they might have on hand into a single pot, usually some combination of game, potatoes, bacon, and beans.

Lake San Cristobal Overlook, with views of the lake and glaciated valley, sits on the slide's south side. The highway runs a mile across the slide and bends northwest down steep slopes to the valley floor. A historic marker commemorating Alferd Packer and his grisly deeds lies just north of the highway before crossing the Lake Fork. Packer, guiding a group of prospectors into the San Juans in the winter of 1873, murdered and ate his five clients. Packer escaped the clutches of the law for nine years before being apprehended in Wyoming under the assumed name of John Schwartze. The cannibal, sentenced to hang in 1883, spent seventeen years in the state prison for his deed before being paroled. Legend says presiding judge Melville Gerry cursed, "Packer, you man-eating son-of-a-bitch, there were seven Democrats in Hinsdale County and you ate five of them." The salty story, made up by local Irish bar-keep Larry Dolan to entertain his customers, was embellished over the years to its current mythological status.

The Alpine Loop Back Country Byway, a Bureau of Land Management drive that climbs over Cinnamon and Engineer passes via jeep roads, begins a half-mile past the Lake Fork crossing. The highway continues north above the river, winding through aspen and pine forests to 8,663-foot Lake City and the drive's end. Lake City, a national historic district, is a picturesque resort and mining community nestled in the valley bottom. The small town is the seat of Hinsdale County, a county of peaks and valleys as big as Rhode Island. Locals boast that if the land was flattened out the county would be as large as west Texas. Hinsdale County is not only the most sparsely populated county in Colorado but in the United States with Lake City as its only town.

Lake City started, like most Colorado mountain towns, as a mining settlement in 1874 after Enos Hotchkiss found gold. The town, a stage and freight hub for surrounding towns, flourished through the 1880s with two banks, seven saloons, two breweries, and the first newspaper and first church on Colorado's western slope. After the boom, Lake City carried on as a mining and ranching center, but today relies on its gorgeous scenery to attract tourist dollars. The town is a great base to explore the natural history of the San Juan Mountains and the area's rich historical legacy. Numerous ghost towns scatter across the mountains, with trails that climb the peaks and traverse nearby wilderness areas. CO 149 continues north for fifty-five miles from Lake City to Gunnison, heading up the Lake Fork before turning inland to Blue Mesa Lake.

22 MILLION DOLLAR HIGHWAY
Durango to Ridgway

General description: This 87-mile drive, part of the San Juan Scenic Skyway, follows U.S. Highway 550 over 3 lofty mountain passes between Durango and Ridgway.

Special attractions: Durango & Silverton Narrow Gauge Railroad, Durango National Historic District, Purgatory Ski Resort, San Juan National Forest, Animas River Canyon, Weminuche Wilderness Area, Molas Pass, Molas Lake, Silverton National Historic District, Red Mountain Pass, Box Canyon Falls, Ouray National Historic District, scenic views, camping, backpacking, fishing, hiking, mountain biking, historic sites, fall colors.

Location: Southwestern Colorado. The drive follows US 550 between Durango and Ridgway.

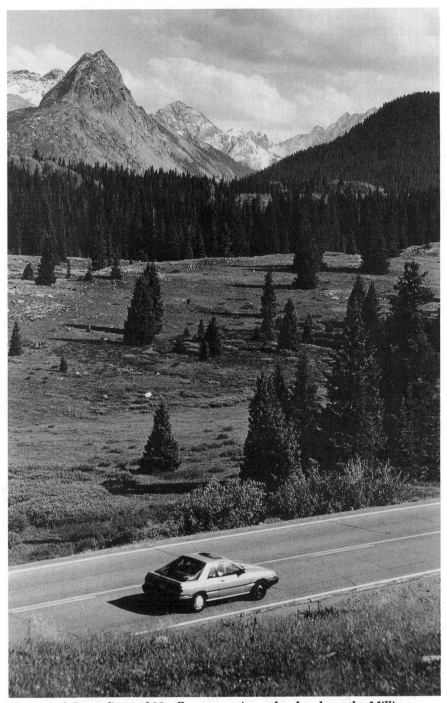

The ragged Grenadier and Needle ranges pierce the sky above the Million Dollar Highway and Molas Pass.

Drive route name and number: Million Dollar Highway, US 550.
Travel season: Year-round. The drive is occasionally closed in winter due to heavy snow and avalanche danger. Chains are often required to drive the highway.
Camping: Several national forest campgrounds lie on or just off the drive, including Chris Park, Haviland Lake, Purgatory, South Mineral, and Ampitheater. Dispersed, primitive camping is permitted on both BLM and National Forest public lands along the drive.
Services: All services are found in Durango, Silverton, Ouray, and Ridgway.
Nearby attractions: Alpine Loop Back Country Byway, Mount Sneffels Wilderness Area, Telluride, Lizard Head Pass, Ophir Pass, Lizard Head Wilderness Area, Unaweep-Tabeguache Back Country Byway, Uncompahgre Plateau, Owl Creek Pass, Lake City, Mesa Verde National Park, La Plata Mountains, Black Canyon of the Gunnison National Monument.
For more information: San Juan National Forest, 701 Camino del Rio, Durango, CO 81301, (970) 247-4874. Durango Chamber Resort Assn., P.O. Box 2587, Durango, CO 81302, (970) 247-0312 or (800) 525-8855. Silverton Chamber, P.O. Box 565, Silverton, CO 81433, (970) 387-5654 or (800) 752-4494. Ouray County Chamber, P.O. Box 145, Ouray, CO 81427, (970) 325-4746 or (800) 228-1876.

The drive: The San Juan Mountains, an immense twelve thousand-square-mile slice of high country, encompasses almost all of southwestern Colorado. The San Juans, with a mean elevation of 10,000 feet, boasts over one hundred peaks topping 13,000 feet and fourteen of Colorado's fifty-four 14,000-foot peaks. This huge range, dissected by sharp canyons and spiked with sky-scraping peaks, is divided into numerous sub-ranges including the San Miguel Range, Rico Mountains, La Plata Mountains, Sneffels Range, West Needle and Needle Mountains, Grenadier Range, La Garita Mountains, and Cochetopa Hills. The heart of the San Juans, however, is the San Juan Range itself, towering above the historic mining towns of Ouray, Silverton, and Lake City. The Million Dollar Highway, following US 550, traverses this rugged, rocky heartland for eighty-seven miles from Durango over 10,910-foot Molas Divide to Silverton and 11,008-foot Red Mountain Pass to Ouray and Ridgway.

The highway, open year-round, is best driven in summer and fall. The wide variation in elevation along the drive from 6,512 feet at Durango to 11,018 feet atop Red Mountain Pass gives a wide diversity of both temperature and precipitation. Summer temperatures in the lower elevations at both ends of the road are typically warm, with highs ranging from seventy to ninety degrees. The mountain heights are cooler. Highs range from fifty to seventy degrees. Afternoon thunderstorms are an almost daily occurrence somewhere along the highway. Watch for slippery roads. Autumn is delightful, with cool, crisp days and spectacular aspen colors.

The first snow falls sometime in October on the high peaks, and winter begins in November with heavy snowfall. As much as four feet of snow can fall in a day, leading to extreme avalanche danger. The highway regularly closes due to avalanches. The steep Uncompahgre Gorge highway section between Ironton Park and Ouray is the most dangerous, with the Riverside and Mother Cline slides. The Riverside Slide, dropping 3,200 vertical feet down abrupt chutes, makes this highway Colorado's deadliest avalanche crossing. Today a snowshed protects the road from the slide's wrath, but not before six highway travelers perished in avalanches. Chains are often required to drive the highway in winter. Watch for the omnipresent snowplows clearing the highway and bring extra clothes and sleeping bags in case of a breakdown. Spring comes slowly to the high country, with the snow cover slowly retreating on warm April and May days. Expect cool, breezy days with occasional snow and rain storms.

The Million Dollar Highway begins in Durango at the junction of U.S. highways 160 and 550. Turn north on US 550 on the town's south side. The road bypasses downtown Durango and heads up Main Avenue. Durango, straddling the broad Animas Valley, was established in 1880 as a Denver & Rio Grande Railroad town. Animas City, the area's first town, started just north of Durango in 1861 as a supply center for San Juan miners. The railroad, wanting to capitalize on the San Juans' rich mines, pushed their narrow gauge tracks west from Alamosa to the Animas River Valley. Animas City seemed the logical choice for their new railroad center, but the town and the railroad couldn't come to terms. Investors then set up the Durango Land and Coal Company and surveyed a new townsite two miles south of Animas City, calling it Durango because of the area's similarity to Durango, Mexico. The town thrived as a railroad hub, hauling valuable ore from mountain mines to Durango's smoke-belching smelter.

Durango, long after the San Juan mines shut down, is still a railroad town. The Durango & Silverton Narrow Gauge Railroad, a National Historic and National Engineering Landmark, begins at the train station on the town's south side and runs north up the old Denver & Rio Grande railbed forty-five miles to Silverton. This spectacular train ride, threading through the steep Animas River gorge, is a living history exhibit that takes the traveler back in time to the railroad's mining heyday. Reservations and advance ticket purchases are advised, particularly during the busy summer months. Durango is also a wonderful outdoor sports town, with nearby mountain bike trails, excellent fly-fishing streams, numerous four-wheel-drive tracks, kayaking and rafting on the Animas River, and a wealth of hiking paths including the terminus of the 469-mile Colorado Trail between Durango and Denver. Durango also offers all visitor services, including hotels, dining, groceries, and service stations.

The highway leaves Durango after three miles and runs north on the western edge of the broad Animas Valley for fifteen miles. The Animas River, a 110-mile-long river originally called *Rio de las Animas Perdidas*, or River of Lost Souls, by early Spanish explorers, meanders in long graceful loops across the wide-bottomed valley past green pastures grazed by horses and cattle. Dense willows and tall narrow-leafed cottonwoods hug the river's rocky

To Montrose

RIDGWAY STATE PARK

Ridgway

550

82

To Placerville

Courthouse Mtn. 12,152 Ft.

UNCOMPAHGRE NATIONAL FOREST

Uncompahgre

Potosi Pk.

Ouray

Wildhorse Pk. 13,266 ft.

MT. SNEFFELS WILDERNESS AREA

Mt. Sneffels 14,150 ft.

Ampitheatre CG

853

River

Abrams Mtn.

UNCOMPAHGRE

NATIONAL

Red Mtn. Pass 11,018 ft.

Storm Pk. 13,487 ft

FOREST

550

Vermillion Pk. 13,894 ft.

Animas River

GUNNISON NAT'L FOREST

Trail

South Mineral CG

Silverton

RIO GRANDE

WEMINUCHE

Sultan Mtn.

Molas Pass

Colorado

NATIONAL

S A N

Engineer Mtn.

Coal Bank Pass

Twilight Pk.

FOREST

Purgatory Ski Area

Purgatory CG

Mt. Eolus 14,083 ft.

NEEDLE MTNS.

WILDERNESS

Electra Lake

J U A N

Chris Park CG

Haviland Lake CG

A R E A

Colorado

N A T I O N A L

Trail

N

0   5   10
Miles

550

Animas River

F O R E S T

To Cortez

160

Durango

160 To Pagosa Springs

To Aztec, NM

•Denver

COLORADO

★

banks. The river did little to excavate this deep valley. Thick glaciers, spilling down from the high mountains, scoured the valley floor, chiseled its steep side-walls, and left a characteristic U-shaped valley behind. Sandstone cliffs abruptly lift from the valley, striping the slopes with diagonal bands.

Durango is on the edge of the Colorado Plateau, a vast geographic province that spreads across the Four Corners region, and the San Juan Mountains. As the highway runs north, it slowly leaves the plateau by traversing upturned sedimentary rock formations—gray Mancos shale, Dakota sandstone, the dinosaur-bearing Morrison Formation, Entrada, Navajo, and Wingate sandstones, and finally old Permian redbeds at Hermosa. Still older formations, including the 300-million-year-old Hermosa Formation, lie farther north. The two thousand-foot-thick Hermosa Formation, laid down as marine sediments in basins off-shore from the Ancestral Rockies, forms lofty gray ramparts above the highway north from Hermosa to Engineer Mountain.

As the highway runs north from Durango it passes Trimble Springs at six miles. This hot springs, located just west of the road, was named for 1874 settler Frank Trimble. He developed two springs, spewing water as hot as 126 degrees, and built a hotel for visitors wanting to sample the spring's "curative value." A new forty-room brick hotel, the Hermosa House, was erected in the late 1890s and offered stables, a gym, bowling alley, golf, and a saloon. After fire destroyed it in 1938, it was replaced by another hotel that burned in 1957. The springs now offers a bathhouse, Olympic-sized outdoor pool, and a smaller hot pool. Hermosa, an old stage and railroad stop, sits just north of Trimble. The town, settled in 1873 as a ranching center for the Animas Valley, now serves as a Durango bedroom community. The highway continues north, skirting the valley's steep wall, and reaches another historic site near the valley head. Baker's Bridge, designated by a state historical society bronze marker, crossed the Animas River here. Charles Baker and several men prospected through the San Juans in 1860, and, after working their way down from Baker's Park at today's Silverton, resolved to spend the winter in the northern Animas Valley. The party laid out a townsite, built rustic log cabins, and suffered through the cold winter. With news of the Civil War, they abandoned the site and returned East. Baker fought in the Confederate Army before Indians killed him while prospecting in 1868.

The flat valley abruptly ends, replaced by forested hills. The Animas River takes leave of the valley and bends northeast into a steep, cliffed gorge. The Million Dollar Highway also leaves the valley, bumping across the narrow gauge railroad tracks and climbing onto wooded slopes below the Hermosa Cliffs. A pullout sits just past the tracks and makes a good stop to watch the train pass by. A side road, La Plata County 75, drops east to a secluded glen and the remains of the old town Rockwood. This town served as the jumping-off point for miners and freighters heading north to Silverton and Rico. An old wagon toll road, now a National Historic Landmark, twisted north from here, with one branch following today's highway up to Purgatory and over Scotch Creek Pass to Rico and the other branch to Silverton.

The highway runs north below the cliffed escarpment and enters San Juan

National Forest. Dense scrub oak thickets line the asphalt and beyond tower ponderosa pines and Douglas-firs. Tamarron, a year-round resort, offers golf on a stunning eighteen-hole course, tennis, swimming, and night skiing on a beginner hill. The road swings past Haviland Lake, a small lake tucked below in thick forest. Haviland Lake Campground, with forty-five sites, sits on its east shore. Three-mile-long Electra Lake, created for electric power, lies to the north. The highway sweeps across a high bench through dense aspen groves. Engineer Mountain, its talus flanks broken by cliff bands, looms to the north and the West Needle Mountains rise roughly to the northeast. Castle Rock, a castellated promontory, juts from the Hermosa Cliffs at twenty-five miles. The road becomes four-lane and reaches Purgatory Ski Area. This popular destination ski resort boasts over three hundred inches of dry powder and thirty-five miles of runs spread over 630 acres. Fifteen miles of groomed cross-country ski trails thread the surrounding woodlands. Purgatory Campground, with fourteen sites, sits just east of the drive.

The highway drops back to two-lanes, crosses Cascade Creek below 12,968-foot Engineer Mountain, and begins steeply ascending above Mill Creek. The blacktop switchbacks through a spruce forest sprinkled with aspen. Potato Hill rises to the east and beyond towers 13,158-foot Twilight Peak in the West Needle Mountains, its rocky flanks chiseled by glaciers into deep cirques, sharp aretes, and flying buttresses. After eight miles the highway emerges on Coal Bank Summit, a 10,640-foot saddle between Engineer Mountain and Potato Hill. The pass name is a misnomer; the apparent coal seams are actually thin shale layers.

The drive winds down from the summit, crosses Deer Creek, and swings up aspen-covered slopes. Most of the rolling country adjoining the highway was consumed in a 26,000-acre forest fire in 1879. Civic groups later replanted much of the Lime Creek Burn. After bending over West Lime Creek, the highway turns east and climbs alongside East Lime Creek. The creek trickles in a shallow valley, with aspens coating the warm south-facing slopes and dense spruce woods blanketing the cooler north-facing hillsides. East Lime Creek Rest Site sits on the east side of the highway. Park here to hike south to Andrews Lake, a popular trout lake. The road continues up East Lime Creek and a mile and a half later reaches 10,910-foot Molas Pass.

Molas Pass yields one of Colorado's most stunning mountain panoramas. Sharp peaks spike the horizon in a wide circle from the summit. The Needle and Grenadier mountains tower to the east, their ragged flanks are strewn with glacier-carved buttresses and cirques, and their pointed summits rip passing clouds. The Animas River gorge, an abrupt forested chasm, hides between the pass and the peaks. Molas Lake, its placid waters reflecting the sky, tucks into a hollow on a broad bench above the canyon. Spruce forest and open willow meadows surround the lake. Snowdon Peak, the 13,077-foot northern outpost of the West Needle Range, looms to the south. Rounded ridges, green with above-timberline tundra grass and broken by rocky crags on the skyline, stairstep up west from the pass. Molas Lake, owned by Silverton and operated by a private concessionaire, offers camping, picnick-

Victorian storefronts line Silverton's main street on the Million Dollar Highway.

ing, and fishing. Good day hikes are found on the Colorado Trail at Molas Pass.

The highway descends sharply for five miles from Molas Lake to Silverton, clinging to steep mountainsides above the Animas River. Thick spruce forest hems in the road, with open slopes offering glimpses north into broad Baker's Park. Finally the road makes a couple hairpin turns, reaches the valley floor, and bends west up Mineral Creek. A right turn here leads to the picturesque mining camp of Silverton. A visitor center, housed in an ornate building, sits on the south edge of town.

Silverton, at an elevation of 9,320 feet, stretches along the Animas River in Baker's Park, a flat two thousand-acre glacial valley encircled by a wall of mountains. Winter blankets the town, one of Colorado's most isolated settlements, with over three hundred inches of annual snowfall. Before modern snow-removal equipment, Silverton was often cut off from the outside world for weeks at a time; even now the Million Dollar Highway shuts down for a few days each winter. The town is undeniably a tough place to live—the year-round average temperature is a mere 35.6 degrees and summer's frost-free growing season may be as short as twelve days. Towering peaks ring Baker's Park, with 13,370-foot Sultan Mountain to the south, 13,068-foot Kendall Mountain on the east, and 13,487-foot Storm Peak to the north.

These mountains, fringed with forest, capped by snow, and filled with mineral riches, attracted the remote valley's first visitors in 1860. Charles Baker and six fellow prospectors trekked over Cinnamon Pass and wandered south down the Animas River to the broad park. These early miners panned the streams for the next couple years, but found little gold to hold their interest. Not until 1870 did miners find promising color and staked their claims on the steep mountainsides. The Little Giant Lode up Arrastra Creek was the first producing mine in the area. The San Juans, however, still remained under Ute Indian control. The Utes protested the miner incursions and federal troops were dispatched to keep the Anglos off Indian land. The Brunot Treaty in 1873, however, removed the Utes from the mountains and opened the San Juans for prospecting.

Miners flocked into the area and by 1873 over fifteen hundred mining claims were filed. Silverton, established in June, 1874, was deemed the county seat. The new town was dubbed Silverton after a miner remarked, "We may not have gold here, but we have silver by the ton." Wagon routes over Stony and Cinnamon passes connected Silverton to the outside world until July 8, 1882, when the Denver & Rio Grande Railroad completed its narrow gauge track from Durango to Silverton. The town boomed through the 1880s with millions of dollars worth of gold and silver mined from the hills, but the 1893 silver crash slowed the growth. At its peak Silverton boasted over thirty mills, two smelters, thirty-seven saloons, and numerous card houses, opium dens, and "pleasure palaces" on its infamous Blair Street.

Silverton today is a quaint village that wears its colorful history well. Most of the town, preserved as a National Historic District, still reflects the mining heyday of a century ago. It appears at first glance like a movie set with false-fronted buildings, opulent Victorian homes, the gold-domed county courthouse, the 1903 brick jail that houses the San Juan County Historical Society Museum, and rustic miners' cabins. The town is also the northern terminus of the Durango & Silverton Narrow Gauge Railroad, the last vestige of Silverton's railway glories. Several hotels dot the town, including the landmark Grand Imperial Hotel. Hillside Cemetery, perched northeast of town, makes an interesting stop. Many of the graves are of miners, snuffed out in their twenties and thirties. Markers reading "Killed in Mine Accident" testify to the underground dangers.

The drive bends west from Silverton on US 550 and heads up Mineral Creek Valley. The North Star Mine and Mill, surrounded by quaking aspens, sits across the creek just west of town. Forest Road 585 turns off the highway and heads west up Mineral Creek's South Fork in a broad, glaciated valley for five miles to twenty-three-site South Mineral Campground. This 9,800-foot campground makes a good base camp for exploring the surrounding high peaks and basins. Ice Lake Basin, three miles to the west, sits amid sheer cliffed peaks including 13,894-foot Vermillion Peak and 13,738-foot Pilot Knob. The highway scales the valley's gentle north flank through mixed aspen and spruce forest and after a couple miles swerves into a valley carved by glaciers and the Middle Fork of Mineral Creek. Numerous avalanche chutes slice through the forest on the steep valley sides.

The Ophir Pass Road, beginning about five miles west of Silverton, takes off from US 550, crosses Burro Bridge, and climbs steeply for four miles to the 11,750-foot summit. The track, one of the area's easier four-wheel-drive routes, continues down the old stage and wagon road six miles to Ophir and

Colorado Highway 145. The drive heads up the valley to the foot of Red Mountain Pass and the old 1883 townsite of Chattanooga. While almost nothing remains now, the town once housed three hundred residents and seventy-five buildings. A fire and disastrous snow slides wreaked the town. Reverend J. Gibbons noted in 1898 that "the ruins of roofs and houses were strewn for half a mile over the valley and the population of this once-flourishing hamlet dwindled down to two."

The highway, traversing the old Silverton Railway's right-of-way, turns west onto the Chattanooga Loop and begins the final three-mile ascent to the summit of Red Mountain Pass. The blacktop, with no guardrail, edges shelf-like along precipitous slopes. Look down the valley for great views of Bear Mountain. Note the forest shape on its flank that appears to be a giant bear licking a honeycomb. The highway bends into a steep gorge, passes the remains of the Silver Ledge Mine, and climbs atop 11,018-foot Red Mountain Pass. Abandoned buildings of the Longfellow Mine and a small, willow-lined tarn sit on the summit. The dangerous, one-way Black Bear Road climbs west from here to Ingram Pass and down to Telluride.

The Million Dollar Highway between Silverton and Ouray follows an old toll road that was started in 1880 and finished in 1884 by road builder and transportation magnate Otto Mears. The road operated as a mail, stage, and freight line until Mears opened his Rainbow Route railway from Silverton to the rich mines at the summit of Red Mountain Pass. The Million Dollar Highway, traversing the old rail and wagon route, was completed in 1924. The road section from Ouray to Red Mountain Pass cost about a million dollars to build, which gave the highway its name.

The highway plunges down from the pass summit twelve miles to Ouray. The first section, a maze of switchbacks and hairpin turns, twists down steep slopes to Ironton Park. Just north of the summit the highway passes the mostly abandoned Idarado Mine, one of this century's largest producers. The mine, nicknamed "Treasury Tunnel," yielded gold, silver, copper, lead, and zinc. Its tunnels bore through the mountains to the Smuggler Mine above Telluride. The surrounding mineralized peaks, including Red Mountain on the east, are tinted yellow and orange with iron oxides, and pockmarked by old mines, weathered buildings, and ore dumps. Several towns once scattered across the slopes here including Red Mountain and Guston. Millions of dollars worth of gold and silver streamed from the area mines. Wealthy producers were the Guston, Yankee Girl, and Robinson mines.

Red Mountain Creek meanders through broad Ironton Park. Aspens blanket the mountainsides above, creating a stunning display of color in late September. The old mining town of Ironton sat near the valley head. After a couple miles the highway leaves the valley and drops into the Uncompahgre Gorge, a deep canyon sliced by the Uncompahgre River. The gorge is simply spectacular. The road angles across steeply tilted cliffs of quartzite, slate, and schist, and scree slopes. Three crosses and a roadside memorial honor Reverend Marvin Hudson and his daughters Amelia and Pauline, and snowplow drivers Terry Kishbaugh and Bob Miller. The deadly Riverside Slide, an avalanche chute now covered with a snowshed, killed the six in

The Million Dollar Highway climbs past mine ruins and tailings to the summit of Red Mountain Pass.

separate winter accidents. The Hudsons died in 1963 after stopping to put on tire chains.

The highway edges north and passes Forest Road 878, the start of the four-wheel-drive Alpine Loop Back Country Byway. Further north the road, clinging to cliffs, crosses Bear Creek Falls. The creek cascades 227 feet down to the river below. The tollgate for Otto Mears' road sat at this narrow site so wagon trains couldn't avoid paying the $3.75 toll for a vehicle with two animals. A nearby monument remembers Mears and his contribution to Colorado history. The drive runs through a short tunnel and emerges at Lookout Point above Ouray. A vast amphitheater of cliffs, formed by volcanic San Juan Tuff, soars above the town to lofty peaks and sharp ridges. Amphitheater Campground, with thirty-three sites, is reached from a side-road past the viewpoint. The highway snakes down into Ouray.

Mountains dominate Ouray. The town, named for a famed Ute chief, sits cupped in a deep canyon. Three waterfalls thunder within shouting distance of Ouray and five creeks dash through town to the Uncompahgre River. Box Canyon, on the southwest edge, is most impressive with Canyon Creek roaring through a narrow gorge. Geothermal hot springs dot the Ouray, filling pools and bathhouses. The springs, named *Uncompahgre* or hot water springs by the Utes, still attracts visitors to Ouray.

Ouray began with rich gold and silver strikes in late 1875. The following year the town was surveyed and quickly boomed. The first building was supposedly a saloon, but by the end of 1876 a school, 214 cabins, two hotels, and a post office also lined the streets. The 1893 silver crash brought Ouray to its financial knees, but Tom Walsh's Camp Bird Mine in Yankee Boy Basin west of town brought new prosperity in 1895. The fabulous lode yielded over twenty million dollars in gold before Walsh sold the mine in 1902 to an English consortium. Through the twentieth century Ouray relied on an economy based on continued mining and tourism.

Now Ouray makes a fabulous base camp to explore what locals call the "Switzerland of America." A legacy of old mining roads lace the mountains and canyons, making Ouray the jeep capitol of America. Some of the best roads are the Corkscrew Road, Poughkeepsie Gulch, Engineer Pass, Yankee Boy Basin, and Imogene Pass. Jeep rentals are available in town. Numerous trails also thread the backcountry, climbing to waterfalls, alpine basins, and sheer peaks. The Ouray Hot Springs Pool, on the north end of town, gives a relaxing soak at day's end. The town, a National Historic District, offers neat streets lined with restored Victorian homes, brick buildings, the haunted Beaumont Hotel, the Ouray County Historical Museum, and a designated walking tour.

The drive's last ten miles connect Ouray to Ridgway, an old railroad hub. The highway runs through a narrow gap lined with towering sandstone walls and takes leave of the San Juan Mountains. The broad glacier-carved valley ahead, flanked by forested slopes, is lush with green pastures, grazing cattle, and immense narrow-leaf cottonwoods. Herds of elk and deer graze in roadside meadows, particularly from late fall to spring. The drive yields great vistas of the ragged Sneffels Range to the west, low-browed Grand Mesa to the north, and Chimney and Courthouse peaks on the east. The drive ends in Ridgway at the intersection of US 550 and Colorado Highway 62. Turn west on CO 62 for the Lizard Head Pass and Unaweep/Tabeguache scenic drives. Montrose lies twenty-six miles north on US 550.

General description: This 110-mile scenic route traverses spectacular 10,222-foot Lizard Head Pass and the Dolores River Valley in the San Juan Mountains between Ridgway and Cortez.

Special attractions: Dallas Divide, Telluride, Telluride Ski Area, Lizard Head Pass, Lizard Head Wilderness Area, Ophir, Dolores River Canyon, Galloping Goose, Escalante Ruins and Anasazi Heritage Center, McPhee Reservoir, camping, hiking, rock climbing, mountaineering, backpacking, four-wheel-drive roads, fishing.

Location: Southwest Colorado. The drive runs west from Ridgway and U.S. Highway 550 to Placerville, south to Telluride, then west over Lizard Head Pass to Dolores and Cortez.

Drive route numbers: Colorado highways 62 and 145.

Travel season: Year-round. Winter conditions can be hazardous. Carry chains, a shovel, and extra clothes.

Camping: Several national forest campgrounds scatter along the drive.

Services: All services are in Ridgway, Telluride, Dolores, and Cortez. Limited services are found in Placerville, Sawpit, and Rico.

Nearby attractions: Million Dollar Highway, Ouray, Silverton, Yankee Boy Basin, Mount Sneffels Wilderness Area, Black Canyon of the Gunnison National Monument, Alpine Loop Back Country Byway, Owl Creek Pass, Unaweep-Tabeguache Scenic Byway, Norwood, Mesa Verde National Park, Hovenweep National Monument, Four Corners, Ute Mountain Indian Reservation and Ute Tribal Park, Durango and Silverton Narrow Gauge Railroad.

For more information: San Juan National Forest, 701 Camino del Rio, Suite 301, Durango, CO 81301, (970) 247-4874. Uncompahgre National Forest, 2250 Hwy. 50, Delta, CO 81406, (970) 874-7691. Telluride Chamber Resort Assn., P.O. Box 653, Telluride, CO 81435, (970) 728-3041. Cortez Chamber of Commerce, P.O. Box 968, Cortez, CO 81321, (970) 565-3414.

The drive: The 110-mile Lizard Head Pass scenic drive, following CO 62 and 145, skirts the majestic Sneffels Range at Dallas Divide, passes the picturesque mining town of Telluride, climbs over Lizard Head Pass, and follows the Dolores River valley to Dolores and Cortez. The drive, one of Colorado's best scenic routes, traverses the rugged San Juan Mountains and the eastern edge of the Colorado Plateau. The San Juans, named by early Spanish explorers, is a huge, confused collection of smaller ranges that drapes across most of southwestern Colorado south of the Gunnison River. The drive winds by three of the sub-ranges—the Sneffels, Rico, and San Miguel ranges.

COLORADO

•Denver

To Montrose

UNCOMPAHGRE
NATL. FOREST

RIDGWAY
STATE PARK

550

Ridgway

To Norwood

Dallas Divide
8,970 ft.

To Ouray

62

UNCOMPAHGRE
NATL. FOREST

San

Miguel

145

Mt. Sneffels
14,150 ft.

Hayden Pk.

Placerville

MT. SNEFFELS
WILDERNESS
AREA

Dallas Pk.

Sawpit

River

145

Telluride

UNCOMPAHGRE
NATL. FOREST

Sunshine CG

Palmyra Pk.

Wilson Pk.
El Diente Pk.

Ophir

Matterhorn CG

Lizard Head Pass

LIZARD HEAD
WILDERNESS
AREA

Cayton
CG

Vermillion
Pk. 13,894 ft.

Sheep
Mtn.
13,188 ft.

Burro
Bridge
CG

Flattop
Mtn.

SAN

535

Eagle Pk.
12,113 ft.

Rico

West Dolores CG

Blackhawk Mtn.
12,681 ft.

JUAN

Mavreeso CG

Stoner

145

River

NATIONAL

Dolores

McPhee
Reservoir

FOREST

Escalante
Ruins

To Dove
Creek

145

Dolores

N

666

MONTEZUMA VALLEY

To Durango

160

160

Cortez

To
Shiprock,
NM

MESA VERDE
NATIONAL
PARK

0   5   10
Miles

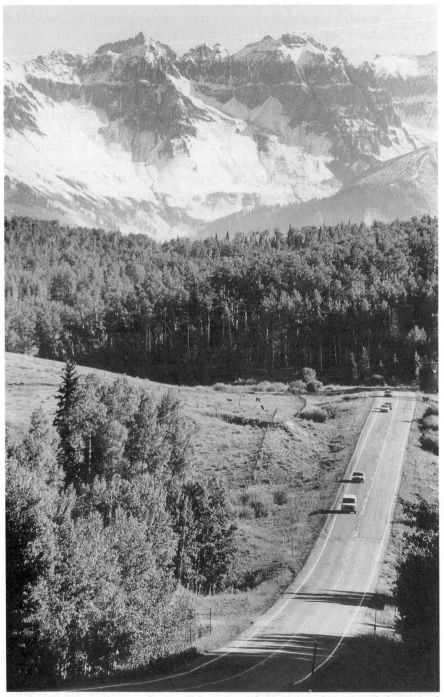

Fresh autumn snow caps the Sneffels Range above aspen forests and the Lizard Head Pass Scenic Drive.

The San Juans formed some 35 million years ago when immense volcanic eruptions spewed some eight thousand cubic miles of lava and thousands of feet of ash over the region. Precious minerals, including gold, silver, lead, copper, and zinc percolated in underground fissures in volcanic calderas. At today's prices the San Juans yielded billions of dollars in riches, and prospectors believe still more lies buried beneath the mountain flanks in the region's fifty mining districts. Periodic glaciation sculpted the mountains with precipitous gorges, broad valleys, and serrated peaks and ridges over the last two million years. The range boasts ten peaks that top 14,000 feet, including Mount Sneffels, Wilson Peak, Mount Wilson, and El Diente Peak along the drive, and is the headwaters of numerous rivers. The drive begins along the Uncompahgre River and follows the San Miguel and Dolores rivers.

The drive, with elevations ranging from 6,200 feet at Cortez to 10,222 feet on Lizard Head Pass, encompasses a diversity of weather. Summer and autumn are the best times to travel the highway. Expect variable summer weather, with highs ranging from ninety degrees at Cortez to the sixties and seventies in the higher mountains. Afternoon thunderstorms can be locally heavy. Autumn days are generally clear and warm, although periods of rain and even snow in the high country occurs through mid-October. Winter sets in by late October atop the pass and the land becomes covered with deep snow. Short winter days are cold with frequent snowfall. The snowpack begins melting off in April, although large drifts remain into early summer at the high elevations. Remnants of the area's once large glaciers, cling to Mount Wilson north of Lizard Head Pass year-round. May is lovely along the drive, with fresh grass covering the ranch land below Mount Sneffels and the myriad aspen forests beginning to leaf out in the Dolores River valley.

The drive begins in Ridgway at the intersection of US 550, twenty-six miles south of Montrose, and CO 62. US 550, the Million Dollar Highway, continues south through Ouray and over Red Mountain Pass to Silverton. Ridgway, at an elevation of 7,003 feet, straddles the Uncompahgre River in its broad, grassy valley. Uncompahgre, meaning "hot water spring," is a Ute word applied to the valley's hot springs frequented by the Indians. Ridgway got its start as a railroad junction and transportation hub in 1890 by road builder Otto Mears and his Rio Grande Southern Railroad. The railroad, which ran 172 miles from Ridgway to Durango via Dolores, linked the isolated mines at Telluride, Ophir, and Rico with the Denver and Rio Grande Railroad's main line in Montrose. The town, earlier known as Dallasville, was renamed by the railroaders for R.M. Ridgway, the superintendent of the Denver and Rio Grande's mountain division. During its heyday the town boasted a huge railroad yard, stockyards, the fifty-five room Mentone Hotel, and a depot that still stands. Today Ridgway thrives as a crossroads for travelers as well as local ranchers. The town serves as a gateway to the San Juan Mountains to the south and 3,260-acre Ridgway State Park four miles to the north. The park by Ridgway Reservoir offers fishing, boating, hiking, and a 187-site campground.

The scenic drive begins in Ridgway and follows CO 62 westward. The road crosses the river and passes through the town. A large city park, with tables

Mt. Sneffels and the rugged Sneffels Range lift above grazing cattle and pastures along the Lizard Head Pass Scenic Drive.

shaded by tall cottonwoods, makes a good picnic site. The highway bends north out of Ridgway, climbing a scrubby slope of gray shale into Dallas Creek's broad, lush valley, aptly named Pleasant Valley. Bales of fresh hay, drying in the autumn sun, and cattle scatter across green, fenced paddocks. Loghill Mesa walls in the valley on the north, while Miller Mesa hems it in on the south. Round Top, a shale knob, guards the valley's eastern entrance north of the highway. The drive rushes southwest past neat ranch homes, crosses cottonwood-lined Dallas Creek, and stumbles onto a magnificent panorama. Mount Sneffels and a long ridge of ragged peaks pierce the southern horizon, forming one of Colorado's most scenic mountain escarpments.

Pastoral ranch land, mostly part of fashion designer Ralph Lauren's Double RL Ranch, spreads across Dallas Creek's broad valley south of the highway. Humped ridges, thick with scrub oak and aspen, climb to spruce-coated hills, rounded by ancient glaciers, along the foot of the Sneffels Range. Above, the mountain wall is marked by sheer cliffs, snow fields tucked under north walls, abrupt gullies of ice, sharp summits, and aiguille-studded ridges. A series of high peaks—13,686-foot Cirque Mountain, 13,786-foot Potosi Peak, and 13,819-foot Teakettle Mountain—sit east of Mount Sneffels, an imposing 14,150-foot peak barricaded by immense cliffs. The long ridge to the west is topped by 13,809-foot Dallas Peak, 13,496-foot Mears Peak, and anchored on the west by pointed 12,987-foot Hayden Peak. The Sneffels

Range, protected in the 16,200-acre Mount Sneffels Wilderness Area, is mostly composed of volcanic rocks. Mount Sneffels was named in 1874 by the Hayden Survey for a mountain in Jules Verne's novel *Journey to the Center of the Earth*. Dallas Peak was designated for former U.S. Vice President George Dallas, Mears Peak commemorates road and railroad builder Otto Mears, while Hayden Peak honors Ferdinand Hayden. Hayden's indefatigable survey team, including pioneer photographer William Henry Jackson and painter Thomas Moran, intensively studied western Colorado from 1873 through 1876. The survey climbed, measured, and named the major mountains and ranges; followed the rivers and traversed the high passes; and gathered data on climate, plants, animals, and future mining and agricultural possibilities. The East Dallas and West Dallas roads head south from the drive to high valleys below the range crest.

Past the Double RL Ranch, the highway ascends the broad flank of a plateau, gaining 1,500 feet in four miles to the 8,970-foot summit of Dallas Divide. Scenic mountain scenes unfold as the road climbs. A couple overlooks, one just below the top, and the other at the summit yield great views of the mountainous wall to the south. Eastward towers Uncompahgre and Wetterhorn peaks (both over 14,000 feet) and blocky Chimney Peak and Courthouse Mountain. The divide's summit, surrounded by aspen-covered hills, was the site of a railroad station, post office, and stock-loading chutes. The dense aspen forests atop Dallas Divide are spectacular in late September when their gold flush brightens the hillsides.

The highway runs west from the summit down a shallow draw. Stands of aspen flutter on rolling hills among open meadows of sagebrush and grass. Low willows huddle along Leopard Creek's roadside trickle. The Last Dollar Road, a rough dirt track connecting Dallas Divide and Telluride, heads south across Hastings Mesa a mile west of the divide summit. The highway, following the old rail bed, begins dropping down Leopard Canyon toward the San Miguel River. The canyon deepens as it descends. The rim looms high overhead and sandstone cliff bands stairstep upward. Dense fir and spruce forest, liberally sprinkled with aspen, march up the shady south slope, while the drier north slope harbors ponderosa pine and scrub oak. The remains of a carnotite claim, the Omega Mine, perch on the south slope above the highway near the canyon mouth. The drive reaches the junction of CO 62 and 145 at Placerville in the San Miguel River canyon twenty-four miles from Ridgway. Turn south on CO 145 toward Telluride.

Placerville, at 7,321 feet, spreads along the highway on the narrow floor of the San Miguel River canyon. Although its origins are uncertain, the town sprang up sometime in the 1870s after prospectors discovered color in gravel deposits along the river floodplain. By 1878 a post office was established and large placer operations lent the name Placerville to the new community. In autumn of 1890, about the time the placer deposits played out, the Rio Grande Southern Railway reached Placerville. The town formed a good railroad junction, with the main line steaming up-river to Telluride, and another line heading down-canyon to other towns. Placerville quickly became a major shipping center for thousands of cattle in western Colorado.

Even as late as 1949, over one thousand carloads of sheep embarked to market from here.

The drive heads south through Placerville on CO 145 and up the canyon. The San Miguel River, beginning in the mountains above Telluride, riffles over cobbles and worn boulders below the highway. Tall narrow-leaf cottonwoods and thick willows line its banks. The river, a favorite of fly fishers and kayakers, offers excellent trout fishing. Red sandstone layers form cliffs bands on the steep canyon walls. The road, following the old railroad grade, winds through a series of small towns that once served as mining centers and railroad stops. At Fall Creek the Fall Creek Road climbs south to Woods Lake, a pretty lake nestled in a high cirque below Dolores Peak. The town of Sawpit boomed as an 1890s mining town after the wealthy Champion Belle Mine yielded $1,800 in silver with its first three carloads. The mill foundations are all that remain of Vanadium, another mining town that dug and milled vanadium, an alloy used in hardening steel. Uranium, used in World War II, was also extracted here. The Silver Pick Road, at Vanadium, heads south up Big Bear Creek to Silver Pick Basin, the base camp for climbers that scale the three fourteeners—Wilson Peak, Mount Wilson, and El Diente Peak—in the San Miguel Range.

The road begins climbing Keystone Hill ten miles from Placerville. The South Fork Road, leading to Ilium and Ames, turns south from the drive up the San Miguel's South Fork just after the ascent begins. The shelf-like highway clings to the steep mountainside under a palisade of sandstone bluffs. Good views of Sunshine Peak and the South Fork valley lie south of the highway. After three miles the drive emerges in a flat-bottomed glaciated valley ringed by towering mountains. Telluride, a picturesque ski community, straddles the box valley's eastern head. The scenic drive crosses the valley mouth, but a highway spur leads three miles to Telluride.

Telluride boasts perhaps the most spectacular setting of any American town. Mountains rise almost a vertical mile out of Telluride's pastoral valley. Cliffs bands, seamed by frothy waterfalls, punctuate the mountain flanks and spruce and fir forests, broken by glades of quaking aspen, spill down the steep slopes. Snowfields whiten the upper alpine cirques and rocky ridges and aretes form bold outlines against the azure sky. This town is a place to savor, to stop and stretch, and gaze in awe at nature's stunning artistry. It's also, despite its contrary intentions, a resort town that offers some of North America's most magnificent skiing terrain.

The town, like most San Juan communities, began as a support center for local mines. Gold was first discovered here in 1875 and the following year J.B. Ingram located the fabulously wealthy Smuggler Mine. The strike produced eighteen ounces of gold and eight hundred ounces of silver per ton. The town, established in 1878, was named for tellurium, a rare element found in association with gold and silver. Colorful locals, however, said the name derived from "To hell you ride," a reference to the town's winter isolation and rowdy reputation. Telluride thrived on its earth riches, eventually yielding almost $400 million from its mines including the Black Bear, Liberty Bell, Cimarron, Japan, Champion, and Snow Drift mines. Almost three hundred miles of tunnels puncture the surrounding mountains. With the 1890 arrival of the railroad, Telluride boomed and reached a population of five thousand. All the excitement also brought ruffians and outlaws. On June 24, 1889 a small-time robber and two of his gang helped themselves to $10,000 at the San Miguel Valley Bank and fled north to Brown's Park near Wyoming. Butch Cassidy had pulled his first hold-up and set off down history's path of infamy. The 1893 silver panic closed Telluride's silver mines and almost bankrupted the new railway. Valuable gold strikes brought new prosperity to Telluride in the late 1890s and with them came trouble between new unions and mine owners.

Telluride, proclaimed a national historic district in 1961, preserves its rich past. The New Sheridan Hotel, built in 1895, still beds visitors and next door stands the two hundred-seat Sheridan Opera House, now a movie theater. The town, despite soaring land prices and encroaching condo developments, maintains a Victorian charm and is trying to avoid becoming another Aspen or Vail. A parade of festivals brings visitors to Telluride, including the premier Telluride Bluegrass Festival in June and September's renowned film festival. The town makes a super base camp for backcountry explorers. Nearby Imogene and dangerous Black Bear passes beckon four-wheelers; numerous hiking trails lace the canyons and climb the mountains; and Telluride Ski Area, with over three thousand feet of vertical drop, offers the expert skier superb bump runs that include the infamous "Plunge." The southern backside hides good beginner and intermediate runs.

The drive crosses the valley mouth west of Telluride and swings up a mountain flank. The highway quickly reaches a rolling bench high above the San Miguel River's South Fork valley. A turn leads to Telluride Ski Area. The road rolls across this high plateau over open grasslands and through thick aspen groves. Marvelous views unfold from every road bend. Wilson Peak, a sharp 14,017-foot mountain, and 12,930-foot Sunshine Mountain tower to the southwest, while lofty peaks loom across the northern and eastern skylines. The Ophir Needles lift a ridge of pinnacles and buttresses above the asphalt. Past Cushman Lake and fifteen-site Sunshine Campground, a side-road climbs to the ghost town of Alta and Alta Lakes. Past the turn the highway steeply drops toward the narrow canyon mouth of the Howard Fork and Ophir.

Ophir started as an 1870s silver camp and flourished as a railroad stop in the 1890s. One of the first roads to Telluride came over 11,750-foot Ophir Pass from Silverton, and today makes a relatively easy, but scenic, four-wheel tour. The one-way track begins on Red Mountain Pass on US 550. Old Ophir, a collection of rustic cabins, sits just east of the drive in a U-shaped hanging valley. The railroad's famed Ophir Loop traversed the canyon entrance where today's highway runs. The great loop spiraled up on wooden trestles to gain elevation to put the train into the upper valley below the final pull up Lizard Head Pass.

Past Ophir, the highway edges above the South Fork valley and bends into a broad, glaciated basin. Matterhorn Campground, with twenty-four sites, sits just off the highway. The basin, floored by the San Miguel's Lake Fork,

The ragged escarpment of the Sneffels Range looms over autumn aspen woodlands on the Lizard Head Pass Scenic Drive.

is surrounded by alpine peaks. After crossing the river the drive begins climbing slopes north of the basin. Trout Lake huddles in the valley below at 9,714 feet. The road steadily ascends through spruce forest, wide meadows, and willow thickets to the summit of 10,222-foot Lizard Head Pass and the drive high point. A small picnic area, parking lot, and overlook lies on the summit. Several interpretative displays explain the area's history, geology, and natural history. The old Rio Grande Southern Railway climbed over the pass here, its bed sitting south of the highway in the broad meadow. The railroad, built by Otto Mears for $9 million, ran from Ridgway to Durango from 1890 until 1951. Indians used the pass for seven thousand years before that. The first known white men in the area were sixty St. Louis Fur Company trappers who spent a summer trapping beaver around Trout Lake in 1833.

The pass is named for Lizard Head, a sharp 13,113-foot tower with a reputation as Colorado's most-difficult-to-reach mountain summit. The crumbling four hundred-foot-high volcanic peak, offering intrepid climbers a three-pitch 5.7 route, was first ascended by pioneer climbers Albert Ellingwood and Barton Hoag in 1920. It was probably the most difficult rock climb in America at the time. Lizard Head sits, along with neighboring 14,017-foot Wilson Peak, 14,246-foot Mount Wilson, and 14,159-foot El Diente Peak, in the 41,496-acre Lizard Head Wilderness Area north of the highway. The wilderness can be accessed via the Lizard Head Trail at the pass summit. Sheep Mountain, a sharp 13,188-foot peak, looms south of the drive. Silverton sits a mere nine miles from the pass over Vermillion Peak to the east.

The highway heads west from the broad pass summit, gently descending along shallow Snow Spur Creek. As the road and creek drop, the valley narrows into a short, steep canyon. The Rico Mountains stud the western horizon and Mount Wilson and Lizard Head lift above rounded, spruce-covered ridges to the north. After a couple miles the drive reaches the Dolores River in a glaciated valley. Beaver ponds block the twisting river. Thick spruce forest blankets the southern hillsides while aspen groves broken by wide meadows coat the steep northern slopes. Cayton Campground, with twenty-seven units, lines the riverbank a couple miles down. Forest Road 535 climbs out of the valley here and leads to Dunton and the West Dolores River. As the highway drops down the river valley, it passes through a succession of tilted sandstone formations, including Dakota and Entrada sandstones and Triassic and Permian redbeds deposited on floodplains over 200 million years ago.

After almost ten miles the valley squeezes into a canyon. Beyond the drive passes a San Juan National Forest Information Station, crosses the Dolores River, and enters the old mining town of Rico. This charming town, at 8,827 feet, spreads along a hillside above the river. The road is lined with old stone and brick buildings and Victorian homes. Gold was discovered here as early as 1866, but Ute Indians drove away the intruding prospectors. Mining, however, began in earnest after the Utes ceded the San Juans in 1873. Rico, Spanish for "rich," boomed with silver after 1879. Later mines extracted lead, zinc, and gold from the area's volcanic rocks.

The highway follows the Dolores River for the next thirty-seven miles to the town of Dolores. The river meanders across a broad valley, riffling over cobbles and placidly flowing between banks lined with willows and narrow-leafed cottonwoods. As the road heads west, the canyon widens and its slopes step back to rocky rims. Bands of sandstone cliffs, first a wave of salmon-colored Entrada Sandstone and then blocky Dakota Sandstone, form abrupt canyon sides. The climate dries as the river and highway run west, with scrub oak and ponderosa pine covering the lower canyon slopes. Stoner sits at the confluence of the Dolores and West Dolores rivers part-way down the canyon.

The 230-mile-long Dolores River originates south of Lizard Head Pass, runs southwest to Dolores, pools in McPhee Reservoir, and twists through spectacular sandstone canyons before emptying in the Colorado River above Moab, Utah. The river's name, given by seventeenth century Spanish explorers, was shortened from the original *El Rio de Nuestra Senora de los Dolores* or "The River of Our Lady of Sorrows" to simply the Dolores River. Franciscan padres Silvestre Escalante and Atanasio Dominguez crossed the Dolores River during their epic 1776 exploration of the American Southwest.

Dolores, a pleasant town spread across the shallow valley at 6,936 feet, sits just above McPhee Reservoir and the river's northward bend. McPhee Reservoir, formed by the only dam on the otherwise free-flowing Dolores River, supplies irrigation water to the nearby Montezuma Valley for crops including pinto beans among others. The 4,470-acre lake, Colorado's second largest when full, is stocked with rainbow trout, bass, bluegill, and crappie. Dolores, established in 1891 along the Rio Grande Southern Railroad, serves as the southwestern gateway to the San Juan Mountains. The Galloping

Goose, alongside the highway in Flanders Park in Dolores, makes an interesting stop. As rail traffic decreased on the railroad, train mechanics devised this ingenious gasoline-powered railcar to continue mail and passenger service. Seven of these silver "railroad buses," made by grafting automobile bodies to railcars, traversed the tracks between Ridgway and Durango from 1931 until the railroad closed down in 1952. The Goose, without breakdowns or snowslides, could travel the route's 175 miles in nine hours.

The drive climbs south out of the Dolores River canyon just past the town. A right turn on CO 184 leads to Escalante Ruin and the Anasazi Heritage Center. The Anasazi ruin, a twenty-five-room pueblo occupied from the late 1000s to about 1300, perches atop a bluff overlooking the Montezuma Valley. The site, excavated in the 1970s as part of the Dolores Archeological Project, is named for its discoverer Padre Escalante. He wrote in his 1776 journal, "upon an elevation of the river's south side, there was in ancient times a small settlement of the same type as those of the Indians of New Mexico." Dominguez Ruin sits nearby. The Anasazi Heritage Center, run by the BLM, houses artifacts from the ruin and interprets the Anasazi and their lifestyle.

The drive heads south for ten miles, running past small ranches and farms shaded by tall cottonwoods. It ends at the highway's junction with U.S. Highway 160 on the east side of Cortez. Mesa Verde stretches its high escarpment to the south. Its entrance and scenic drive begins ten miles east on US 160. Sleeping Ute Mountain hems in the broad Montezuma Valley on the west. Cortez, seat of Montezuma County, still thrives as an agricultural and ranching town, and offers all traveler amenities.

24 FLAT TOPS TRAIL
Meeker to Yampa

General description: The 82-mile-long Flat Tops Trail, a National Forest Scenic Byway, traverses the scenic upper White River valley and crosses Ripple Creek and Dunckley passes on the wild White River Plateau.

Special attractions: Meeker, White River, White River National Forest, Routt National Forest, Flat Tops Wilderness Area, Trappers Lake, Ripple Creek Pass, autumn colors, fly fishing, hiking, camping, backpacking, scenic views.

Location: Northwestern Colorado. The drive begins in Meeker 41 miles north of Interstate 70 and Rifle, and ends in Yampa 31 miles south of Steamboat Springs.

Drive route name and numbers: Flat Tops Trail Scenic Byway, Rio Blanco County 8, Routt National Forest Road 16, Routt County 17.

Travel season: Only the lower road section outside Meeker is open year-round, otherwise the drive closes after the first heavy snow and opens after the spring thaw. Check with the national forest office for road conditions and closures.

24   FLAT TOPS TRAIL

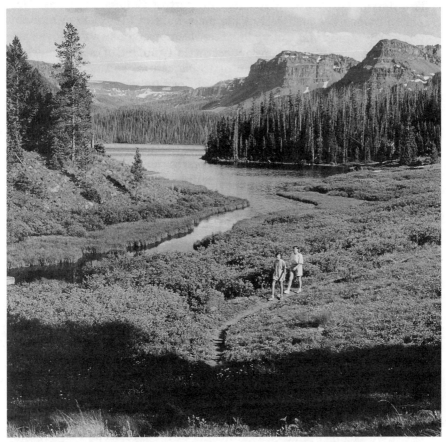

Hikers follow an arm of Trappers Lake on the edge of the Flat Tops Wilderness Area off the Flat Tops Trail drive.

Camping: Campgrounds along the drive are 39-site North Fork and 6-site Vaughn Lake. 11-site Himes Peak Campground sits on Forest Road 205 to Trappers Lake and 12-site Trapline, 10-site Bucks, 14-site Cutthroat, and 20-site Shepherds Rim campgrounds cluster near Trappers Lake. Other forest campgrounds lie on side roads off the drive.

Services: All services are found in Meeker and Yampa at either end of the drive. Limited services in Buford.

Nearby attractions: Rifle Falls State Park, Rifle Mountain Park, Grand Hogback, Stagecoach State Recreation Area, Steamboat Springs, Gore Pass, Finger Rock, Upper Yampa River, Craig, Dinosaur National Monument.

For more information: Blanco Ranger District, White River National Forest, 317 E. Market, Meeker, CO 81641, (970) 878-4039. Yampa Ranger District, Routt National Forest, 300 Roselawn, P.O. Box 7, Yampa, CO 80463, (970) 638-4516. Meeker Chamber of Commerce, 710 W. Market, P.O. Box 869, Meeker, CO 81641, (970) 878-5510.

The drive: The White River Plateau, part of Colorado's plateau geographic province lies just west of the main bulk of the Rocky Mountains between the Yampa and Colorado rivers. Deep canyons and valleys excavated by swift rivers and streams dissect this lofty upland of raised sandstone layers. Ancient lava flows top the plateau's central section, forming the magnificent Flat Tops Wilderness Area. The eighty-two-mile-long Flat Tops Trail scenic drive, beginning in Meeker west of the plateau, follows the White River's deep gash eastward almost to the heart of the Flat Tops before swerving northeast over Ripple Creek and Dunckley passes to the Yampa River's broad upper valley. The road crosses the ancestral homeland of the Ute Indians, the second oldest national forest in the United States, and some of Colorado's best aspen colors and most dramatic scenic views.

Temperatures along the drive, open spring through fall, vary according to elevation. Summer highs in the lowlands near Meeker climb into the low nineties, while four thousand feet higher atop the passes the temperatures range in the sixties or seventies. Expect chilly nights at the higher elevations, particularly near Trappers Lake, with lows dipping to the thirties and forties. Insect repellent checks ubiquitous mosquitoes along the drive's moist creeks, beaver ponds, and lakes. Expect thunderstorms almost every afternoon, some locally heavy. Drive carefully during and after rain—the gravel roads can be slippery. Side roads are often muddy. September and early October brings cool, crisp days with generally clear skies. The first snow falls on the higher mountains by late October and the road closes in early November until spring thaw. Check with the forest office in either Meeker or Yampa for road closing and opening dates. The drive's upper reaches accumulate as much as ten feet of snow, allowing excellent snowmobiling and cross-country skiing conditions.

The drive begins a mile east of Meeker at the intersection of Colorado Highway 13 and Rio Blanco County 8. Turn east on County 8. Meeker, a pleasant off-the-beaten-track town, nestles in the broad White River Valley. The fertile bottomlands along the river has long attracted settlers. The earliest residents were Ute Indians who camped among cottonwoods along the river and grazed their horses in the lush pastures. The Utes, Colorado's mountain tribe, ranged across the Rocky Mountains gathering edible plants and hunting plentiful game. Summer camps in the high mountains offered superb hunting, while winter camps were made in mild valleys. After gold was discovered in Colorado's high country in the 1860s, a collision between the Utes and incoming prospectors and settlers became inevitable. A series of treaties drove the Utes from their ancestral mountain homeland. An 1868 treaty ceded central Colorado from the San Luis Valley to North Park to incoming Anglo settlers. Western Colorado remained reserved for the Utes. Rich mineral discoveries in the San Juan Mountains, however, precipitated another pact and the Utes were relocated to southwestern and northwestern Colorado. Settlers still chafed that almost a third of Colorado remained in Ute hands and by 1876 the state legislature asked Congress to relocate the Utes to an Oklahoma reservation. In 1879 Colorado Governor Frederick Pitkin wrote that, "if this reservation could be extinguished, and the land thrown open to settlers, it will furnish homes to thousands of the people of our State who desire homes." The beginning of the end of Ute domination in western Colorado came near Meeker in 1879.

The green river bottom just west of Meeker, originally known as Powell Park for Major John Wesley Powell who explored here in 1868, was the site of the White River Indian Agency. The agency, established in 1869, had a succession of agents until Nathaniel C. Meeker came in 1878. Meeker, who established the town of Greeley as an agricultural utopia in the early 1870s, arrived with the idea of domesticating the Utes, changing them from a nomadic people to sedentary Christian agriculturists. Conflict became inevitable after Meeker forbid hunting, fishing, gambling, and the pursuit of other traditional activities. The Indians reached the boiling point after Meeker dug an irrigation trench across their racetrack and plowed under a prime winter horse pasture. On September 29, 1879, the Utes rebelled by killing Meeker and eleven white men at the agency, and taking Meeker's wife, daughter, and three others as captives. A military force led by Captain Thomas Thorburgh was also defeated by the Utes. After the hostages were released, a new agreement was signed in 1880 that pushed the White River Utes onto today's reservation in Utah. The Meeker Massacre site lies four miles west of Meeker on Colorado Highway 64.

Today Meeker, the 6,180-foot-high seat of Rio Blanco County, remains a real western town that serves as a supply center for area sheep and cattle ranches. The town, established in 1883, bills itself as the "Gateway to the Flat Tops." The town thrives on hunters who flock here in October and November and recreationists who come for the surrounding wilderness and spectacular mountain scenery. Meeker's White River Museum, housed in an original 1879 log cabin built by U.S. cavalry troops, offers displays of pioneer and Indian artifacts, and historical photos. Annual events include the fifty-five-mile-long Almost Meeker to Rangely Canoe Race in May and the July 4th Range Call Celebration, Colorado's oldest continuous rodeo since 1885.

The scenic drive heads east from Meeker along County 8 on the northern edge of broad Agency Park. The White River meanders gracefully across the grassy valley, past hay fields and grazing cattle. Low hills, coated with juniper and sagebrush, flank the flat-bottomed valley. After six miles the road passes eight thousand-acre Oak Ridge State Wildlife Area and the valley narrows into a canyon. The White River Agency Monument, marking the original agency site, sits alongside the road seven miles from Meeker. Meeker floated the buildings downstream to Powell Park in 1878, thinking it a better farming area. Ranches spread across the canyon floor, with thick stands of cotton-woods and willows lining the river bank. Spruce and fir darken the moist north-facing slopes above the river while juniper stud the dry south-facing hillsides. The drive passes Lake Avery State Wildlife Area at twenty miles. This large reservoir offers great fishing year-round, as well as camping and picnicking facilities. The drive enters 7,009-foot Buford a mile later. A store offers supplies and gasoline, the last services until Yampa. The New Castle/ Buford Road, Forest Road 244, begins here and twists south across the White River Plateau's western edge to New Castle on the Colorado River.

The drive continues northeast, following the north bank of the White River. Large aspen groves spill down the south canyon slopes and dense scrub oak thickets blanket the north hillside. The pavement ends at thirty-one miles and becomes gravel for the next forty-seven miles. White River National Forest, an immense two-million-acre slice of public land, borders the river above the road. The drive enters the forest eleven miles east of Buford and becomes Forest Road 8. North Fork Campground, with thirty-nine sites at 7,750 feet, spreads across grassy meadows among towering aspens a half-mile into the forest. The canyon narrows as the road runs east. After a few miles the road climbs away from the river up a shallow valley, swings across wooded slopes to Ripple Creek, and reaches a junction with FR 205 forty miles from Meeker.

FR 205 leads south above the placid North Fork of the White River eight miles to Trappers Lake Recreation Area, passing eleven-site Himes Peak Campground on the way. Trappers Lake, the headwaters of the White River, glistens like a shiny jewel cupped in a high basin surrounded by majestic flat-topped mountain peaks. Trappers Lake, sometimes called the "Cradle of Wilderness," figures prominently in the preservation of public lands as wilderness. The area was first protected by President Harrison in 1891 as the 1.2-million-acre White River Plateau Timberland Reserve, the nation's second national forest. In 1919 the USDA Forest Service decided to develop the recreational potential of Trappers Lake by building summer cabins, lodges, guest ranches, a loop road around the lake, and other civilized amenities. A young landscape architect, Arthur Carhart, was hired to study the plan. After viewing the scenic site, Carhart made the radical assertion that the area should be preserved as untrammeled wilderness and any development should be made at least a half-mile from the lake shore. The Forest Service, with Carhart's recommendation, dropped plans for the lakeside road and refused private homesites. Carhart went on, with famed naturalist Aldo Leopold from the Forest Service's Albuquerque office, to establish the nation's first wilderness area in New Mexico's Gila National Forest. In 1929 the area became the newly formed Flat Tops Primitive Area, which, after the establishment of the national wilderness system in 1964, became the 235,000-acre Flat Tops Wilderness Area in 1979.

Trappers Lake serves as a popular jumping-off point for hikers and horseback riders venturing into the wilderness area. The wilderness includes over thirty fishable lakes and 160 miles of trails that lace its remote backcountry. Four forest campgrounds—twenty-site Shepards Rim, fourteen-site Cutthroat, ten-site Bucks, and twelve-site Trapline, perch on hummocky ridges north of the lake. Several trails drop down to Trappers Lake, offering scenic views and fishing access. The lake houses native cutthroat trout that reproduce naturally in its clear, cold water. Fishing is allowed only with flies or one-hook lures; native trout between eleven and sixteen inches must be released; and fishing is not permitted in the lake's inlets and outlet to allow trout to spawn from January 1 through July 31. An excellent hike climbs east from the lake on Forest Trail 1814 to the lofty Chinese Wall, an above-timberline cliffed escarpment.

The drive, continuing east on County 8 from the intersection, begins switchbacking up a broad ridge through lush aspen stands and open meadows. After five miles of climbing the road, now in spruce and lodgepole pine forest, reaches Ripple Creek Overlook. This high viewpoint yields expansive views west down the White River Valley and south into the heart of the Flattops. Interpretative signs discuss the wilderness concept, watchable wildlife, and the area's geology. The drive crosses 10,343-foot Ripple Pass and enters 1.2-million-acre Routt National Forest a mile and a half later. The road drops east down spruce-clad slopes above Poose Creek and reaches Vaughn Lake almost three miles later. A six-site forest campground at 9,720 feet nestles under trees along the edge of the small reservoir. The drive spirals down through thick aspen and conifer forest into the broad upper valley of the East Fork of the Williams Fork River. Pyramid Ranger Station, built by the Civilian Conservation Corps in 1934 near the valley head, continues to serve as a busy Forest Service center in summer.

The aspen-lined lane runs north from the station in the broad river valley. Tall cottonwoods and green meadows clot the river's banks, and gray sagebrush colors the dry hillsides above. The road crosses the river at the old townsite of Pyramid, now a collection of summer cabins, and begins ascending steep slopes above the valley. After twisting up for three miles the drive swings under the Dunckley Flat Tops, a long ridge broken into flat-topped summits. The road threads along steep slopes, passing through thick aspen forest, and reaches the broad summit of 9,763-foot Dunckley Pass. An overlook yields superb views southward to pointed 11,532-foot Pyramid

A truck nears the top of Ripple Creek Pass on the Flat Tops Trail Scenic Drive.

Peak, the Little Flat Tops, and 12,133-foot Orno Peak in the Flat Tops Wilderness Area. In mid-summer wildflowers, including columbines, carpet the meadows on the pass summit.

The drive drops east from the pass, dipping through several drainages before bending northeast down Oak Creek's broad valley. A side road, Forest Road 959, leads three miles south to Sheriff Reservoir. A primitive campground and trailhead for the wilderness area sits here. The road bumps through the shallow valley for a couple miles past beaver ponds and a thick fir and spruce woodland, before turning up a grassy side-canyon. A half-mile later it crosses a low divide and the turnoff to Chapman Reservoir, a popular camping and fishing site.

The last leg of the scenic drive drops east above Spronks Creek into a wide valley. The climate and vegetation change as the road descends, with sagebrush coating the drier slopes and aspens clinging to the moist north-facing hillsides. Rolling hills and scattered cattle ranches border the road after it leaves the creek. Keep right at the intersection with Forest Road 925 and head south on Routt County 17. The now-paved road dips and rolls beneath towering Rattlesnake Butte and Devils Grave Mesa. Sharp volcanic outcrops mingle with sagebrush on the steep mesa slopes. After a couple miles the road bends east through hay fields and cattle pastures, passes the Byrd Homestead, the first recorded homestead in the Yampa Valley, and enters the small hamlet of Yampa perched on the banks of the Yampa River. The 170-mile-long Yampa River, Colorado's longest free-flowing river, begins in the Flat Tops, heads north to Steamboat Springs, and flows west through broad valleys and abrupt canyons to its confluence with the Green River in the heart of Dinosaur National Monument. The Utes called an edible potato-like root that grew on the river's banks *Yampa*, and the name was applied to the river and town. The town offers all visitor services. The Royal Hotel Visitor Center dispenses information on the Yampa Valley. The drive ends at Colorado Highway 131. Steamboat Springs sits thirty-one miles to the north and I-70 lies thirty-nine miles to the south.

25 GRAND MESA SCENIC DRIVE
Delta to Grand Junction

General description: The 75-mile Grand Mesa scenic drive climbs from desert canyons and ranch lands to the subalpine summit of 11,000-foot-high Grand Mesa, the world's largest flat-topped mountain.
Special attractions: Grand Mesa National Forest, Cedaredge Pioneer Town, Crag Crest National Recreation Trail, Land's End, Powderhorn Ski Area, 300+ lakes, fishing, camping, hiking, spectacular views, excellent fall colors, cross-country skiing, snowmobiling.
Location: Western Colorado. The drive begins 4 miles east of Delta at the

intersection of Colorado highways 92 and 65, and ends at the junction of CO 65 and Interstate 70 just east of Grand Junction.

Drive route names and numbers: Grand Mesa Scenic Byway, Lands End Road, CO 65, Forest Road 100.

Travel season: Year-round. The paved drive section is open all winter and plowed and sanded after snowstorms. The Land's End Road closes in winter.

Camping: 8 national forest campgrounds—26-site Jumbo, 16-site Spruce Grove, 41-site Island Lake, 36-site Little Bear, 27-site Ward Lake, 12-site Kiser Creek, 6-site Eggleston Lake, and 11-site Crag Crest—sit on or just off the drive on the mesa top.

Services: All services are found in Grand Junction, Delta, and Cedaredge. Limited services at Mesa.

Nearby attractions: Colorado National Monument, Uncompahgre Plateau, Unaweep Canyon, Black Canyon of the Gunnison, West Elk Scenic Drive, Paonia State Recreation Area, West Elk Wilderness Area, Gunnison National Forest, Grand Junction attractions, Vega State Recreation Area, White River National Forest, Debeque Canyon, Island Acres State Recreation Area.

For more information: Grand Mesa National Forest, 2250 Hwy 50, Delta, CO 81416, (970) 874-7691. Delta Chamber, 301 Main Street, Delta, CO 81416, (970) 874-8616. Surface Creek Valley Chamber, P.O. Box 278, Cedaredge, CO 81413, (970) 856-6961.

The drive: The Grand Mesa, lying between the Gunnison and Colorado rivers in western Colorado, hides a remote, off-the-beaten-track landscape. It's a place studded with lakes that nestle among spruce woodlands, undulating meadows carpeted with summer wildflowers, trickling creeks lined with willows, and a basalt rim formed by ancient lava flows. The seventy-five-mile-long Grand Mesa scenic drive traverses this massive island in the sky. The mesa, with its high point, 11,237- foot Leon Peak, boasts an average elevation of 10,000 feet. The rolling mesa-top, called the "world's highest flat-topped mountain," is a summer oasis of cool temperatures and plentiful rainfall that towers over surrounding desert valleys. Over three hundred lakes stud the upland, and thick woodlands and broad meadows carpet the mesa's hillocks and swales. The drive yields stunning views— golden aspens that cascade over the mesa rim; the broad Grand Valley flanked by upturned cuestas and plateaus; and vistas of distant snow-capped peaks that gleam in the summer sun.

Temperatures along the drive vary greatly from the semi-arid river valleys at either end and the road's 10,839-foot summit, an almost 6,000-foot elevation difference. Precipitation varies from a scant eight or so inches in the desert lowlands to over thirty inches atop the mesa. Summer daytime temperatures regularly climb into the nineties in the lower elevations, while temperatures atop the mesa remain in the sixties and seventies. Summer nights are cool, and occasionally drop into the thirties. Expect regular afternoon thunderstorms during the summer months, with locally heavy rain

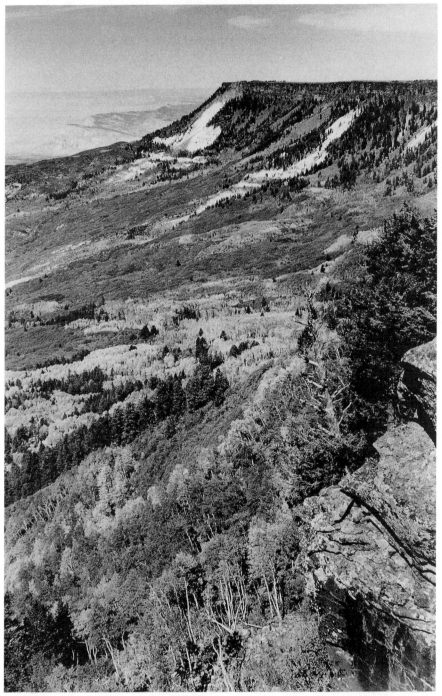

Steep basalt cliffs at Land's End abruptly fall away below the Grand Mesa Byway.

and possible hail. September brings warm days and cold nights, with infrequent rainshowers. October begins the cool-down, with occasional dustings of snow on the higher elevations. The upper mesa road becomes locked under a mantle of snow from November through April. The Land's End Road closes in winter, but the rest of the drive remains open. Excellent cross-country skiing and snowmobiling trails thread the mesa-top, while Powderhorn Ski Area offers downhill runs. Most of the snowdrifts melt away by late May.

The scenic drive begins at the intersection of CO 92 and 65 four miles east of Delta. Delta, at 4,980 feet, sits at the confluence of the Gunnison and Uncompahgre rivers. It's a pleasant Western town, with all visitor services. Points of interest include the Delta County Historical Museum with displays of ranch and farm tools and a butterfly collection, and the Ute Council Tree, a spreading two hundred-year-old cottonwood on the town's north side used by Ute Indians, including Chief Ouray, as a meeting place. Grand Mesa National Forest's office sits on U.S. Highway 50 on Delta's south side and offers visitor information and maps. The drive begins by heading east from Delta and CO 92 for four miles. Turn north on CO 65 near the end of the four-lane highway stretch.

The drive's first eleven miles run north from the highway intersection to Cedaredge. The road goes over flat, corn fields on the broad valley floor and after 0.8 mile crosses the Gunnison River. Tall cottonwoods and Russian olives line the river banks. The highway climbs north into scrubby hills of gray Mancos shale, a deposit laid down on an ancient seabed some seventy million years ago. The Mancos shale stretches along the foot of Grand Mesa, forming a wide, brightly colored band of dissected badlands, broad valleys, and hump-backed ridges. The Adobes, a shale area west of the highway beyond Tongue Creek's lush valley, offers excellent backcountry hiking through austere, barren hills.

The highway ascends a low shale hill onto a broad, gently tilted mesa seamed by Surface Creek's shallow valley. Orchard City spreads along the creek at 5,800 feet. Orchard City is not actually a town at all but rather a collection of three separate towns—Cory, Austin, and Eckert—each with its own post office. The trio incorporated in 1912 to obtain bonds to build a water system so residents could tap into Grand Mesa's spring run-off for irrigation and home water. The road runs through Orchard City, passing the small towns, old stone buildings, and grassy paddocks with grazing horses and cattle. Surface Creek parallels the blacktop, with cottonwoods, willows, and Russian olives lining its lush banks. After crossing the creek a couple miles north of Eckert, the highway follows the broad Surface Creek valley and reaches 6,100-foot-high Cedaredge.

Cedaredge, the valley's commercial center, is a lovely backroads town. It began as the headquarters for the Bar-I Ranch in the 1890s. Sophie Kohler, the foreman's wife, called the place Cedar Edge and when the post office was established the name became Cedaredge. All that remains of the ranch are three wooden multi-sided silos. These sit in Pioneer Town, a picturesque outdoor museum operated by the Surface Creek Valley Historical Society.

The site is open during the summer, and there is no charge. Visitors enjoy a look back at western Colorado's colorful past. Pioneer Town features many historic buildings and houses, including the Lizard Head Saloon, Wells-Fargo Express, barber shop, livery stable, the Cedaredge Town Jail, an Indian museum, blacksmith shop, schoolhouse, and Chapel of the Cross. All are painstakingly furnished and outfitted with period artifacts and antiques. Cedaredge also offers numerous craft shops and hosts the country's longest running Little Britches Rodeo each July. The town's annual Applefest occurs the first Saturday in October each year.

Cedaredge marks the official beginning of the national forest's Grand Mesa Scenic and Historic Byway. The highway passes downtown Cedaredge and climbs north past scattered homes and apple orchards. The Surface Creek Valley, along with the North Fork Valley at Paonia, is one of Colorado's renowned fruit-growing areas. Orchards were first planted in 1882 near Cory and by the 1920s fruit farming became a major industry. Thousands of acres in the Surface Creek Valley yield cherries, apricots, plums, peaches, nectarines, pears, and apples between July and October. Roadside stands sell fresh in-season fruit and vegetables at bargain prices.

The drive passes apple orchards, drops over Youngs Creek, and climbs onto a rolling benchland blanketed with sagebrush and a pinyon pine and juniper woodland. Grand Mesa towers overhead with steep aspen-covered slopes spilling over its cliffed rim and down abrupt ravines. The drive's ascent travels through four distinct biological life zones that represent a telescoped journey from Mexico to northern Canada's boreal forest. The highway bends northwest and skirts the edge of a long ridge. After a few miles the road turns east, climbs onto the ridge, and begins sharply ascending hills thick with Gambel oak copses. Magnificent views unfold as the road climbs. The long snow-capped escarpment of the San Juan Mountains parades across the southern horizon, with several 14,000-foot peaks—Uncompahgre and Wetterhorn peaks, Mount Sneffels, Mount Wilson, and Wilson Peak—poking against the azure sky. The humped Uncompahgre Plateau spreads to the southwest above the Gunnison River valley. To the southeast towers the West Elk Range and the dark rim of the Black Canyon of the Gunnison. The highway finally leaves the oak woods behind and enters immense aspen groves. A paved overlook offers spectacular views just before the road enters 346,000-acre Grand Mesa National Forest.

After entering the forest the drive turns away from the aspen-clad rim up Ward Creek's shallow vale. Spruce dominates the forest atop the mesa, with only scattered patches of aspen. Willows cling to the creek's banks. The road swings past small Ward Creek Reservoir and bends northeast to Grand Mesa Recreation Area. A series of jewel-like lakes hides among the spruce forest here, including Eggleston Lake, Ward Lake, Carp Lake, Baron Lake, and Island Lake, the largest on the Grand Mesa. All give excellent fishing for native cutthroat, rainbow, and brook trout. This popular scenic area, lying above 10,000 feet, offers campers Island Lake, Little Bear, Ward Lake, Kiser Creek, Eggleston Lake, and Crag Crest campgrounds. Other recreation here includes hiking, four-wheeling, and boating. The national

To Rifle

•Denver

★

COLORADO

To Collbran

70

65

330

Plateau Cr.

Mesa

The Beehive
6,282 ft.

To Grand
Junction

70

Chalk Mtn.
8,092 ft.

65

GRAND

MESA

Crag Crest National
Recreation Trail

Powderhorn
Ski Area

Skyway
Point

MESA

Mesa
Lakes

GRAND

Land's End

100

Island
Lake

To Grand
Junction

End

Road

NATIONAL

Land's

FOREST

50

Cedaredge

Orchard
City

To Hotchkiss

Adobe
Buttes

65

92

Gunnison

River

Delta

N

50

0   2   4   6   8   10
Miles

To Montrose

forest operates Grand Mesa Visitor Center at Cobbett Lake and three lodges sit near the lakes.

The drive bends west above spruce-fringed Island Lake and runs along a bench below a cliffed ridge. Crag Crest National Recreation Trail begins from a roadside 10,375-foot-high trailhead above the lake, and threads for seven miles along the narrow, rocky Crag Crest and through quiet forests and wildflower-sprinkled meadows. The trail, climbing over 11,000 feet, yields breathtaking views of the glistening emerald lakes scattered across the mesa-top as well as vistas of distant mountain ranges.

Grand Mesa, named Mesa Grande by the Spanish, is a huge layer-cake of horizontal rock layers. Late Cretaceous rocks—the Mancos shale and above-lying Mesa Verde Formation—form the bottom layers at Cedaredge, while more recent sandstones and shales called the Green River and Wahsatch formations form the upper mesa slopes. The mesa top is capped by a thick layer of erosion-resistant basalt laid down as lava flows in ancient river valleys ten million years ago. The lava spewed from vents on the mesa's east side, forming twenty-five separate flows between ten and seventy feet thick. Grand Mesa's lava cap varies between two hundred and six hundred feet thick. Later erosion swept away the softer hills that surrounded the lava-filled valleys, leaving them as a high, isolated plateau. Glaciers also blanketed the mesa-top and the mesa's northern slopes, leaving piles of boulders and etching depressions that later formed lakes.

The drive runs west below broken cliffs and tumbled boulder fields before climbing higher onto the flattened mesa. A rest area sits at the 10,839-foot drive high point on the Mesa-Delta county line. The road rolls through open meadows with willow-lined tarns tucked amid boulders and Englemann spruce woods. At just over thirty-two miles the highway intersects the Land's End Road, FR 100.

This twelve-mile-long gravel road travels west to Land's End, one of Colorado's most stunning viewpoints. The road heads southwest across the undulating mesa, traversing the west rim of shallow Kanah Creek's canyon for a few miles before bending west along the edge of a gigantic amphitheater. Wide meadows broken by sparse spruce woodlands and small aspen groves characterize the mesa top. A dense aspen forest spills down steep slopes below the cliffs along the rim and road. As the road runs west the mesa's climate becomes more temperate, moderated by warm winds that sweep up from the Grand Valley to the west. Sagebrush replaces the thick grasses and the forest disappears altogether. After ten miles the road bends northwest, dipping through shallow ravines and crossing hillocks. A short spur leads to Coal Creek Overlook, a spectacular point perched atop black basalt cliffs. Small waterfalls drop over nearby cliffs. A couple miles later the road reaches Land's End.

A magnificent panorama stretches away from the point. Steep slopes, colored brilliant yellow with changing aspen in September, cascade down to barren hills. The Grand Valley, seamed with the meandering Colorado River and divided into green fields, reaches west to Utah. The Book Cliffs and a host of broken ridges march north from the valley, while the Uncompahgre

Plateau, its northern edge eroded into Colorado National Monument's red rock canyons, looms to the southwest. The pointed La Sal Mountains in Utah pierce the sky above the plateau. The national forest's Land's End Visitor Center, open in summer, sits at the overlook. To continue the drive, head twelve miles back east to the road's junction with CO 65. The Land's End Road, however, continues west and twists downward for more than 5,000 feet to US 50 through numerous hairpin turns.

The scenic drive continues north from Land's End Road over the rolling mesa-top. After about a mile the highway reaches Skyway Point and the northern edge of Grand Mesa. The road descends east in the shadow of tall basalt cliffs and boulder fields to a broad bench before making a U-turn westward. A thick spruce forest borders the asphalt. The road passes sixteen-site Spruce Grove Campground and drops down to Mesa Lakes Recreation Area. The Mesa Lakes, scattered through the forest, are a popular overnight and fishing destination. Another campground, twenty-six-site Jumbo, two picnic areas, and Mesa Lakes Resort surround the lakes.

The highway drops past a small reservoir and turns onto the abrupt northern flank of Grand Mesa. A couple paved pullouts give great views north down the aspen-covered slopes to the Colorado River's salmon-colored Debeque Canyon. The road descends steep slopes for the next four miles, running through a spectacular aspen forest. Drive this road section in late September when the colors run from orange and rust to gold and yellow. At the bottom of the steepest slopes, the highway leaves Grand Mesa National Forest. The turn to Powderhorn Ski Area sits just north of the boundary. Powderhorn gives great intermediate runs, with wide views of the surrounding plateau country. It offers four lifts, 240 skiable acres, 220 inches of annual snow, and a 1,659-foot vertical drop. The area has a lodge, lessons, and ski rentals.

The highway swings into a broad tilted basin, flanked by high ridges on the east and west and the lofty rim of Grand Mesa on the south. The road curves down through a scrub oak woodland and after a few miles reaches pastures, ranchettes, and sagebrush hills. The Breaks form a ragged ridge on the east, eroded into a red rock badlands. Chalk Mountain lifts a twin-summited peak with bare white cliffs to the west. The drive descends along Coon Creek and runs down sloping pastures to the small ranching town of Mesa. The Beehive, a 6,282-foot butte, is a prominent landmark east of Mesa. Past Mesa the highway plunges into Mesa Creek's narrow canyon and reaches a junction with Colorado Highway 330 at Plateau Creek. A right turn on CO 330 leads to Collbran and Vega State Recreation Area. The drive bends left on CO 330, crosses the creek, and heads toward I-70 and Grand Junction.

The drive's last ten miles twist down Plateau Creek's deepening canyon to its confluence with the Colorado River. This is dry, dusty country. Cliff bands of tawny Mesa Verde sandstone tower above the highway, broken by erosion into bulging buttresses and tumbled boulders. Sagebrush, saltbush, dry grass clumps, and occasional pinyon pines and junipers scatter over the rocky canyon walls. The creek, lined by scraggly cottonwoods and tamarisks, riffles through cobbled rapids. The highway follows the canyon's immense curves and finally the road divides. The right branch continues on the creek's north bank to eastbound I-70 while the left branch crosses to the opposite shore and heads to the westbound interstate and Grand Junction.

26 BLACK CANYON SOUTH RIM DRIVE
Montrose to High Point on the South Rim Road

General description: A 13-mile road that follows the lofty south rim of the Black Canyon of the Gunnison National Monument.

Special attractions: Black Canyon of the Gunnison, Tomichi Point, Pulpit Rock Overlook, Chasm View, Painted Wall View, High Point, Visitor Center, East Portal, camping, picnicking, hiking, wildlife, rock climbing, scenic views.

Location: West-central Colorado. The drive begins 6 miles east of Montrose on U.S. Highway 50.

Drive route name and number: Colorado Highway 347, South Rim Road.

Travel season: Spring, summer, and fall. Heavy snow occasionally blocks the drive from Gunnison Point Overlook to High Point during winter months. Check with monument headquarters in Montrose for road closure and opening.

Camping: The South Rim Campground, just inside the monument's southern boundary, offers 102 campsites spread among scrub oak. It operates on a first-come, first-served basis and is closed in winter.

Services: A concessionaire operates the Rim House at Pulpit Rock Overlook in summer, offering food and souvenirs. Otherwise no services are found along the drive. Montrose offers all traveler services including restaurants, groceries, lodging, and RV parks.

Nearby attractions: Curecanti National Recreation Area, Gunnison Gorge, Montrose, Montrose County Historical Museum, Ute Indian Museum and Ouray Memorial Park, Uncompahgre National Forest, Gunnison National Forest, Owl Creek Pass scenic drive, San Juan Scenic Skyway, Ouray National Historic District.

For more information: Black Canyon of the Gunnison National Monument, 2233 E. Main St. Suite A, Montrose, CO 81401, (970) 249-7036. Montrose Chamber of Commerce, 550 N. Townsend, Montrose, CO 81401, (800) 873-0244.

The drive: Colorado is a land of surprises. It's a land that appears at first glance to be ravishingly pure, untouched, and unchanging. But underneath that pristine veneer lies a landscape that is in constant motion and change. It's just that life is too short to recognize geologic change when we see it. The land's shape alters over eons of unfathomable time—millions of years pass

The Black Canyon's Narrows, seen here from the North Rim, lie below the South Rim Drive and precipitous cliffs.

in the creation of a single mountain peak or a desert canyon. The Black Canyon of the Gunnison River, lying on the edge of the Colorado Plateau in western Colorado, teaches the fundamental geologic lesson that nothing ever remains the same. There is no status quo on this dynamic earth.

The thirteen-mile-long South Rim Drive explores the southern edge of the Black Canyon, a deep, precipitous gorge hacked out of ancient bedrock by the Gunnison River in the Black Canyon of the Gunnison National Monument. The monument protects twelve miles of the fifty-mile-long canyon. The drive offers not only geologic lessons, but a wealth of scenic views, outdoor activities, and opportunities for nature study. Trails lead to observation points perched along the canyon rim. Soaring cliffs provide adventure for intrepid rock climbers and homes for raptors, swallows, and swifts. The forested canyon rim yields glimpses of life: a porcupine-gnawed pinyon pine; the underbrush rustlings of rufous-sided towhees; the hoofbeats of an alarmed mule deer; and the jubilant howl of a distant coyote.

The Black Canyon slices through an uplift that reaches elevations above 8,000 feet, well over 2,000 feet higher than Montrose in the nearby Uncompahgre Valley. The canyon rim, with its higher elevation, consequently receives more precipitation than adjoining valleys with an average of twenty inches annually. Each canyon rim season is distinct. Spring arrives in May with windy weather, rain showers, and cool nights. Summer days can be hot, occasionally reaching ninety degrees, but regular afternoon thunderstorms and breezes moderate the temperatures. Night temperatures can be very cool, dipping into the forties. Autumn brings a succession of clear, glorious days and cold nights. Winters are frigid, with snow blanketing the rim and shaded canyon walls from late November into April. The drive is open in winter only to Gunnison Point Overlook. Check with monument headquarters in Montrose for information on road closures in winter.

The Black Canyon scenic drive begins six miles east of Montrose at the junction of US 50 and CO 347. Turn north on CO 347. The road climbs up dry Pinon Springs Draw, a shallow canyon carved into Mancos Shale, a dark gray formation deposited in a quiet seaway some 75 million years ago during the Cretaceous Period. The shale forms sharp, barren badlands on the flanks of the Uncompahgre Valley around Montrose and Delta. After a mile-and-a-half of climbing, the highway emerges onto a wide, level bench covered with green farm fields, before again steeply ascending slopes coated with pinyon pine and juniper. Five miles from US 50 the road reaches Jones Summit on the crest of a rolling ridge between Pinon Springs and Jones draws. The state highway ends here at the national monument border and the drive becomes South Rim Road.

East Portal Road, a good side-trip, begins just inside the monument boundary. This five-mile road winds east down steep slopes to East Portal on the canyon floor just upstream from the Black Canyon itself. East Portal, part of Curecanti National Recreation Area, offers camping, fishing, boating, picnicking, and a feel for the canyon's inner gorge. Vehicles with an overall length exceeding twenty-two feet are not allowed down this steep, switchbacked road.

The entrance station to 20,766-acre Black Canyon of the Gunnison National Monument sits one-tenth mile past the East Portal turn. The monument, like most national park areas, is a fee area. The three-loop South Rim Campground, with 102 campsites spread among a dense scrub oak woodland, lies just beyond the entrance at 8,320 feet. The campground, open April through October, operates on a first-come, first-served basis.

The drive heads north from the campground and after a mile reaches Tomichi Point and the first view of the Gunnison's stupendous chasm. Nothing prepares the first-time visitor for the inaccessibility and sheerness of the canyon. The road to this point has climbed and traversed rolling ridges, with distant peaks and low-slung mesas poking above the landscape. But here the land falls away into abrupt, sudden space. Broken side canyons, sweeps of menacing rock buttresses, and gullies and ledges mantled with fir trees fill the gorge below.

Gunnison Point Overlook and the monument's visitor center sit just down the road from Tomichi Point. The center displays the monument's geology, natural history, and history, and provides information, maps, books, and daily ranger-led programs. Gunnison Point, sitting atop an erosion-resistant pegmatite dike, yields good views into the canyon's somber interior. Other pink pegmatite bands slice through the canyon walls across from Gunnison Point. Gneiss and schist, the softer metamorphic rocks that surround the pegmatite, weather more quickly and leave the resistant rock jutting into the canyon.

The Black Canyon's geologic story is divided into two chapters: the existing rocks and their history, and the Gunnison River's erosion of the canyon. Much of the exposed rock is gneiss and schist, metamorphic rocks originally deposited as layers of sand, silt, and mud on the floor of a primordial sea some two billion years ago. Intense heat and pressure later "metamorphosed" or transformed the rock to their present contorted state. Molten magma, later injected into cracks and fissures in the gneiss and schist, slowly cooled into pegmatite, a coarse-grained igneous rock. Pegmatite forms the striking dikes and bands that criss-cross the canyon walls, particularly the Painted Wall. Other large magma bodies intruded into the metamorphic bedrock and form quartz monzonite, a hard, granite-like rock found on the sheer walls at Chasm View.

Time and the flowing river created the Black Canyon. The canyon, a recent topographic feature, is between two and three million years old. Its story, however, began with the uplift of the Rocky Mountains sixty million years ago. As the mountains slowly rose, erosion swiftly tackled them with glaciers chiseling at the high peaks and snowmelt-laden rivers, including the ancestral Gunnison, carving into the uplift in western Colorado. Volcanism in the West Elk Range to the north and the San Juan Mountains to the south also affected the course of the Gunnison River by channeling it between narrow highlands. The river, cutting through layers of volcanic ash and sedimentary rock, established a course atop the buried metamorphic basement rock. By the time volcanism ceased, the Gunnison was firmly entrenched in its bedrock canyon.

The Gunnison River, Colorado's fourth largest river, originates on the Continental Divide far to the east of the Black Canyon. West of the town of Gunnison it drops into the fifty-mile-long Black Canyon before emerging in the Uncompahgre Valley near Delta. Three dams—Blue Mesa, Morrow Point, and Crystal—impound the river water in the upper canyon for flood control, water storage, recreation, and electric power. Below Crystal Lake the Gunnison plunges twelve miles through its narrow canyon in the national monument, before entering Gunnison Gorge, its lower canyon. The Gunnison River owns one of the nation's steepest river gradients, dropping 2,150 feet from the canyon head at Sapinero (now under Blue Mesa Reservoir) to its North Fork junction—an average fall of forty-three feet per mile. By contrast the Green River drops only twelve feet a mile in Dinosaur National Monument. In the national monument below the scenic drive, the Gunnison's average gradient is ninety-five feet a mile. But in the two miles from Pulpit Rock to Chasm View it descends an astounding 480 feet. That steep gradient, combined with the abrasion of tumbling boulders on its riverbed, gives the Gunnison a sharp cutting edge. Geologists estimate the river deepens the canyon about one inch every century.

Past the visitor center the drive heads northeast, following the rim's contours. Dense thickets of Gambel or scrub oak line the road, with occasional open meadows. Other shrubs mix in the pygmy woodland, including serviceberry and mountain mahogany, a favorite deer food. Mule deer flourish along the canyon rim. Keen eyes can sight them in roadside meadows and near the campground. Other mammals include porcupines, marmots, rock and ground squirrels, coyotes, grey foxes, and bobcats. Mountain lion, black bear, bighorn sheep, and elk occasionally wander through. The road reaches Pulpit Rock Overlook two miles from the visitor center. The viewpoint offers a good view of the V-shaped upper canyon and Pulpit Rock, a semi-detached pinnacle. The Rim House, operated by a private concessionaire, sells snacks and souvenirs.

The canyon narrows past Pulpit Rock and a series of overlooks scattered along the drive yield excellent views. Cross Fissures View, Rock Point, and Devils Lookout all perch atop the canyon rim and are reached by short trails from the drive. Chasm View, the monument's most spectacular and airy overlook, sits a mile past Devils Lookout. The cliffs fall abruptly away from the overlook railings to the frothy river 1,800 feet below. North Chasm View Wall dominates the canyon here, its gray bulk seamed with cracks and fissures. The opposite north rim lies a scant eleven hundred empty feet across the abyss from the viewpoint, yet by car it's eighty-two miles away. Upstream lies The Narrows. Towering cliffs hem the river into a cleft only forty feet wide, forming the most forbidding section of this somber canyon.

At Chasm View the road swings south and begins climbing toward High Point. Painted Wall View sits one-tenth mile past Chasm View. This point offers views of the Painted Wall, Colorado's highest cliff with a 2,240-foot vertical rise from base to rim. Numerous pink pegmatite bands slash across the wall. Cedar Point and Dragon Point, the next two stops, also yield outstanding views of the Painted Wall. A short nature trail wanders out to

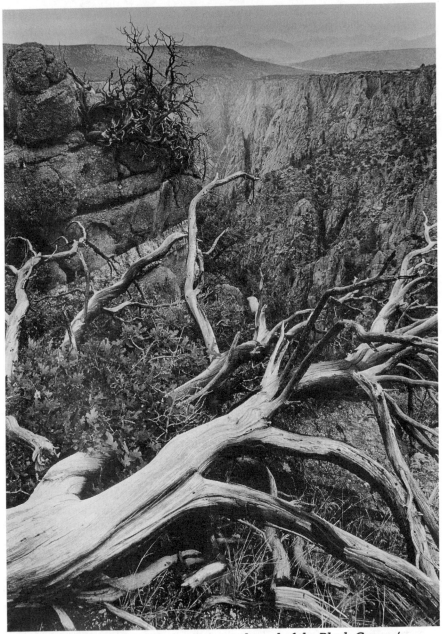

A pinyon pine skeleton at Warner Point at the end of the Black Canyon's South Rim Drive.

Cedar Point, with typical rim plants identified along the path.

The Black Canyon's rims once offered the nomadic Utes cool summer camps and plentiful game and edible plants. The Utes, however, rarely entered the precipitous canyon and called the depths *Tomichi* or "Land of cliffs and water." Captain John Gunnison first explored the canyon region and river now bearing his name on an 1853 railroad survey. Shortly afterwards Gunnison was killed by Indians in western Utah. The canyon itself was first traversed in 1901 by William Torrance and A.L. Fellows on a water survey expedition. The duo endured nine days and seventy-two river crossings before climbing out of the canyon. Fellows described the trek: "Our surroundings were of the wildest possible description. The roar of the water falls was constantly in our ears, and the walls of the canyon, towering half mile in height above us, were seemingly vertical. Occasionally a rock would fall from one side or the other, with a roar and crash, exploding like a ton of dynamite when it struck bottom, making us think our last day had come."

The road continues ascending gentle slopes past Dragon Point and soon reaches Sunset View. This viewpoint, with a small picnic area, looks down-canyon into Gunnison Gorge. This lower canyon, composed of softer rocks, is wider and lower than the monument's narrow abyss. Likewise more side-canyon erosion has widened the gorge and the Gunnison River's gradient drops to thirty-five feet per mile. A mile farther lies 8,289-foot High Point and the drive's turn-around point. Douglas-fir, mixed with pinyon pine and juniper, blanket this lofty ridge and spill down the canyon side. A 0.6-mile trail heads west from here to Warner Point. The point, the south rim's highest spot, is named for Reverend Mark Warner who pushed the canyon's designation as a national monument. Warner Point yields great vistas of the surrounding land. Southward stretches the snow-capped San Juan Mountains and ragged Mount Sneffels; Grand Mesa's dark bulk lingers to the northwest; and the pointed West Elk Range forms a jagged horizon to the northeast. This privileged view, reserved for those who walk out here, forms a fitting end to this short but spectacular scenic drive.

General description: This 133-mile-long open loop drive traverses western Colorado's lonely plateau country, threading through Unaweep Canyon and following deep canyons along the Dolores and San Miguel rivers.

Special attractions: Unaweep Canyon, Taylor Quarry Overlook, Driggs Mansion, Thimble Rock, Palisade Wilderness Study Area, Dolores Canyon, Sewemup Wilderness Study Area, The Hanging Flume, Norwood, San Miguel Canyon, rock climbing, camping, hiking, fishing, scenic views, historic sites, Indian rock art, rafting.

Location: Western Colorado. The drive begins at Whitewater on U.S. Highway 50 just south of Grand Junction and ends in Placerville 25 miles west of Ridgway.

Drive route name and numbers: Unaweep-Tabeguache Scenic & Historic Byway, Colorado Highways 141 and 145.

Travel season: Year-round.

Camping: No established campgrounds lie along the drive. Primitive camping is allowed, however, on adjoining BLM public land. Camp well off the road and practice "no trace" camping. The BLM's Dominguez Campground, reached via the Divide Road from CO 141 in Unaweep Canyon, offers shaded campsites above Big Dominguez Creek. A national forest campground sits further south on Divide Road.

Services: All services are found in Grand Junction, Naturita, Nucla, Norwood, and Placerville. Limited services in Gateway.

Nearby attractions: Colorado National Monument, Grand Mesa, Lands End Road, La Sal Mountains, Black Ridge Wilderness Study Area, Dominguez Canyon Wilderness Study Area, Uncompahgre Plateau, Divide Road, Dry Mesa Dinosaur Quarry, Canyonlands National Park (UT), Mt. Sneffels Wilderness Area, Lizard Head Wilderness Area, Telluride National Historic District, Dallas Divide, Lizard Head Pass scenic drive, Million Dollar Highway, Ouray.

For more information: BLM, Grand Junction Resource Area, 764 Horizon Drive, Grand Junction, CO 81506, (970) 243-6561. Uncompahgre National Forest, Main Street, Norwood, CO 81423, (303) 327-4261. Norwood Chamber, P.O. Box 528, Norwood, CO 81423, (970) 327-4406.

The drive: The 133-mile-long Unaweep-Tabeguache Scenic and Historic Byway threads across the splendid Colorado Plateau country along the dissected western fringe of the humpbacked Uncompahgre Plateau. It discovers a remote, hidden landscape along a couple off-the-beaten-track

To Grand Junction

Whitewater

50

To Delta

PIÑON MESA

Unaweep Divide

UNAWEEP CANYON

Gunnison River

THE PALISADE

UNAWEEP CANYON

141

Divide Road

Dominguez Canyon CG

Gateway

UNCOMPAHGRE

UNCOMPAHGRE PLATEAU

•Denver

★ **COLORADO**

DOLORES

Dolores River CANYON

Sewumup Mesa

MANTI LA SAL NATL. FOREST

NATIONAL

Hanging Flume

Uravan

To Montrose

PARADOX VALLEY

San Miguel

FOREST

To La Sal Junction, UT

70

SLICKROCK CANYON

Dolores River

141

Nucla

Naturita

Miguel

WRIGHTS MESA

Norwood

145

To Ridgway

UNCOMPAHGRE NATL. FOREST

River

62

Placerville

145

To Telluride

N

0   5   10
Miles

225

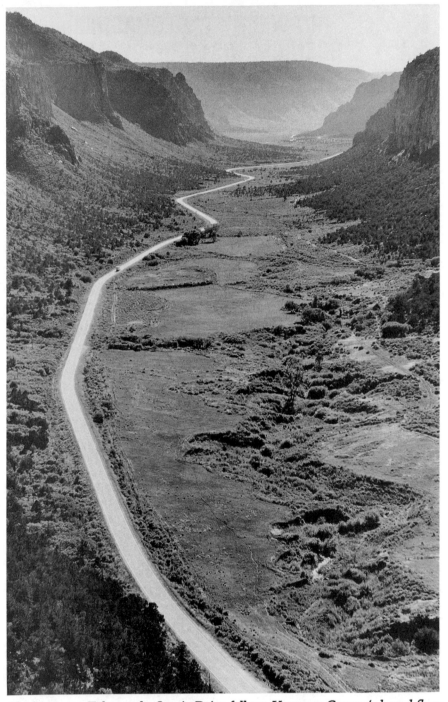

The Unaweep-Tabeguache Scenic Drive follows Unaweep Canyon's broad floor beneath abrupt granite crags.

state highways, exploring wondrous Unaweep Canyon and the harshly eroded canyons of the Dolores and San Miguel rivers. The drive passes precipitous granite cliffs and sandstone battlements, twists along dusky red rivers, and crosses a land rich in prehistoric geologic activity.

Mild weather dominates along the drive year-round. The highways run over high desert country characterized by sparse precipitation, hot summers, and short chilly winters. Occasional thunderstorms rumble through in summer, with most of the rain dousing the drive's higher elevations in Unaweep Canyon and near Norwood. Expect hot summer temperatures, with daily highs in the nineties along the rivers. Higher elevation temperatures are cooler, but can still reach into the eighties. Autumn, beginning in late September and running to early November, offers pleasant drive weather. Days are usually clear and warm with only occasional rainstorms. Winter begins in November and ends by March in the lower elevations. Snow blankets Unaweep Canyon, Wrights Mesa, and the shady slopes in the San Miguel Canyon in winter, but otherwise quickly melts away under the warm sun. Days are cool with highs generally between thirty and fifty degrees, and nights are cold. Spring creeps onto the plateau in late March, with dry, windy weather punctuated by occasional rain, sleet, and snow storms. The weather begins warming in April, and May brings wildflowers and grass to the sere lowlands.

The scenic drive begins fifteen miles south of Grand Junction at the intersection of US 50 and CO 141 at Whitewater. Turn west on CO 141. The drive's first leg runs forty-four miles west through Unaweep Canyon to Gateway and the Dolores River Canyon. The paved road swings over the Gunnison River after a quarter-mile, crosses a corn field on the river floodplain, and turns west up a shallow canyon. East Creek trickles through cottonwoods on the canyon floor. Pinyon pine and junipers scatter over the dry, rocky slopes above.

East Creek, beginning on Unaweep Divide in Unaweep Canyon, cuts east through upturned rock layers on the edge of the Uncompahgre Plateau. The Uncompahgre Plateau, a broad, flattened highland crested with dense forests and meadows, stretches northwest one hundred miles from the San Juan Mountains to the Grand Valley and the Colorado River. The plateau reaches heights of 10,000 feet. Numerous canyons crease the twenty-five-mile-wide uplift, slicing deeply through sandstone layers that drape over its Precambrian basement rocks. The plateau's most dramatic canyons lie in Colorado National Monument's northern end and Unaweep and Dominguez canyons in its mid-section.

Lower Unaweep Canyon slowly widens as the highway climbs west. After three miles the road swings away from the creek and begins ascending a tilted bench on the south canyon slope. Dakota sandstone, forming a long tawny band of cliff, rims the canyon. Immense boulders tumble down slopes above the highway. As the road climbs, the creek cuts deeply into soft shale layers, forming an abrupt canyon below. After eight miles the highway reaches Grand Valley Overlook, a dramatic viewpoint that peers north to the Book Cliffs and the fertile Grand Valley and east to imposing basalt-rimmed Grand

Mesa, the largest flat-topped mountain in the world. Portions of the first stage and wagon route to Gateway thread along the bouldery slopes north of East Creek below the overlook.

The six-mile highway section from the canyon's lower gate to Grand Valley Overlook ascends Ninemile Hill. The highway roughly follows an old Ute Indian trail that later became "Uranium Road," the only route that connected Grand Junction's processing mill with uranium mines along the Dolores River. In the early 1900s, teamsters used the trail up Ninemile Hill to carry mail and supplies to Gateway and several now-abandoned mining camps in Unaweep Canyon. This long hill offered vicious eighteen percent grades that required doubled horse teams. When autos began using the winding shelf road, passengers usually walked ahead to lighten the load and warn the driver of on-coming traffic as the track was too narrow for two vehicles. The road was widened and improved in the 1930s for trucks hauling uranium. It was finally paved in 1958.

The canyon widens and flattens past the overlook, with tall cottonwoods and willow thickets lining the creek. Low sandstone cliffs and slopes covered with pinyon pine and juniper trees stairstep back to a high rim. A mile past the overlook a dirt road heads south to Cactus Park. This dry open valley, flanked by low hogbacks, was the channel of the ancestral Gunnison River between one and five million years ago. The Gunnison Gravels Natural Research Area, a half-mile south of the drive, protects these ancient river deposits. As the drive runs west, the sandstone walls are replaced by cliffs of Precambrian metamorphic rock, the basement rock layer of the Uncompahgre Plateau. Unaweep Canyon's granite and metamorphic rocks, dated between 1.4 and 1.7 billion years old, are among Colorado's oldest exposed rocks. Some three hundred million years ago the plateau was the site of "Uncompahgria," an ancestral Rocky Mountain range. Over ensuing millennia the range weathered down to its bedrock roots, and its eroded cobbles, gravels, and sands were deposited to the west, forming today's canyon country layers. Later sandstone was deposited on the old bedrock, forming the "Great Unconformity" with some five hundred million years of geologic history missing.

Two abandoned towns sit near the drive at Nancy Hanks Gulch. Copper City and Pearl City both began in 1897 with the discovery of copper, gold, and silver in Unaweep Canyon. Both quickly flourished with populations of about one hundred each. Copper City took the lead, building two schools, stores, and cabins. Pearl City, however, kept the rustic look, and in its seventeen-year existence remained a community of tents. The Pearl City Hotel offered the town's deluxe accommodations with three tents joined together. No permanent structures were ever erected. Area fortunes sagged after a 1901 mining downturn, but the pair lingered on. Pearl City folded up its tents in 1912 and Copper City followed suit in 1914. Nothing remains of either today, save a few old photographs.

As the drive heads west the canyon deepens. Rosy sandstone caps the dark gray bedrock along the sidewalls. The creek becomes entrenched in a deep arroyo filled with reeds, cattails, tall grass, and cottonwoods. Broad ranches with grazing cattle and wide hayfields grace the flat valley floor, offering a pastoral counterpoint to the rugged walls. Divide Road begins just past a ranch. This gravel road twists over one hundred miles down the spine of the Uncompaghre Plateau, giving access to a vast swathe of remote backcountry. Take a left turn here for a short drive up Divide Road to a stunning viewpoint above Unaweep Canyon. The gravel road climbs a couple miles up to the site of abandoned Taylor Granite Quarry, a rock quarry that operated in 1928. Park and walk down to the cliff edge for one of western Colorado's most spectacular overlooks.

Unaweep Canyon stretches westward. The highway below uncoils like a long snake up the sagebrush valley floor. Gentle slopes, forested with scrub oak, pinyon pine, and juniper, slant upwards to abrupt, towering granite cliffs. Above, steep slopes lean back to the valley's sandstone rim high above the floor. Unaweep Canyon, slashing across the entire Uncompahgre Plateau, is a unique canyon. The U-shaped canyon is supposedly the only canyon in the world drained by two creeks. A divide in mid-canyon separates the East Creek and West Creek drainages. The Ute Indian name *Unaweep* itself means "Canyon with Two Mouths." This deep canyon's formation has long been a geological enigma. Geologists agree the two small streams in today's canyon could not have chiseled the deep chasm, leading to several theories that explain its origin. Some say it was carved along a massive fault line while others argue that glaciation alone excavated the gorge. The most credible explanation concludes that the canyon was the ancestral river bed of the Gunnison and Colorado rivers. The Colorado River drained southward from Debeque Canyon through Unaweep Canyon and the Uncompahgre Plateau before an eroding tributary breached a divide northwest of the plateau and diverted the river flow into today's Grand Valley. This action, called stream piracy, left Unaweep Canyon high and dry.

The drive continues west up the canyon past steel gray cliffs seamed by black water streaks. The cliffs, ranging up to 500 feet high, yield excellent rock climbing on steep faces and cracks. Popular crags include the Quarry Wall just past Divide Road, and Mothers Buttress, Television Wall, and Sunday Wall farther west on the canyon's north slopes. The American Alpine Club's Access Fund owns sixty-one acres of the canyon to preserve access to the more popular crags. Otherwise, almost all the canyon floor is privately owned. Unaweep Divide, a broad 7,048-foot saddle in mid-canyon, separates East and West creeks. Past the divide the highway begins gently dipping west, running through fields of grass and sagebrush. Several shallow lakes dot the canyon floor. Look for Fall Creek Waterfall plunging off a cliff three miles west of the divide. The falls is on private land.

The highway drops past Thimble Rock, a prominent pyramid towering south of the blacktop. Ledges studded with tall trees interrupt the rock's steep cliffs. The stone ruin of Driggs Mansion sits just off the highway in the morning shadow of Thimble Rock. Lawrence K. Driggs, a wealthy New York lawyer, constructed this huge mansion between 1914 and 1918. Masons, using sandstone blocks cut from nearby Mayflower Canyon, carefully built the eight-room house including a stone arch that mirrors an arch on Thimble

Thimble Rock towers over the ruins of Driggs Mansion in Unaweep Canyon along the Unaweep-Tabeguache Scenic Drive.

Rock. The mansion boasted chandeliers and hard-carved stone mantles above the fireplaces. Despite its expensive construction, no existing record verifies the house was ever occupied. The building was acquired as a hunting lodge and named Chateau Thimblerock. It later became part of the Craig Ranch. The badly vandalized house, on private property, remains a weathered outpost of graceful opulence.

The road continues down the valley through lush Gill Meadows and bends through a rock portal. The canyon widens as it descends, with broken granite crags scattered on the steep mountainsides above. The southern canyon walls and the plateau beyond lies in Ute Creek Wilderness Study Area, a forty-four thousand-acre proposed wilderness of canyons and mesas blanketed with pinyon pine, juniper, aspen, fir, and spruce forest. The northern canyon walls from here west to Gateway are part of the remote twenty-six thousand-acre Palisade Wilderness Study Area. The northern slopes step almost 4,000 thousand feet above the canyon floor to high mesatops. After forty miles the canyon begins to narrow, its walls steepen, and the drive reaches Unaweep Seep.

Unaweep Seep, a collection of springs percolating from hillsides northwest of West Creek, offers an astounding diversity of plant and animal life. This unusual ecosystem, preserved as a registered Colorado Natural Area, displays numerous wildflowers as well as box elder, alder, smooth sumac, blackberry, and ground cherry. The fifty-five-acre site also protects the rare Nokomis Fritillary butterfly. This endangered butterfly, with orange four-inch wings, is gorgeous as it flutters across the wet meadow. The Unaweep colony is seen from mid-July to early September. Other animals inhabiting the canyon and surrounding mesas include mountain lion, black bear, elk, mule deer, and many small mammals. A roadside interpretative BLM sign explains Unaweep Seep.

Past the seep the canyon pinches inward. The creek dashes over worn cobbles and boulders below rocky ridges and granite buttresses. The highway twists through the canyon and passes West Creek Picnic Area. This site, sitting in West Creek Narrows, offers picnic tables shaded by cottonwoods. A sign displays area riparian habitats. The road sharply curves through the canyon, and after a mile and a half crosses the Uncompahgre Fault. The scenery abruptly changes after crossing the fault. The fault vertically displaces some eight thousand feet of rock, and the drive passes from the ancient bedrock to easily eroded sandstones in the Paradox Basin.

The deep canyon ends at the fault, and the highway runs west down a broad, shallow valley. Soft mudstone slopes climb upwards to high, vertical cliffs of Wingate sandstone. The La Sal Mountains, a laccolithic mountain range in Utah, towers to the west above carved canyons and mesas. Immense old cottonwoods spread over the creek along the road. The blacktop gently drops and enters 4,595-foot-high Gateway, the lowest town on Colorado's Western Slope. Gateway, established in 1890, sits at the canyon gateway of an old Ute trail. Settlers built cabins, irrigated fields with ditches full of Dolores River water, planted orchards, and ran cattle over the dry mesas. The first road reached Gateway in 1906 and the first bridge spanned the river in 1912. Electricity finally came to town in 1952, but long-distance telephone service wasn't available until 1965. Gateway boomed with uranium mining in the 1940s and 1950s. Today it's a quiet garden spot on the edge of the wilderness. The town offers a few services including a store and gas, and a town park with shaded picnic tables and restrooms. The Palisade, an immense fin of salmon-colored Wingate sandstone capped with Kayenta sandstone, looms above scree and boulder slopes north of Gateway. The Palisade, part of a proposed wilderness area, also lies in the BLM's fourteen thousand-acre Palisade Outstanding Natural Area.

The next drive segment runs fifty-two miles from Gateway to Naturita along the Dolores and San Miguel rivers. The highway crosses the Dolores River and bends south in the river canyon. The 230-mile-long Dolores River begins high in the San Miguel Range near Lizard Head Pass, runs southwest to Dolores, and arcs north through a series of deep canyons along the western edge of the Uncompahgre Plateau to Gateway. Here it bends northwest, enters Utah, and empties into the Colorado River. The river was named *El Rio de Nuestra Senora de Dolores* or "The River of Our Lady of Sorrows" by Spanish explorer Juan Rivera on a 1765 expedition.

The highway runs south along a wide canyon floor. The river loops in broad, chocolate-colored meanders and riffles over gravel bars. Tamarisk trees, an Asian import, and occasional cottonwoods line the sandy riverbank. The canyon slopes rise above in a series of step-like benches to a castellated rampart of ruddy Wingate sandstone that forms an unbroken palisade. Ten miles south of Gateway the road passes a dirt track that bumps west up Salt

Creek to Sinbad Valley, a salt basin that reminded early miners of Sinbad the Sailor's Valley of Diamonds in the book *A Thousand and One Arabian Nights*. Past the turn the canyon narrows, with the river and highway making great horseshoe loops beneath immense red and black cliffs. Sewemup Mesa, a nineteen thousand-acre proposed wilderness area, hems in the canyon on the west. This huge mesa, isolated by towering cliff bands, preserves a pristine high-desert ecosystem. The mesa acquired its unusual name from the McCarty Gang's cattle rustling operation. The outlaws brought stolen cattle here, cut off the old brands, sewed up the wounded hide, and rebranded the cattle with their own iron. As the canyon narrows the sheer Wingate cliffs begin dipping into the river. The highway makes graceful loops along the glassy river through this spectacular canyon section. Past RocK Creek, the southern end of Sewemup Mesa, and its fertile hayfields and cottonwoods the road makes one more grand horseshoe bend and exits the narrow gorge.

The canyon widens and the drive passes Mesa Creek and the Lone Tree Placer Gravels. The gravels, washed from ore-bearing deposits high in the San Juan Mountains, attracted prospectors with their glittering gold in 1887. These placer miners hauled the gravels by wheelbarrows, chutes, and wagons down to the river's edge where they could be washed in machines. The highest bench held the most riches said knowledgeable miners, but it was too far from the river to be profitable and the technology to pump water up-hill did not yet exist. Engineers designed and built a six-mile ditch and seven-mile hanging flume to carry upstream water to the placer site. The highway climbs south on a broad bench, passes a coke oven used by blacksmiths during the flume's construction, edges under a sweeping band of rosy Entrada sandstone, and reaches the Hanging Flume Overlook.

The Hanging Flume, a national engineering landmark, clings to Wingate sandstone walls in the Dolores River canyon below. The flume, constructed between 1889 and 1891, snakes along the cliffs 100 to 150 feet above the river. The flume, six-feet wide and four-feet deep, used 1.8 million feet of lumber, cost over $100,000, carried 80-million gallons of water a day to the mine, and turned out to be an engineering marvel. The mine, however, turned out to be a total bust. Most of the gold was unrecoverable leaf gold and the St. Louis-based mining company closed the mine in 1893 after turning an $80,000 profit on a million-dollar investment. Area ranches stripped some of the flume, reusing the lumber for fences, cabins, and ranch buildings.

The highway continues south on a broad bench above the river canyon and after a mile swings east. A short dirt track bumps south to the airy confluence of the Dolores and San Miguel rivers. The rivers merge far below in a crimson-colored gorge flanked by towering sandstone cliffs. The drive bends southeast and follows the edge of the San Miguel's abrupt canyon. A wave of Entrada sandstone overhangs the asphalt. The canyon broadens and the road reaches the now-abandoned townsite of Uravan. The town, its name a contraction of uranium and vanadium, sprang up in 1936 as a company town for U.S. Vanadium Corporation, part of Union Carbide. Area mines yielded rich deposits of yellow carnotite, with radium, vanadium, and uranium ores. Vanadium, used to harden steel, was mined during both world wars, while

A palisade of Wingate sandstone cliffs line the Dolores River Canyon along the Unaweep-Tabeguache Scenic Drive.

uranium, recovered from mill tailings, went to the Manhattan Project in World War II to develop the world's first nuclear weapons. Only the mill ruins remain today on the old Club Ranch property, stairstepping up the hillside above settling ponds. The town, its houses, stores, post office, and school, has vanished. Everything was removed during environmental reclamation because of radioactive contamination.

The drive runs southeast along the San Miguel River in a broad, picturesque canyon. Steep slopes rise in step-like benches dark with pinyon pine and juniper, each rimmed with sandstone strata. Tawny Dakota sandstone forms a prominent battlement atop the canyon rim, its cliffs creased with cracks. Huge boulders cascade down steep slopes above the road. Fourteen miles from Uravan the highway intersects Colorado 90, which heads west up the Paradox Valley to Utah. A roadside monument here commemorates the passage of Franciscan padres Francisco Dominguez and Silvestre Escalante, who explored this area in 1776 in search of an easy route to the California missions from New Mexico.

Naturita perches on terraced benches a couple miles up the highway. Naturita Creek and this small 5,431-foot-high town, established in 1882 as a ranching and mining supply center, were named by pioneer settler Rockood Blake with a Spanish word meaning "close to nature." Five miles north is Nucla, a utopian agricultural community founded in 1896 as a communal experiment by the Colorado Cooperative Company. The highway leaves the San Miguel River just west of Naturita and bends up Naturita Creek's shallow canyon. CO 141 intersects CO 145 in the canyon. The drive continues southeast on CO 145. Past the junction the highway climbs onto Wrights Mesa, a long, flattened tableland between Naturita Creek and the San Miguel River canyon.

Majestic views of the snow-capped San Juan Mountains spread away from the highway. The San Miguel Range looms to the south; Mount Sneffels and its ragged crest studs the southeastern horizon; the Uncompahgre Plateau lifts its whiskered flanks to the east; and Utah's La Sal Mountains pierce the northwestern sky. The highway runs across the fertile mesatop, passing lush paddocks filled with grazing cattle and horses and green hay fields. The road passes Redvale, a small town founded in 1910 by an orchard company. Its high elevation coupled with a short growing season doomed the orchards. Norwood lies nine miles up the highway. This genuine Western community, named for a Missouri town by founder I.M. Copp in 1885, serves as a supply hub for area ranchers and farmers. The town, offering all visitor services, boasts an excellent bookstore—Bear Paw Books—housed in a historic stone building on Main Street.

Past Norwood the highway crosses fields, enters a pinyon woodland, and drops onto the lip of the San Miguel River's deep canyon. The road twists two miles down Norwood Hill to the canyon floor, passing a couple scenic overlooks. The drive's last twelve miles wind along the river to Placerville. Much of the canyon's diverse riparian habitat is preserved in the San Miguel River Nature Conservancy Preserve. This lush riverside environment, one of Colorado's last undisturbed, mid-elevation riparian areas, is rich in plant and animal life. The San Miguel River, falling over 8,000 feet in eighty miles from its mountain headwaters to the Dolores River, tumbles over cobbles and boulders. Tall cottonwoods and willow thickets clot its grassy banks. Cliff bands, punctuated by steep slopes dense with Gambel oak, pinyon, fir, spruce, and pine, stretch along the canyon walls. The drive quietly ends at Placerville, an old placer-mining town, and the junction of CO 145 and Colorado 62. CO 145, part of the Lizard Head Pass scenic drive, continues up the canyon fifteen miles to Telluride, while CO 62 climbs east over scenic Dallas Divide to Ridgway.

28 MESA VERDE NATIONAL PARK DRIVE
Cortez to the Soda Canyon Rim

General description: The drive runs 21 miles across mesa-tops and canyons in Mesa Verde National Park to the park museum. Ruins Road, formed by 2 additional 6-mile-long self-guiding loops, explores the cliffed cities and mesa-top remains of the Anasazi culture on Chapin Mesa.
Special attractions: Mesa Verde National Park, Far View Visitor Center, Mesa Verde Museum, Far View Ruins, Cedar Tree Tower, Spruce Tree House, Cliff Palace, Balcony House, Long House, Step House, Badger House, pithouse and pueblo ruins, Spruce Canyon and Petroglyph Point

28 MESA VERDE NATIONAL PARK DRIVE

To Dove Creek

666

Cortez

160

To Four Corners

160
666

To Mancos

MONTEZUMA VALLEY

Point Lookout
8,427 ft.

Morefield CG

Park Point
8,571 ft.

MESA

VERDE

Far View
Visitor Center

Far View Ruins

Wetherill Mesa Rd.

CHAPIN MESA

NATIONAL

WETHERILL MESA

PARK

Cedar Tree
Tower

Long
House

Museum
and Spruce
Tree House

Cliff Palace

Mancos

River

UTE

MOUNTAIN

INDIAN

N

RESERVATION

•Denver

COLORADO

0   2   4   6   8   10
Miles

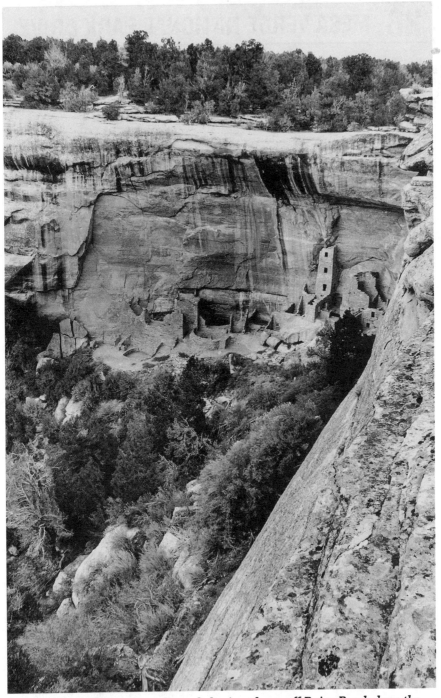

Square Tower House sits under a sheltering alcove off Ruins Road along the Mesa Verde National Park drive.

trails, panoramic overlooks, hiking, camping, interpretative programs, guided tours.

Location: Far southwestern Colorado. The drive begins 10 miles east of Cortez on U.S. Highway 160. Durango is 30 miles east on US 160.

Drive route name: Ruins Road.

Travel season: Year-round. The park and drive are open all year. Many services are curtailed in the off-season between November and the end of April. The Ruins Road loop drive is open 8 a.m. to sunset and the museum is open 8 a.m. to 5 p.m. daily in winter. Check for times of off-season tours of Spruce Tree House and Cliff Palace. Expect hazardous road conditions during and after snowstorms. Ice lingers on shaded corners on the road's upper elevations.

Camping: Morefield Campground, operated by a private concessionaire, is generally open early May through mid-October. The 452-site campground, spread across scenic Morefield Canyon, sits 4 miles south of the park entrance. The campground offers tables, fireplaces, comfort stations, trailer dumping stations, and summer evening programs.

Services: Services, including supplies, groceries, gasoline, laundromat, and showers, are found in Morefield Village at the campground between May and October. Far View has gas station, restaurant, cafeteria, gift shop, and lodge. There are omplete visitor services in Cortez and Mancos.

Nearby attractions: Wetherill Mesa, Ute Mountain Tribal Park, Sleeping Ute Mountain, Cortez, Four Corners Monument, Hovenweep National Monument, Anasazi Heritage Center, Escalante Ruins, McPhee Reservoir, Dolores River Canyon, Mancos State Recreation Area, La Plata Mountains, San Juan National Forest, Durango, Lizard Head Pass scenic drive, Million Dollar Highway scenic drive, Durango and Silverton Narrow Gauge Railroad.

For more information: Mesa Verde National Park, CO 81330, (970) 529-4475. Cortez Chamber, P.O. Box 968, Cortez, CO 81321, (970) 565-3414.

The drive: Anasazi, a Navajo word meaning "the ancient ones" or "enemy ancestors," describes a loose aggregate of Indian cultures that once inhabited the Colorado Plateau province in northern New Mexico and Arizona, southern Utah, and southwestern Colorado. Sharp, unfinished edges fill the plateau's distinctive landscapes. It's a harsh land of bare-bones sandstone, sliced by deep canyons and arroyos, lorded over by towering mesas and buttes, and traversed by rivers of history and character. Sparse rainfall, a fierce temperature range, and a storm of sunlight dictates the plateau's environment and, in turn, shaped the destiny and cultures of the peoples who have lived here over the last ten thousand years.

The Anasazi, one of southwest America's three main cultural groups, developed, flourished, and vanished centuries before Columbus set foot in the New World. The hallmark trait of the Anasazi are the great stone cities built during their "classic" era almost a thousand years ago. The Anasazi erected massive, above-ground pueblos like those seen today at their descendants' villages in Taos, Acoma, and Hopiland. They also built pueblos nestled under the protective eaves of immense caves. Mesa Verde National Park in far southwestern Colorado preserves these startling cliff towns and the thirty-three-mile-long Mesa Verde scenic drive explores and interprets this lost world of the Anasazi. The 52,000-acre national park, established in 1906, protects more than four thousand prehistoric sites, including almost six hundred cliff dwellings.

Mesa Verde made an ideal place for human habitation. More rain falls on this highland than surrounding lowland valleys and its gentle tilt to the south keeps winter temperatures moderate. Rainfall on the semi-arid mesa averages eighteen inches a year, with the bulk of that coming in the eighty to one hundred inches of annual winter snow. A long, 171-day frost-free growing season ensured good summer crops for the Anasazi farmers. Expect cold, snowy winters and warm, dry summers when visiting the national park. Daily highs during the busy season, June through September, reach into the eighties and nineties. Thunderstorms often occur on July and August afternoons. Winters at Mesa Verde are a delight, with low visitation and clear, cold days. The road's upper elevations can be snow-packed and icy, particularly in shaded areas. Spring brings warm, breezy days and occasional rain, sleet, and snow.

The drive begins ten miles east of Cortez on US 160. Exit south to Mesa Verde National Park. The paved road runs south up a shallow draw bordered by shale hills studded with pinyon pines and junipers. A trailer parking area sits alongside the road. Because of the narrow, winding road no trailers are permitted past Morefield Campground. Visitors not camping are required to leave their rigs here. The park entrance station is reached after a mile. Entrance fees are paid here and park information is dispensed.

The road continues south and begins switchbacking upward under 8,427-foot Point Lookout, an abrupt cliff-lined promontory. This airy lookout, reached via a 2.3-mile trail from Morefield Campground, marks Mesa Verde's northernmost point. The Mesa Verde, Spanish for "Green Table," lifts sharply from the broad Montezuma Valley in southwestern Colorado. The high plateau, bordered by sheer cliffs and precipitous shale slopes, forms a natural fortress. Only the Mancos River, following a sinuous canyon, penetrates the lofty sandstone barrier. Mesa Verde is a textbook example of what geologists call a cuesta—a tilted mesa with a steep escarpment on one side and a gently dipping slope on the other. Deep canyons, draining southward to the Mancos River, dissect the Mesa Verde between long finger-like mesas laden with fertile, windblown soil deposits.

Past Point Lookout the road swings onto the mesa's east flank, edging south high above the broad Mancos Valley. This road section crosses gray Mancos Shale, a two thousand-foot-thick layer of consolidated mud deposited sixty-five-million years ago in a quiet, shallow sea. The shale weathers into the towering badlands that dominate the Mesa Verde's steep edges. The formation, which swells and contracts with moisture, is prone to landslides and subsidence. The road here has been erased and closed several times by landslides. The area above the road has since been reworked and anchored to avoid future problems.

Above the Mancos Shale lies the Mesa Verde Group. Three distinct formations—Point Lookout Sandstone, the Menefee Formation, and Cliff House Sandstone—compose this grouping of rock layers. Both the Point Lookout and Cliff House sandstones are cliff-forming units laid down as shoreline sand deposits as the Mancos Sea alternately retreated and advanced. Point Lookout Sandstone forms the massive ramparts above the drive's first miles, while the Cliff House Sandstone caps the mesa's interior canyons and provides the open alcoves used by the Anasazi. The easily-eroded Menefee Formation, squeezed between the two sandstones, resulted from silt and sand being deposited in swampy marshes and lagoons along an ancient shoreline.

The Mancos Valley Overlook sits near the end of the shelf road. A great panorama spreads out beyond this lofty viewpoint. Below spreads the broad Mancos Valley, divided by ranches and green pastures. At its head sits the town of Mancos and above looms the La Plata Mountains, a small, ragged range topped by 13,232-foot Hesperus Mountain. Past the overlook the drive bends through a saddle and enters Morefield Canyon four miles from the park entrance.

This wide canyon, rimmed by low cliffs and fringed by scrub oak-covered slopes, houses most of the park's visitor services. Morefield Village offers a laundromat, gas station, refreshment center, store with supplies and souvenirs, and coin-operated showers. Morefield Campground, operated by a concessionaire between April and October, boasts 452 campsites, 17 group sites, and 4 handicap-accessible sites. Camping, available on a first-come, first-served basis, is limited to fourteen days. Evening campfire programs are presented nightly June through Labor Day in the Morefield Ampitheatre.

The Morefield Campground area also offers excellent hiking trails. Hiking is limited to only a few areas in Mesa Verde National Park to protect the park's unique archeological treasures. Visitors hiking away from developed areas and off designated trails are subject to stiff penalties. Three trails roam the Morefield area. The 1.5-mile Knife Edge Trail follows the old road from the campground to the Montezuma Valley Overlook. The 2.3-mile Point Lookout Trail treks out to the point's precipitous edge and yields spectacular views. The 7.8-mile Prater Ridge Trail climbs west from the campground onto lofty Prater Ridge.

The drive drops down, crosses Morefield Canyon, and enters a quarter-mile-long tunnel through Prater Ridge. After exiting the tunnel the road climbs up flat-bottomed upper Prater Canyon to 7,820-foot-high Montezuma Valley Overlook. Look for mule deer grazing on the canyon floor, particularly in early evening. The viewpoint, with picnic tables and ramadas, looks west across the broad Montezuma Valley. Numerous farms and ranches dot the valley around Cortez, one of southwest Colorado's largest towns. Beyond towers 9,977-foot Ute Peak and Sleeping Ute Mountain, a small laccolithic range formed when intrusive volcanic rock blistered up through the surrounding sedimentary strata.

The road winds south from the overlook, ascending steep slopes covered with scrub oaks, pinyon pines, and occasional Douglas-firs. For the next nine miles the road follows the North Rim of the Mesa Verde, climbing over high ridges, dipping across shallow canyon heads, and edging along steep slopes that plunge down to the Montezuma Valley. These upper elevations are heavily forested. Gambels or scrub oak heavily coats the hillsides and Douglas-fir, ponderosa pine, and even quaking aspen tuck into cool, moist ravines. Abundant wildlife populates Mesa Verde's diverse, wild habitats. Mule deer are abundant, while transient elk occasionally wander onto the escarpment. Mountain lion, black bear, coyote, bobcat, and gray fox roam this upland plateau, and scattered bighorn sheep inhabit the rocky canyons. The more than 160 birds species seen include turkeys, golden eagles, hawks, owls, turkey vultures, ravens, Stellers jays, chickadees, nuthatches, and hummingbirds. Rattlesnakes hide on warm, rocky canyon slopes.

After four miles the road reaches 8,571-foot Park Point, the park's highest elevation. This lookout yields a spectacular overview of the surrounding Colorado Plateau. To the northeast lie forested plateaus topped by the snow-capped San Miguel and La Plata ranges. Utah's canyon country stretches westward beyond Ute Peak to the Abajo and La Sal mountains. The Chuska and Lukachukai ranges, straddling the Arizona and New Mexico border, recede to the southwestern horizon, while the immense San Juan Basin, punctuated by the volcanic peak of Shiprock, basks south of Mesa Verde in New Mexico.

The drive winds another five miles along the North Rim to Far View. Here, perched on a flattened ridge, sits the Far View Visitor Center. The center, open June through September, displays contemporary Indian arts and crafts and historic lifestyles. Nearby is Far View Motor Lodge and a restaurant, cafeteria, and gas station. An excellent summer side-trip begins at Far View and travels twelve miles southwest to Wetherill Mesa via a narrow, winding road with sharp curves and steep grades. Wetherill Mesa offers a good, uncrowded alternative to the busy Chapin Mesa ruins. Visitors can follow a self-guided tour through Step House or an hour-long ranger-led excursion into Long House, the park's second largest ruin.

The drive bends onto upper Chapin Mesa at Far View Visitor Center, begins descending southward, and a mile later reaches Far View Ruin. This large mesa-top village, located just east of the road, is best visited on the return trip. Far View House, a rectangular pueblo with about fifty rooms, was a possible trading center inhabited from A.D. 1100 to 1200. A large population lived in the area surrounding Far View with over fifty dwelling sites within the pueblo's immediate area. While this area is colder in winter than farther south on the mesa, it receives more annual rainfall—an important consideration for these early farmers.

Water became the blood of the Anasazi lifeway when they became agriculturists. By controlling water, the Anasazi controlled their destiny. Without water they would remain locked into a basic hunting and gathering economy, following game and harvesting seasonal plants. The miracle of water, however, grew nutritious crops like corn, beans, and squash that in turn made social and religious growth possible. Water, in a sense, created Mesa Verde's vibrant Indian cities and gave their inhabitants the leisure time to develop crafts like basketry, pottery, and weaving. The Anasazi became masters of water exploitation in this semi-arid land by utilizing floodwater and subsurface irrigation, planting crops near seepage springs, and building ditches and reservoirs to transport and store water.

Mummy Lake, sitting alongside the drive just north of Far View Ruin, testifies to the Anasazi's reliance on water. A fan of uphill channels could have diverted runoff from rain and snow into a main ditch that drained into Mummy Lake. The stone-lined lake is possibly a reservoir ninety feet in diameter and twelve feet deep with a 500,000-gallon storage capacity. A distribution channel ran south from the reservoir to nearby fields for irrigation. The Far View Ditch, another canal, ran five miles down Chapin Mesa to the head of Spruce Tree Canyon. That water was probably used for irrigation, although no clear evidence indicates water ever flowed that far down the ditch. Some archeologists also dispute that Mummy Lake was a reservoir or was used for water collection. Mummy Lake is reached via a short trail from Far View Ruin.

The road continues south on Chapin Mesa and reaches Cedar Tree Tower after three miles. This small ruin, composed of a tower connected to a "kiva" or underground ceremonial chamber, lies east of the road. Prehistoric farming terraces scatter along a short trail south of the site. A major road intersection is a half-mile further south. A mile-long loop road continues south to the Mesa Verde Museum, park headquarters, and Spruce Tree House. The museum offers an excellent introduction to the evolution of the Anasazi culture through a series of dramatic dioramas and displays numerous artifacts including pottery, basketry, jewelry, and weaving. A picnic area spreads along the rim of Spruce Canyon on the west side of the loop opposite the museum.

A self-guiding paved trail begins at the museum and drops east into Spruce Tree Canyon to Spruce Tree House, the park's third largest cliff dwelling. This well-preserved ruin, protected from weathering by an immense alcove, boasts 114 rooms and eight kivas and housed as many as 150 people. The site was named by its discoverers Richard Wetherill and Charlie Mason after a large Douglas-fir tree that grew in front of the village. The tree was cut down in 1891. A booklet, available at the trailhead and museum, explains Spruce Tree House's important features. Two other trails explore the park headquarters area. The 2.8-mile Petroglyph Point Trail follows Spruce Tree Canyon's eastern edge to Petroglyph Point, passing several rock art panels, before climbing onto the rim for the return walk. The 2.1-mile Spruce Canyon Trail winds into Spruce Canyon before climbing onto Chapin Mesa near the picnic area.

The Ruins Road, consisting of two six-mile-long loops, begins at the intersection with the headquarters road. The drive heads down Ruins Road and goes straight on the Mesa Top Ruins drive loop. This loop explores the architectural development of the Anasazi by stopping at a succession of sites. Few places are found in the Southwest where the Anasazi's long march to civilization can be seen so clearly as along this loop. The first stop is a pithouse, a roofed semi-subterranean pit, built about A.D. 575 during an era archeologists call the Modified Basketmaker Period. The next viewpoint overlooks deep Navajo Canyon, containing over sixty cliff dwellings, including Echo House across the chasm. Square Tower House, one of Mesa Verde's most elegant ruins, nestles in a shallow cavern below the next stop. The seventy-room pueblo boasts Mesa Verde's tallest structure with one wall measuring thirty-three feet high.

The next three stops include pithouses erected before A.D. 700 and several above-ground villages dating from the Developmental Pueblo Period between A.D. 800 and 1100. Sun Point Pueblo, at the next pull-off, dates from 1200 during the Classic Pueblo Period, a time when the Anasazi culture reached its zenith. The Anasazi began leaving the mesa-tops shortly after the pueblo's construction and building their villages in caves tucked under the canyon rims. Why they retreated into the cliffs is an enduring mystery. Defense reigns as the common explanation. A village built in a protective alcove was undoubtedly easily defended, particularly with bow and arrows and stockpiles of food and water. Little evidence exists, however, that these were people at war. But whatever the reasons, the move to their cliffed aeries was the first step toward the total abandonment of the Mesa Verde by A.D. 1300.

Sun Point Overlook yields cross-canyon views of numerous ruins built during the thirteenth century. The next two viewpoints look into Fewkes Canyon and several impressive sites including Oak Tree House, Fire Temple, and New Fire House. Sun Temple, the last stop, sits on a narrow promontory above Fewkes Canyon. This large D-shaped building, while never completed, is thought to be a ceremonial structure. Another overlook just north of Sun Temple yields marvelous views of Cliff Palace, North America's largest cliff dwelling.

It was near this spot that two cowboys from the Mancos Valley stumbled upon this "magnificent city" on a cold snowy December day in 1888. Richard Wetherill and his brother-in-law Charlie Mason were searching this rough country for stray cattle when they happened upon the grandest cliff dwelling of all and transformed Mesa Verde from a remote plateau to America's greatest archeological wonder. After their initial astonishment, they lashed several trees together, descended to the canyon bottom, and clambered up to the silent chamber. The ruin appeared almost undisturbed from the passage of centuries. Pots and stone tools lay on walls, awaiting the return of their owners. Parts of human skeletons scattered across the ground. The men dubbed their amazing discovery Cliff Palace.

Why the Anasazi abandoned their ancestral homeland at Mesa Verde and across the Four Corners region is an enduring mystery. While they left a rich legacy of crumbling ruins from their golden years, a time of growth, trade, and frenzied construction, they left few clues as to their disappearance. By the A.D. 1200s Mesa Verde's Indians had built a sophisticated society with all the tools for success in this arid country, including water-control projects, solar calendars that marked the solstices and equinoxes, multi-storied apartment houses, and a flourishing trade network with the rest of the Southwest and Mexico. But something happened, and between A.D. 1270

Visitors explore Cliff Palace on the Mesa Verde scenic drive.

and 1300 the Anasazi homeland of a thousand years was emptied. Archeologists speculate a combination of factors forced the perplexing migration from the Four Corners area to New Mexico's Rio Grande Valley and Arizona's Hopi Mesas. A prolonged drought stunted crops by shifting moisture from spring and summer to autumn. The mesa's large population depleted ground cover and trees for construction and firewood, and centuries of farming robbed mesa soils of their productivity. Disease, internal bickering, social fragmentation, and raids by outside enemies also made compelling reasons to abandon the mesa for greener pastures elsewhere.

The drive continues back to the intersection with the other Ruins Road loop. Turn east. The new road drops southeast through dense pinyon pine and juniper forest and reaches Cliff Palace just after turning to one-lane. Cliff Palace is viewed from a mesa-top overlook and a self-guiding loop trail descends into the ruin. Visitors must climb stairs and four ten-foot ladders along the trail. An excellent trail guide, available at the trailhead, details Cliff Palace and the Anasazi. Park rangers are stationed in the ruin to answer questions and ensure visitors stay on the trail.

Cliff Palace, the park's largest cliff dwelling, housed over two hundred people in its 217 rooms and twenty-three kivas. The village, built between A.D. 1209 and 1273, exhibits superb construction and masonry skills. Cliff Palace was built by accretion rather than from a grand plan—rooms were added on as they were needed. Stones, often pecked with harder hammerstones into usable shapes, were laid with a mud mortar before being carefully plastered over. Painted designs often brightened the walls.

Willa Cather aptly described Cliff Palace in her novel *The Professor's House* as "a little city of stone, asleep. It was as still as sculpture.... It all hung together, seemed to have a kind of composition: pale little houses of stone nestling close to one another, perched on top of each other, with flat roofs, narrow windows, straight walls, and in the middle of the group, a round tower...I had come upon the city of some extinct civilization, hidden away in this inaccessible mesa for centuries, preserved in the dry air and almost perpetual sunlight like a fly in amber, guarded by the cliffs and the river and the desert."

The road continues south, skirting the sandstone rim of Cliff Canyon. Several roadside overlooks view ruins including the House of Many Windows tucked into shallow caves across the canyon. The road bends east across the mesa, briefly dipping into Ute Mountain Tribal Park, a 125,000-acre park preserving the remote canyons to the south and numerous Anasazi ruins, on the Ute Mountain Indian Reservation.

The next stop atop the Soda Canyon rim offers Balcony House, one of the park's most popular ruin tours. This forty-five room pueblo nestles under an arching cave beneath the parking area. Regular ranger-led tours, available only by first-come, first-served basis, explore the site in summer. Line up under the ramada for a place on the tour. The hour-long tour descends a paved trail and climbs a thirty-two-foot-high ladder into Balcony House. Exit back to the rim is via a crawl tunnel, several wooden ladders, and steps chopped into the cliff face. Visitors with health problems or fear of heights should by-pass this tour. Balcony House, perched above abrupt cliffs, is the park's most defensible large ruin with only one entry and exit path. An excellent year-round spring undoubtedly made this aerie attractive to its inhabitants.

The Soda Canyon Overlook Trailhead, the drive's last stop, sits a little farther up the road. This quiet 0.75-mile trail winds through pinyon pine and juniper to a jutting promontory that yields a good view of Balcony House and Soda Canyon. The loop road continues northwest back to the main intersection. Turn north for the twenty-one-mile journey back to the park entrance and US 160.

29 RIM ROCK DRIVE
Colorado National Monument

General description: A 22-mile drive that explores the lofty sandstone rim and canyons of Colorado National Monument on the northern edge of the Uncompahgre Plateau.

Special attractions: Sandstone cliffs and spires, Monument Canyon, Alcove Nature Trail, Independence Monument, Window Rock Nature Trail, visitor center, John Otto's Trail, numerous overlooks, Coke Ovens, Ute Canyon, Cold Shivers Point, Devils Kitchen, hiking, camping, backpacking, rock climbing, wildlife, interpretative programs.

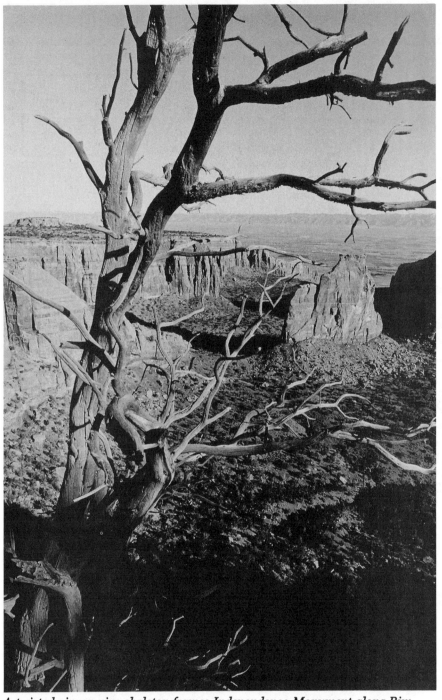

A twisted pinyon pine skeleton frames Independence Monument along Rim Rock Drive.

Location: West-central Colorado. The national monument and drive lie just west of Grand Junction near the Utah border.

Drive route name: Rim Rock Drive.

Travel season: Year-round. Although the road is regularly plowed in winter, snow and ice may persist on shaded road sections.

Camping: Saddlehorn Campground offers 80 sites near the visitor center on the drive's west end. The campground is open year-round, although the restrooms and water are shut off in winter.

Services: All services are found in Fruita and Grand Junction, including lodging, private campgrounds, gas, food, and medical facilities.

Nearby attractions: Grand Junction, Museum of Western Colorado, Highline Lake State Recreation Area, Island Acres State Recreation Area, Grand Mesa Scenic Byway, Lands End Road, Rattlesnake Canyon and arches, Ruby and Horsethief canyons, Colorado River, Kokopelli's Trail, Rabbit Valley Paleontology Area, Grand Mesa National Forest, Uncompahgre National Forest, Unaweep-Tabeguache Scenic and Historic Byway.

For more information: Colorado National Monument, Fruita, CO 81521, (970) 858-3617. Grand Junction Visitor & Convention Bureau, 360 Grand Ave., Grand Junction, CO 81501, (970) 242-3214 or (800) 962-2547.

The drive: Thick sandstone layers drape across the Uncompahgre Plateau, a long humpbacked highland that stretches across western Colorado from the San Juan Mountains to the Colorado River on the eastern edge of the immense Colorado Plateau. Colorado National Monument, on the plateau's northern edge, protects a 20,450-acre wonderland of dipping sandstone strata chiseled by erosion into precipitous canyons, abrupt buttresses, sharp spires and buttes, and soaring cliffs. This rugged monument relates a spectacular lesson in geology. It spreads open like a textbook that illuminates forgotten chapters in the earth's long history. The monument's 1.5-billion-year-old basement rocks once floored a primeval ocean. The horizontal rock strata above—the Chinle, Wingate, Kayenta, Entrada, and Morrison formations—tell more recent tales of immense dune fields, meandering rivers, and swamps alive with dinosaurs. The twenty-two-mile Rim Rock Drive traverses the monument's canyons and airy rims, explores its geologic history, offers nineteen scenic overlooks, and passes several trails that plunge into the canyons, leading to spring-fed oases of grass, birdsong, and solitude.

Colorado National Monument offers a generally pleasant year-round climate. Temperatures, however, range from below zero in winter to one hundred degrees in summer. Most summer days are sunny and warm with highs in the eighties and nineties. Hikers should carry a gallon of water per day and wear a hat. Temperatures in the canyons, with heat radiating off bare rock surfaces, can be extreme. Occasional afternoon thunderstorms douse the monument's rim and canyons in July and August. Autumn brings gorgeous warm days and clear nights. Expect highs in the seventies and eighties with cool evenings. Winter days are cold and crisp, but highs often reach into the forties. Snow occasionally blankets the monument under a mantle of white. Spring offers warm weather, windy afternoons, light rain showers, and wildflowers.

Rim Rock Drive is accessed at two points—at Grand Junction on the east and at Fruita on the west. The drive description begins at Colorado National Monument's west entrance on Colorado Highway 340-Redlands Road almost three miles south of Fruita and Interstate 70's Exit 19 on the southern edge of the broad Grand Valley west of Grand Junction. The Colorado River, formerly called the Grand River, drifts lazily across the valley, meandering past cottonwood-lined banks, fruit orchards, and a series of towns including Palisade, Grand Junction, and Fruita. Grand Junction, western Colorado's largest city, was named because the Gunnison River joins the Colorado River here. Mountains and cliffs hem in Grand Valley—the lofty plateau of Grand Mesa dominates the eastern horizon, the bare cliffs and eroded badlands of the Book Cliffs march across the northern edge, and the national monument's ragged cliffs and canyons mark the southern skyline.

CO 340 swings south from Fruita, a small agricultural town, passes a Colorado Welcome Center with maps and brochures, and crosses the Colorado River's muddy channel. The road climbs away from the river through the multi-colored siltstones and mudstones of the Morrison Formation. This 150-million-year-old formation preserves the skeletons of great dinosaurs that roamed the region's dense forests and swamplands as well as some of the oldest mammal fossils found in the Western Hemisphere.

Numerous dinosaur bones are found in the Morrison rocks below the uplifted Uncompahgre Plateau between Fruita and Grand Junction. The barren hill east of the highway and above the river is the site of paleontologist Elmer Riggs' 1901 discovery of an *Apatosaurus* skeleton. A bronze plaque honors the event. A short trail also loops through the area, exploring this famed dinosaur locale. Riggs Hill, another notable dinosaur quarry, lies a few miles east of here. There, in 1900, Riggs excavated the first known skeleton of the immense *Brachiosaurus*.

The highway bends southeast from the dinosaur site and climbs to Colorado National Monument's west entrance almost three miles from Fruita. Rim Rock Drive begins here. After passing the entrance station the paved road crosses the maroon-colored Chinle Formation and quickly reaches steep Wingate sandstone cliffs. The road ascends a tight switchback on the west side of Wedding Canyon, with the rounded tower of the Praying Monk sitting east of the loop. Redlands View, a quarter mile up the drive, offers a look at the Grand Valley and a fault zone below the escarpment.

Past the overlook the road bends south and enters Fruita Canyon, a deep box canyon sliced into the plateau rim. The road swings under towering sandstone cliffs on the canyon's east flank. A turnout near the canyon's head yields a great view of Balanced Rock, a short pinnacle topped with an overhanging block of precariously balanced Wingate sandstone. The road climbs steeply past Balanced Rock, passes through two tunnels, and reaches Historic Trails View near the cliffed rim. An interpretative sign details the area's early explorations including the famed Spanish padres Dominguez and Escalante's 1776 expedition in search of a trail from New Mexico to the

California missions. The drive continues climbing and finally reaches the lofty rim above Fruita Canyon and Fruita Canyon Viewpoint. Past the canyon the drive bends south and reaches the visitor center.

The visitor center, at an elevation of 5,787 feet, details the natural history, geology, and history of Colorado National Monument. The center also offers ranger-led walks and talks in the warmer months, an introductory audio-visual program, restrooms, books, and maps. A paved, one-way side road heads north from the visitor center and loops around Saddlehorn Rock, a prominent monolith of pale Entrada sandstone. Eighty-site Saddlehorn Campground spreads along the road north of the rock. The widely spaced sites lie in a pinyon and juniper woodland. The campground, open year-round on a first-come, first-served basis, offers water, restrooms, and nightly campfire programs in the warmer months.

Window Rock Trail, an excellent 0.3-mile loop trail, begins at an overlook where the campground road reaches the western lip of Wedding Canyon. The short trail winds past twisted junipers and slickrock gardens tucked in alcoves and bays above abrupt cliffs. The path leads to a magnificent viewpoint poised on the canyon rim above Window Rock, an elongated opening carved by water and ice on the cliff edge. The view encompasses broad Wedding Canyon, its sides walled with towering cliffs, and the pastoral Grand Valley. The Colorado River uncoils below. Farther north stretch the Book Cliffs, with bare shale slopes, long cliff bands, and forested summits. Evening is a great time to hike to this overlook. Silence shrouds the canyon and valley at sunset. In growing darkness, the valley below twinkles with a thousand points of light. A small pamphlet, available at the visitor center, identifies plants along the trail. The half-mile Canyon Rim Trail, another good path, runs from Window Rock along the rim of Wedding Canyon to the visitor center. Hikers should beware of steep cliffs and keep children under control. A large picnic area lies just beyond the campground and Window Rock trailhead.

Rim Rock Drive runs south from the visitor center and after a half-mile edges along a narrow bench above an overhanging cliff. At the canyon head the road bends east and continues along a broad rimrock bench. At the next pullout, John Ottos Trail runs a 0.25-mile across a narrow promontory above Wedding Canyon to a lofty lookout perched above the Pipe Organ. John Otto, a trailblazer, promoter, patriot, and outdoorsman, worked tirelessly for the establishment of Colorado National Monument. He first settled in a canvas tent in Monument Canyon in 1906. The next year he wrote, "I came here last year and found these canyons, and they feel like the heart of the world to me. I'm going to stay and build trails and promote this place, because it should be a national park. Some folks think I'm crazy, but I want to see this scenery opened up to all people." Otto devoted himself to building trails, writing the Grand Junction Chamber of Commerce and President Taft to establish a "Monument National Park" here, and guiding local citizens through the wondrous sandstone canyons of his proposed park. Otto was appointed custodian at one dollar a month after the monument was established in 1911.

Three spectacular viewpoints—Independence, Grand View, and Monument Canyon—lie along the next few road miles. All yield spectacular views into Monument Canyon, a wide canyon flanked by sandstone cliffs and floored with ancient bedrock. Independence Monument View overlooks Independence Monument, a five hundred-foot-high monolith that sits atop a soft sandstone cone between Monument and Wedding canyons. Independence Monument, the monument's most distinctive landmark, formed after water and ice eroded walls that once connected the pinnacle to mesas on the northeast and southwest. Wingate sandstone, a buff-colored sandstone deposited as immense sand dunes 210 million years ago during the Triassic Period, forms Colorado National Monument's dramatic cliffs and spires. Atop the Wingate lies the Kayenta Formation, a thin layer deposited by rivers and streams. The Kayenta sandstone, a coarse erosion-resistant rock, forms a capstone atop the softer underlying Wingate Formation and slows its erosion. Independence Monument, with a large, flat summit, is capped and protected by Kayenta sandstone. By contrast, the nearby Coke Ovens weathered into rounded domes with small summits after they lost their Kayenta cap. Independence Monument, today a moderate four-pitch rock climb, was first ascended by John Otto on July 4, 1910, to celebrate Independence Day. Otto scaled a ladder of pipes laboriously drilled into the spire. On the flat summit he hoisted Old Glory. Later Otto displayed the flag every Independence Day giving Independence Monument it's name.

Grand View Point, another half-mile up the drive, offers a spectacular view of Monument Canyon, Independence Monument, and the fertile Grand Valley from a fenced overlook. Past Grand View, the drive twists for a mile

The Grand Valley spreads out below Grand View Point along Colorado National Monument's Rim Rock Drive.

along the Kayenta sandstone rim and reaches Monument Canyon View, another scenic overlook perched atop tall sandstone cliffs. The sinuous road bends south following the rim of a spur canyon to Coke Ovens Overlook. A pullout views the Coke Ovens, several domed rocks shaped like old-time coke ovens. A quarter-mile up the drive is the Monument Canyon Trailhead. This popular 6.3-mile-long trail, built by John Otto in 1910, descends six hundred feet from the rim to Monument Canyon's wide floor, traversing almost a billion years of geologic history from Entrada sandstone to ancient Precambrian gneiss and schist. The trail, a walker's delight, winds past rusty sandstone cliffs and soaring towers like the Kissing Couple and Independence Monument before dropping to a lower trailhead on CO 340. Hikers should carry plenty of water and wear in the warmer months. The short quarter-mile Coke Ovens Trail also begins at the parking area and traverses to an overlook above the Coke Ovens.

Artist's Point sits high above Monument Canyon a half-mile up the road. This lofty viewpoint offers a marvelous panorama of canyons, mesas, and valleys. The drive winds upward through a pygmy forest of pinyon pine and juniper, passes Highland View Overlook, and reaches the 6,593-foot-high divide between Monument and Ute canyons on Monument Mesa. The monument's scant eleven inches of annual precipitation and an extreme temperature range limits plant and animal life on this high desert. The pinyon pine and juniper woodland dominates the monument's mesas and canyons. Both trees blanket moist, north-facing slopes. Junipers also scatter across the desolate rimrock along the drive, sending sturdy taproots down through cracks in pursuit of water. Several stands of quaking aspen and Douglas-fir hide on moist, sheltered slopes in No Thoroughfare Canyon. A sparse understory of shrubs spreads over the forest's sandy floor, including mountain mahogany, a favorite deer food, and open meadows of sagebrush and saltbush. Late spring and early summer brings a colorful display of wildflowers including Indian paintbrush, phlox, yellow mustard, evening primrose, and yucca stalks laden with bulbous white blossoms.

Common animals found in the monument include coyote, mule deer, kangaroo rat, bat, porcupine, rock squirrel, bobcat, and occasional mountain lion, black bear, and elk. Bighorn sheep, reintroduced into the monument in 1979, are sometimes sighted in the canyons. Numerous reptiles and amphibians, including the uncommon midget-faded rattlesnake, as well as 126 bird species inhabit the monument's varied habitats.

Past the divide, the road swings into upper Ute Canyon, a broad valley coated with sagebrush and pinyon. The trailhead for seven-mile Liberty Cap Trail lies just before the valley floor on the road's east side. The path, a favorite cross-country ski tour in winter, threads across undulating Monument Mesa to Liberty Cap before dropping to the lower trailhead below the monument's rocky escarpment. A side road, beginning on the south slope of Ute Canyon, heads south and west across Glade Park five miles to the small hamlet of Glade Park. Rough, four-wheel-drive tracks head west from here to the BLM's Black Ridge Wilderness Study Area, a rough country seamed by deep canyons and studded with hidden arches.

Rim Rock Drive turns sharply east and follows shallow Ute Canyon. The canyon's intermittent stream, flowing only after snowmelt or heavy rain, slowly sliced a V-shaped canyon into the Entrada and Kayenta sandstones. After a mile the canyon abruptly deepens at Suction Point, an airy 350-foot-high pour-off where the creek cut through soft Wingate sandstone. The drop makes a spectacular waterfall after a summer thunderstorm.

The drive traverses the south rim of Ute Canyon and passes two excellent rimrock viewpoints, Upper Ute Canyon and Fallen Rock overlooks. Fallen Rock Overlook gives a great view down-canyon to Fallen Rock, a giant sandstone slab that fell off the sheer canyon wall above. Short, steep Ute Canyon Trail, one of the monument's best hikes, begins at the parking area and plunges into Upper Ute Canyon. A primitive path continues down Lower Ute Canyon to a trailhead seven miles down-canyon. The trail, flanked by rosy cliffs, passes sagebrush meadows, tall cottonwoods that offer welcome summer shade, and cattail-lined potholes alive with spadefoot toads and singing birds.

The road swings around the east arm of Ute Canyon and climbs to 6,640 feet, the drive's highest point. A mile farther sits Lower Ute Canyon View, a fenced viewpoint that looks down the canyon to the distant Book Cliffs. The road turns away from Ute Canyon, traverses a narrow mesa, and after a half-mile emerges at Red Canyon Overlook. This short, deep canyon extends northeast from the viewpoint. The drive twists along Kayenta sandstone on Red and Columbus canyons' airy south rims and after two and a half miles reaches an intersection with DS Road, a county road that heads southwest above No Thoroughfare Canyon to Glade Park. No Thoroughfare Canyon offers wild terrain and primitive trails.

Cold Shivers Point, a barrier-free overlook, lies just north of the road junction. This aptly-named overlook perches atop vertical cliffs hundreds of feet above the floor of Columbus Canyon. The drive begins descending past Cold Shivers Point, and after a half-mile switchbacks steeply down the uplifted escarpment of the Ladder Creek monocline. Serpents Trail begins above the north entrance of a long tunnel. This historic route follows the old road bed of what was nicknamed "the crookedest road in the world." The road, built by John Otto and Glade Park ranchers, was completed in 1921 and closed to vehicular travel in 1950 after the lower section of Rim Rock Drive was completed. Rim Rock Drive was built in the 1930s by work crews with the Civilian Conservation Corps, National Park Service, and WPA. Some twenty-three miles of the drive were handmade, with help only from pickaxes and dynamite. Just before Christmas in 1933 a massive rock fall near Grand View killed nine workers. Serpents Trail uncoils 2.5 miles down a steep sandstone rib. It's best to hike one-way with a driver meeting the walkers at the lower trailhead at Devils Kitchen.

The drive twists through the dark red Chinle formation below the tunnel, switchbacking across steep slopes strewn with tumbled boulders and twisted junipers. Devils Kitchen, a collection of tilted Wingate sandstone towers and buttes, makes a good stop. A short trail climbs 0.7 mile to the bulky rocks.

A picnic area sits down the drive from the trailhead. Nearby hides a panel of Indian petroglyphs or rock drawings carved onto a slab of Wingate sandstone. From the picnic area the drive descends to the monument's east entrance station and the park boundary. Continue northeast down the road to its junction with CO 340. Across the Colorado River lies Grand Junction, US 50, and Interstate 70's Business Route.

30 HARPERS CORNER ROAD - DINOSAUR NATIONAL MONUMENT

General description: This 31-mile-long scenic drive climbs from the headquarters of Dinosaur National Monument over a high, rolling plateau to a lofty lookout atop Harpers Corner above the confluence of the Green and Yampa rivers.

Special attractions: Dinosaur National Monument, Plug Hat Butte, Willow Creek BLM Wilderness Study Area, Bull Canyon BLM Wilderness Study Area, scenic overlooks, Echo Park Road, Whirlpool Canyon, Harpers Corner, Ruple Point, hiking, bicycling, picnicking.

Location: Far northwestern Colorado. The drive begins a 1.5 east of Dinosaur on U.S. Highway 40.

Drive route name: Harpers Corner Road.

Travel season: Late spring through late fall. The road generally opens by late May and closes after the first heavy winter snows, usually sometime in November. Call monument headquarters for information on road closing and opening dates.

Camping: No camping is available on the drive. Primitive camping is permitted on surrounding BLM lands. Dinosaur National Monument campgrounds are located at the Quarry area in Utah almost 30 miles west of monument headquarters via US 40 and Utah Highway 149.
A primitive campground is in Echo Park below the drive. Check at headquarters for road information and site availability. A park campground at Deerlodge Park lies 53 miles east of Dinosaur off US 40.

Services: All services are found in Dinosaur and Rangely.

Nearby attractions: Dinosaur National Monument Quarry (UT), Deerlodge Park, Gates of Lodore, Cross Mountain Canyon, Skull Creek BLM Wilderness Study Area, White River National Forest, Meeker, Flattops Trail Scenic Byway, Uinta Mountains, Flaming Gorge National Recreation Area, Brown's Park.

For more information: Dinosaur National Monument, P.O. Box 210, Dinosaur, CO 81610, (970) 374-2216.

★ •Denver

COLORADO

Wild Mtn. 8,380 ft.

Zenobia Pk. 9,006 ft.

DINOSAUR

Harpers Corner 7,510 ft.

Mitten Fault

WHIRLPOOL CANYON

Green

ISLAND PARK

Green River

NATIONAL

Echo Park Overlook

Echo Park

Rd.

Yampa

Island Park Overlook

Iron Springs Bench Overlook

Park

YAMPA BENCH

River

Echo

Canyon Overlook

MONUMENT

Round Top Mtn. 8,575 ft.

STUNTZ RIDGE

16

To U.S. 40

16

Escalante Overlook

To Vernal, UT

UTAH

COLORADO

BUCKWATER RIDGE

Plug Hat Butte

40

Dinosaur

■Visitor Center

40

To Maybell

N

64

0 1 2 3 4 5
Miles

To Rangely

The drive: Dinosaur National Monument spreads across Colorado's empty quarter—a remote, wild land of sagebrushed valleys, sandstone canyons, and high mesas and mountains. The Green and Yampa rivers meet in secluded Echo Park beneath soaring sandstone walls in the middle of this immense 326-square-mile parkland, their placid waters mingling before edging around Steamboat Rock and spinning down Whirlpool Canyon into Utah. Two distinct natural features comprise Dinosaur National Monument—the unique deposit of dinosaur bones across the border in Utah and the wonderland of canyons incised by the mighty rivers. Most visitors, deluded by the name, come only to gaze at the extraordinary bas-relief of ancient life buried in sandstone, but out there in the monument's backcountry stretches an equally spectacular natural world. The thirty-one-mile-long Harpers Corner Road, beginning at monument headquarters, explores the heart of Dinosaur. It climbs onto the rounded crest of the Yampa Plateau before twisting out to Harpers Corner, a airy viewpoint perched high above Echo Park and Whirlpool Canyon.

Snow determines the drive's season, generally June through October. The road opens after snow drifts melt off the higher elevations, usually sometime in May, and closes in November after heavy snowfall blocks the asphalt. Check at the monument for road closing and opening dates. Expect hot temperatures in the lower elevations near Dinosaur, with highs reaching into the nineties. Temperatures on the high plateau at Canyon Overlook and at Harpers Corner are cooler, ranging from sixty to eighty degrees. Heavy thunderstorms occur on summer afternoons. Watch for lightning on isolated ridges and viewpoints. Autumn offers warm days and cool nights, with occasional storms that bring rain and snow.

The drive begins at the Dinosaur National Monument Visitor Center a mile and a half east of Dinosaur on US 40. The small town of Dinosaur, decorated with scattered sculptures of its namesake including a stegasaurus outside the town hall, is the gateway to northwestern Colorado and Dinosaur National Monument. The town offers visitor services, including lodging, dining, and gas. More complete services are found in Rangely eighteen miles to the south. The Dinosaur Quarry section of the monument lies thirty miles west of Dinosaur near Vernal, Utah. Split Mountain and Green River campgrounds spread along the Green River near the quarry.

The monument visitor center, at the junction of US 40 and the Harpers Corner Road, offers interpretative displays on the area's geology, archeology, and natural history, and a ten-minute introductory slide show. Maps, books, brochures, and restrooms are available. A guide to the Harpers Corner road and trail are sold for a nominal cost here and at kiosks at the road start and end. The quarter-mile, self-guiding Cold Desert Trail begins at the visitor center and explores the natural history of the cold desert community.

The drive heads north from the visitor center, passing an interpretative booth, and begins the sixty-two-mile-long round-trip. The road corridor, while bordered by Bureau of Land Management public lands, is part of the national monument and administered by the National Park Service. A roadside sign notes, "Fossil bones are not found in this section." The road leaves the dry Mancos shale country and passes through a gateway chiseled through an upturned hogback of Dakota sandstone. The road ascends Dripping Rock Creek's shallow draw. Junipers, pinyon pines, and sagebrush cover the hillsides and gangly cottonwoods line the dry streambed below. After a half-mile the road climbs onto a broad ridge. Farther up, the drive crosses fire-ravaged hills. Dense grass coats the ground amid blackened tree skeletons. Lightning caused this fire in 1972.

The road climbs across a divide and winds along the southern base of Plug Hat Butte. A viewpoint below the butte looks south across broad basins broken by ribbed hogbacks. Rangely and the Rangely Oil Field lie to the south and beyond stretch forested plateaus. Two distinct rock layers form the butte—the Entrada and Carmel formations. The salmon-colored Entrada sandstone, forming the butte's hat and brim, was deposited some 200 million-years ago as windswept sand dunes. Mud deposits on an ancient shallow seafloor form the butte's hatband of red Carmel mudstone. The road climbs up through a break in the cliffs to a broad bench atop the butte. The Plug Hat Butte Picnic Area sits on the road's north edge, while the quarter-mile-long Plug Hat Trail begins across the road. This level trail yields easy walking, marvelous views across the cliffed plateau edge, and exhibits on history, plants, and geology.

The drive bends northeast across a high, rolling benchland. Thick sagebrush and scattered junipers blanket the landscape. Sagebrush, *Artemisia tridentata*, coats much of western Colorado. This common plant, identified by its gray-green color and aromatic scent, withstands cold temperatures and provides important browse for mule deer in winter. Overgrazing of native grasses by cattle and sheep and the supression of natural fires expanded the historical range of sagebrush over much of the West during the last one hundred years. The pinyon pine and juniper woodland also forms excellent animal habitat. Mule deer, porcupines, birds, rodents, and mice use the pygmy forest for both food and cover.

Two BLM wilderness study areas—Willow Creek and Bull Canyon—abut the drive as it ascends above Plug Hat Butte. Willow Creek WSA sprawls across ridges and canyons to the east, and Bull Canyon WSA encompasses the cliff-lined drainages below the road on the west. Both offer solitude and good hiking opportunities. After eight miles the road swings past 7,710-foot-high Escalante Overlook on Buckwater Ridge. Marvelous views unfold west from this lofty point—Cliff Ridge stairsteps up from the desert to the plateau crest and dry washes and canyons drain down to the Green River's broad shale valley. A party of Spaniards, including Franciscan padres Escalante and Dominguez, camped among cottonwoods in the rocky valley directly below the overlook.

Frays Velez de Escalante and Francisco Atanasio Dominguez were charged with finding a possible overland route from Santa Fe, New Mexico to new Spanish settlements at Monterey, California. The two priests and eight companions explored north from New Mexico, skirting the ragged San Juan Mountains and the precipitous canyons of the Colorado River. On September 12 and 13, 1776 they traversed the broad valley below, stopping overnight

The Green River drops westward into Utah through cliff-lined Whirlpool Canyon below Harpers Corner.

along a dry wash. On September 14 they bivouacked on the Green River's bank below Split Mountain Canyon just across today's Utah border. Escalante noted in his journal: "In this place there are six large black cottonwood trees...Near them is another, standing alone, on whose trunk, on the side facing the northwest, Don Joaquin Lain with an adz cleared a small space in the form of a rectangular window, and with a chisel carved on it the letters and numbers of this inscription, *The Year 1776*; and lower down in different letters the name *Lain*, with two crosses outside...." The Spaniards turned west and followed the southern edge of the Uinta uplift to snowy passes before returning to Santa Fe. Interpretative displays at the overlook discuss air pollution at this relatively pristine parkland.

The road continues climbing past the overlook, swinging through thick sagebrush stands, onto a high upland plateau. Slight valleys, floored with meandering ribbons of water and grass, dip east through rounded ridges. Cattle graze on these high meadows. Moffat County 16E is reached after eleven miles. This dirt road twists east over the plateau and through canyons and valleys to US 40. Moffat County 16W begins 0.5-mile up the road. This scenic backroad drops west into Utah to US 40. The drive climbs north up a low draw that separates Stuntz Ridge and Round Top Mountain. Here the road crosses the Wolf Creek Fault where two huge blocks of land slipped against each other. The northern block pushed higher, exposing older rocks than those found on the drive's lower elevations. The road wends north across an undulating plateau, dropping through dry washes and skirting humped hills and sagebrush-strewn plains. Groves of quaking aspen huddle

The Yampa River winds through deep canyons east of Harpers Corner Drive.

in moist ravines on north-facing slopes, their golden leaves lending bright patches to the dull-colored landscape. Mule deer frequent the roadside on this highland; be watchful for them in early morning and evening.

After a couple miles the road sweeps onto a wide bench and reaches the turnoff to Canyon Overlook. A short road curves a mile to the overlook and the first view of the Yampa River's sinuous canyon carved from gleaming Weber sandstone almost 3,000 feet below. The overlook perches on the edge of the broad Yampa Plateau, a high rounded uplift that is an eastward extension of the Uinta Mountains. The Uintas, lifted some sixty-five-million years ago along with the rest of the Rocky Mountains, are North America's only major east-west trending mountain range. Erosion attacked the mountains as they rose, dissecting abrupt gorges and canyons into the uplift and sweeping eroded sand and gravel into surrounding basins. Geologists estimate over twenty-five thousand feet of overlying rock washed off the rising mountains. Zenobia Peak, the monument high point at 9,006 feet, lies to the northeast above Yampa Canyon. A picnic area sits among firs at the overlook.

The drive crosses into Utah a couple miles later and drops onto the broad ridge of Harpers Plateau. Shallow draws fall away from the road into steep canyons. The road passes a large corral used in spring and fall round-ups when area ranchers move cattle and sheep to and from high pastures. A parking area and lookout sits alongside the drive at twenty-eight miles. Two major faults are seen from here. The Yampa Fault forms the wide bench below Round Top in a textbook example of step-faulting. The Mitten Park Fault drops down and around the east side of Harpers Plateau before before bending east at dramatically tilted strata north of Steamboat Rock. Faults are fractures in the earth's crust caused by extreme stress and strain. Movement along the fracture results in jarring displacements, causing earthquakes. Faults formed some of Dinosaur's most spectacular scenery.

The Echo Park Road leaves the Harpers Corner scenic drive just past the overlook. The thirteen-mile-long dirt road loops over 2,000 feet down to Echo Park, a sunken hole of looming cliffs, cottonwoods poised on the crumbly river bank, and the confluence of the Green and Yampa rivers. A park campground spreads along the bank opposite jutting Steamboat Rock. Echo Park, the lovely secret heart of Dinosaur's backcountry, was named and explored by one-armed Civil War veteran John Wesley Powell, who, with ten men and four boats, floated down the Green and Colorado rivers in 1869. After running disastrous rapids and making laborious portages through the Canyon of Lodore on the Green River, Powell's expedition lingered in the bucolic hollow for a few days. Repetitious echoes off Steamboat Rock gave the park its name. Powell wrote, "Standing opposite the rock, our words are repeated with startling clearness, but in a soft, mellow tone, that transforms them into magical music. Scarcely can one believe it is the echo of his own voice." Echo Park later became the home of Irishman Pat Lynch, another Civil War veteran, in the early 1880s. Lynch lived as a hermit in cabins and caves here and in the Yampa Canyon until his death in 1918. The Echo Park area still bears the name Pats Hole.

The drive enters Dinosaur National Monument just past the Echo Park turnoff. Island Park Overlook lies beyond the monument boundary. This point looks west to Island Park, a broad basin between Whirlpool Canyon and Split Mountain Gorge. The Green River threads across the emerald-colored park between numerous cottonwood-studded islands. Hills and badlands, etched with dry washes and arroyos, fringe the river's floodplain. The Ruple Point Trail, beginning at the overlook, follows an abandoned road west across Ruple Ridge eight miles to Ruple Point, a spectacular viewpoint above Split Mountain Gorge.

The road bends east and swings past Iron Springs Bench Overlook. The point yields excellent views down Pool Creek and across Iron Springs Bench, the historic Chew Ranch, Pearl Park, and Red Rock Bench to Blue Mountain's rounded uplift. The road twists northeast on an ever-narrowing ridge, re-enters Colorado, and reaches Echo Park Overlook. Echo Park and the mingling of the two great rivers lies far below the overlook. Echo Park, now a peaceful retreat, was a battleground in the 1950s. A massive dam, creating a 107-mile-long, 43,000-acre lake, was proposed for Echo Park. The project would flood the gorgeous river canyons, destroy wildlife habitat including the muddy river waters used by endangered fish species, and set a dangerous precedent that no national parkland could remain inviolate and undeveloped. A heated debate between conservationists and the Bureau of Reclamation resulted in Dinosaur National Monument and its valuable natural values being preserved for posterity.

The drive twists through gnarled junipers, becomes one-way, and reaches a parking area a mile and a half north of Echo Park Overlook. This marks the end of the drive, but not the end of the scenery. The Harpers Corner Trail begins here and threads along a narrow ridge to 7,510-foot Harpers Corner, a jutting promontory high above Echo Park and the Green River. An informative brochure, found at the trail's beginning, explains the area's natural history and geology. As the trail gently descends from the road, glimpses of the canyons unfold below. Finally the path reaches a slight saddle and clambers over bedrock to a magnificent fenced overlook.

Echo Park lies to the east, with the muddy Green River making a tight horseshoe bend around Steamboat Rock. Beyond, lost in the ivory-tinted Weber sandstone, hides the sinuous canyon of the Yampa River. The 170-mile-long Yampa River, Colorado's last major free-flowing river, arises from snow atop the Flat Tops on the White River Plateau. In Dinosaur National Monument, the Yampa winds forty-six miles through a serpentine maze of pale sandstone before merging with the Green River.

The Green River plunges through eighteen-mile-long Lodore Canyon above Echo Park. This somber gorge, its stairstepped upper walls visible northeast of Harpers Corner, possesses the monument's oldest rock formation—billion-year-old Uinta Mountain quartzite. A host of frothy rapids, with terrifying names given by Powell's 1869 expedition like Hells Half Mile and Disaster Falls, challenge river rafters.

The Green River changes character below Echo Park as its makes a wide loop around Harpers Corner. The Mitten Park Fault's upturned rock layers are exposed in a dramatic cross-section above the river. The river enters

Rafters glide by the Tiger Wall on the Yampa River below Harpers Corner Road in Dinosaur National Monument's pristine backcountry.

Whirlpool Canyon at the fault, a spectacular abyss of somber rocks deposited on ancient seabeds. The cliff-lined river flows quickly through here, tumbling over water-worn boulders and passing secret alcoves and sand beaches. John Wesley Powell named and described the canyon: "The Green is greatly increased by the Yampa, and we now have a much larger river. All this volume of water, confined, as it is, in a narrow channel and rushing with great velocity, is set eddying and spinning in whirlpools by projecting rocks and short curves, and the waters waltz their way through the canyon, making their own rippling, rushing, roaring music." An earlier passer-by, a French fur trapper, etched his name and date, "D. Julien 1836," on a rock panel below Harpers Corner.

Before starting the walk and the drive back to US 40, sit and linger atop the lofty aerie of Harpers Corner. Listen to the deep river currents far below, spinning the time-worn music heard by Major Powell. Rivers and time are alike in their relentless resolve and single-minded purpose. To be here now. To hear the flow of the river. That's important. We've left our cultural baggage back in the parking lot and begun to let the consciousness of these rivers and canyons seep in. That's the enchantment of rivers—they're disarmingly simple, yet they teach great lessons.

ABOUT THE AUTHOR

Stewart M. Green is a freelance photographer and writer living in Colorado Springs, Colorado. His photographs appear in many national publications. He is the author and photographer of *Pikes Peak Country: The Complete Guide, Colorado Parklands, Back Country Byways, Arizona Scenic Drives,* and *California Scenic Drives.*

FALCON GUIDES ® Leading the Way

FIELD GUIDES
Bitterroot: Montana State Flower
Canyon Country Wildflowers
Central Rocky Mountains
  Wildflowers
Great Lakes Berry Book
New England Berry Book
Ozark Wildflowers
Pacific Northwest Berry Book
Plants of Arizona
Rare Plants of Colorado
Rocky Mountain Berry Book
Scats & Tracks of the Pacific
  Coast States
Scats & Tracks of the
  Rocky Mountains
Southern Rocky Mountain
  Wildflowers
Tallgrass Prairie Wildflowers
Western Trees
Wildflowers of Southwestern
  Utah
Willow Bark and Rosehips

FISHING GUIDES
Fishing Alaska
Fishing the Beartooths
Fishing Florida
Fishing Glacier National Park
Fishing Maine
Fishing Montana
Fishing Wyoming
Fishing Yellowstone
  National Park

ROCKHOUNDING GUIDES
Rockhounding Arizona
Rockhounding California
Rockhounding Colorado
Rockhounding Montana
Rockhounding Nevada
Rockhound's Guide to New
  Mexico
Rockhounding Texas
Rockhounding Utah
Rockhounding Wyoming

MORE GUIDEBOOKS
Backcountry Horseman's
  Guide to Washington
Camping California's
  National Forests
Exploring Canyonlands &
  Arches National Parks
Exploring Hawaii's Parklands
Exploring Mount Helena
Exploring Southern California
  Beaches
Recreation Guide to WA
  National Forests
Touring California & Nevada
  Hot Springs
Touring Colorado Hot Springs
Touring Montana & Wyoming
  Hot Springs
Trail Riding Western
  Montana
Wild Country Companion
Wilderness Directory
Wild Montana
Wild Utah

BIRDING GUIDES
Birding Minnesota
Birding Montana
Birding Northern California
Birding Texas
Birding Utah

PADDLING GUIDES
Floater's Guide to Colorado
Paddling Minnesota
Paddling Montana
Paddling Okefenokee
Paddling Oregon
Paddling Yellowstone & Grand
  Teton National Parks

HOW-TO GUIDES
Avalanche Aware
Backpacking Tips
Bear Aware
Desert Hiking Tips
Hiking with Dogs
Leave No Trace
Mountain Lion Alert
Reading Weather
Route Finding
Using GPS
Wilderness First Aid
Wilderness Survival

WALKING
Walking Colorado Springs
Walking Denver
Walking Portland
Walking St. Louis
Walking Virginia Beach

■ *To order any of these books, check with your local bookseller*
or call FALCON ® *at 1-800-582-2665.*
Visit us on the world wide web at:
www.FalconOutdoors.com

FALCON®

FALCONGUIDES® Leading the Way™

FALCONGUIDES® are available for where-to-go hiking, mountain biking, rock climbing, walking, scenic driving, fishing, rockhounding, paddling, birding, wildlife viewing, and camping. We also have FalconGuides on essential outdoor skills and subjects and field identification. The following titles are currently available, but this list grows every year. For a free catalog with a complete list of titles, call FALCON toll-free at 1-800-582-2665.

SCENIC DRIVING GUIDES

Scenic Driving Alaska and the Yukon
Scenic Driving Arizona
Scenic Driving the Beartooth Highway
Scenic Driving California
Scenic Driving Colorado
Scenic Driving Florida
Scenic Driving Georgia
Scenic Driving Hawaii
Scenic Driving Idaho
Scenic Driving Michigan
Scenic Driving Minnesota
Scenic Driving Montana
Scenic Driving New England
Scenic Driving New Mexico
Scenic Driving North Carolina
Scenic Driving Oregon
Scenic Driving the Ozarks
Scenic Driving Pennsylvania
Scenic Driving Texas
Scenic Driving Utah
Scenic Driving Washington
Scenic Driving Wisconsin
Scenic Driving Wyoming
Scenic Driving Yellowstone and
   the Grand Teton National Parks
Scenic Byways East
Scenic Byways Far West
Scenic Byways Rocky Mountains
Back Country Byways

HISTORIC TRAIL GUIDES

Traveling California's Gold Rush Country
Traveling the Lewis & Clark Trail
Traveling the Oregon Trail
Traveler's Guide to the Pony Express Trail

WILDLIFE VIEWING GUIDES

Alaska Wildlife Viewing Guide
Arizona Wildlife Viewing Guide
California Wildlife Viewing Guide
Colorado Wildlife Viewing Guide
Florida Wildlife Viewing Guide
Indiana Wildlife Viewing Guide
Iowa Wildlife Viewing Guide
Kentucky Wildlife Viewing Guide
Massachusetts Wildlife Viewing Guide
Montana Wildlife Viewing Guide
Nebraska Wildlife Viewing Guide
Nevada Wildlife Viewing Guide
New Hampshire Wildlife Viewing Guide
New Jersey Wildlife Viewing Guide
New Mexico Wildlife Viewing Guide
New York Wildlife Viewing Guide
North Carolina Wildlife Viewing Guide
North Dakota Wildlife Viewing Guide
Ohio Wildlife Viewing Guide
Oregon Wildlife Viewing Guide
Puerto Rico & the Virgin Islands
   Wildlife Viewing Guide
Tennessee Wildlife Viewing Guide
Texas Wildlife Viewing Guide
Utah Wildlife Viewing Guide
Vermont Wildlife Viewing Guide
Virginia Wildlife Viewing Guide
Washington Wildlife Viewing Guide
West Virginia Wildlife Viewing Guide
Wisconsin Wildlife Viewing Guide

FALCON®